THE AUSTRALIAN TRAVELLERS ATLAS

EXPLORE AUSTRALIA

CONTENTS

VICTORIA

SOUTH AUSTRALIA

WESTERN AUSTRALIA

NORTHERN TERRITORY

QUEENSLAND

TASMANIA

MAP SYMBOLS

	Freeway, with tunnel and toll
	Freeway under construction
M31 31	Highway, sealed, with National Highway Route Marker
A1 1	Highway, sealed, with National Route Marker
5	Highway, sealed, with Metroad Route Marker
	Highway, unsealed
	Highway under construction
C141 26	Main road, sealed, with State Route Marker
	Main road, unsealed, with Tourist Route
	Main road under construction
	Secondary road, sealed, (suburbs maps only)
	Secondary road, unsealed, (suburbs maps only)
	Other road, sealed, with traffic direction arrow
	Other road, unsealed, with gate
	Mall
	Vehicle track
	Walking track
Paratoo	Railway, with station
Flagstaff	Underground railway, with station
114	Total kilometres between two points
45	Intermediate kilometres
	State border
	Fruit fly exclusion zone boundary
SYDNEY	State capital city
GEELONG	Town, over 50 000 inhabitants
Bundaberg	Town, 10 000–50 000 inhabitants
Katherine	Town, 5 000–10 000 inhabitants
Narrogin	Town, 1 000–5 000 inhabitants
Robe	Town, 200–1 000 inhabitants
Miena	Town, under 200 inhabitants
BELCONNEN	Suburb, on state and region maps
Acton	Suburb, on capital city map
Williamsford	Locality (area name)
Alroy Downs	Pastoral station homestead
Galiwinku	Major Aboriginal community
Murgenella	Aboriginal community
Fortesque Roadhouse	Roadhouse
	Commercial airport
	Place of interest
	Landmark feature
	Hill, mountain, peak
	Mine site
	Lighthouse
	River, with waterfall
	Lake, reservoir
	Intermittent lake
	Mangroves
	Coastline, with rocks
TO BIRDWOOD	Route destination
31	Adjoining map page number
	National park
	Other reserve
	Other named area
	Aboriginal / Torres Strait Islander land
	Prohibited area

AUSTRALIA AT A GLANCE

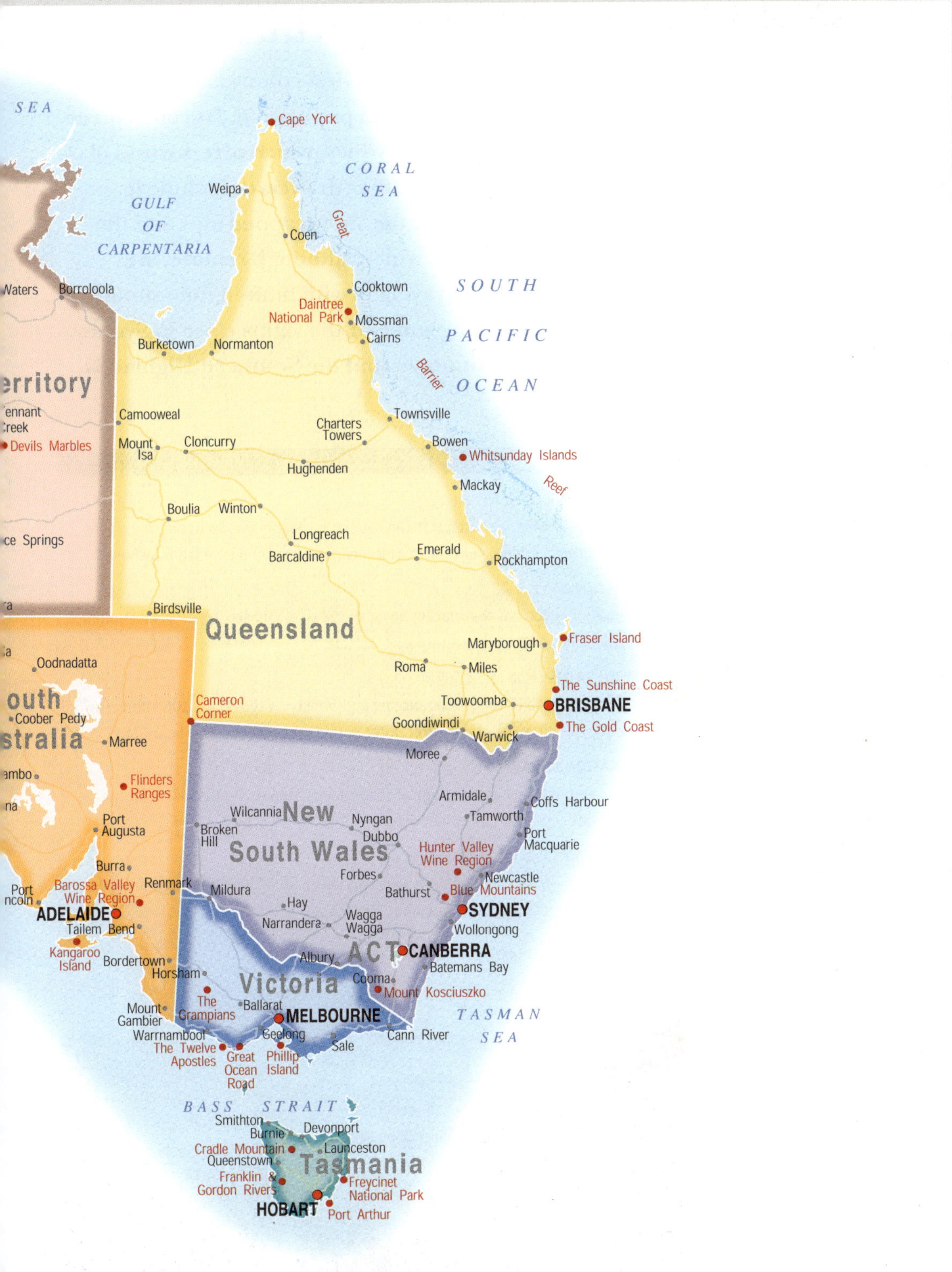
SEA
Cape York
CORAL SEA
Weipa
GULF OF CARPENTARIA
Coen
Great
Waters
Borroloola
Cooktown
SOUTH PACIFIC OCEAN
Daintree National Park
Mossman
Cairns
Burketown
Normanton
Barrier
erritory
Camooweal
Townsville
ennant Creek
Charters Towers
Devils Marbles
Mount Isa
Cloncurry
Bowen
Whitsunday Islands
Hughenden
Mackay
Reef
Boulia
Winton
ce Springs
Longreach
Barcaldine
Emerald
Rockhampton
Birdsville
Queensland
Maryborough
Fraser Island
Oodnadatta
Roma
Miles
outh stralia
Coober Pedy
Cameron Corner
The Sunshine Coast
Toowoomba
BRISBANE
Goondiwindi
The Gold Coast
Warwick
Marree
Moree
Flinders Ranges
Armidale
Coffs Harbour
Tamworth
Wilcannia
New South Wales
Nyngan
Port Augusta
Broken Hill
Dubbo
Port Macquarie
Hunter Valley Wine Region
Burra
Forbes
Newcastle
Barossa Valley Wine Region
Renmark
Mildura
Bathurst
Blue Mountains
Port ncoln
ADELAIDE
Hay
SYDNEY
Narrandera
Wagga Wagga
Wollongong
Tailem Bend
Kangaroo Island
Bordertown
Albury
ACT
CANBERRA
Batemans Bay
Horsham
Victoria
Cooma
Mount Kosciuszko
The Grampians
Ballarat
Mount Gambier
MELBOURNE
TASMAN SEA
Warrnambool
Geelong
Cann River
Sale
The Twelve Apostles
Great Ocean Road
Phillip Island
BASS STRAIT
Smithton
Burnie
Devonport
Cradle Mountain
Launceston
Queenstown
Tasmania
Franklin & Gordon Rivers
Freycinet National Park
HOBART
Port Arthur

FACTFILE

Population: 6 600 000

Land area: 800 628 sq km

Percentage of total area of Australia: 10.4%

Highest mountain: Kosciuszko (2228 m)

Key event: Australian Country Music Festival (Tamworth, January)

CAPITAL CITY

SYDNEY
(Map ref: 3 E6)

Australia's international gateway has a population of four million, and plays host to two million overseas visitors each year. It is a modern and intensely urban city, but also boasts substantial historic areas like The Rocks as well as famous surf beaches, bushland and the glittering waters of Sydney Harbour. It has a range of world-class cultural institutions such as the Powerhouse Museum, located in the popular Darling Harbour precinct, and the Art Gallery of New South Wales, on the edge of the city's historic Botanic Gardens. Top experiences include a ride on a harbour ferry and a visit to the observation deck of Sydney Tower.

VISITOR INFORMATION

Sydney Visitors Centre
106 George Street, The Rocks
(02) 9255 1788

New South Wales Visitor Information Line
13 2077
www.visitnsw.com.au

NEW SOUTH WALES

New South Wales is Australia's first colony and its largest state in terms of economy and population. Its centerpiece is its cosmopolitan capital Sydney, which offers world-class attractions and facilities. Other drawcards include its 2000-kilometre coastline, the snow-capped alps and the vast outback territories, which, although remote, are relatively accessible. Travellers with limited time should concentrate on visiting some of the sights close to Sydney, such as the Blue Mountains and the Southern Highlands.

STATE HIGHLIGHTS

SYDNEY HARBOUR (Map ref: 3 G1)
The world's most beautiful harbour is the setting for landmarks including the Opera House and Harbour Bridge, along with glorious beaches and bush-clad foreshores

BYRON BAY (Map ref: 9 R2)
This international coastal destination has a subtropical climate, top-class restaurants, great surf beaches and a lively alternative culture

BLUE MOUNTAINS (Map ref: 4 I6)
A World Heritage area of rugged mountains and forested valleys just 100 kilometres from Sydney, the Blue Mountains offer great dining and accommodation options

MUNGO NATIONAL PARK (Map ref: 12 G5)
Off the beaten track, the archaeological sites of this arresting outback landscape preserve 40 000 years of Aboriginal history

HUNTER VALLEY (Map ref: 7 M4)
This historic wine-producing region is just two hours from Sydney and has around 60 wineries set across a picturesque rural landscape

Three Sisters, Blue Mountains

AUSTRALIAN CAPITAL TERRITORY

The Australian Capital Territory was created in 1911 as the seat of federal government in Australia. It lies at the southern end of New South Wales in the foothills of the Australian Alps. Its capital Canberra and surrounding suburbs take up almost a quarter of the territory, while the magnificent bush and mountain landscape of Namadgi National Park occupies most of the rest. An easy three-hour drive from Sydney, Canberra offers excellent access to the Snowy Mountains, the Southern Highlands and the tranquil South Coast.

Parliament House, Canberra

TERRITORY HIGHLIGHTS

PARLIAMENT HOUSE (Map ref: 15 C11)
The workings of federal government are on display within the massive, architecturally acclaimed building, completed in 1988 at a cost of 1.1 billion

NAMADGI NATIONAL PARK (Map ref: 16 E4)
This subalpine mountain wilderness is a haven for campers, trampers and inland anglers

TIDBINBILLA (Map ref: 16 F3)
This area is home to the Canberra Deep Space Communications Complex (visitors welcome) as well as the 5000-hectare Tidbinbilla Nature Reserve

AUSTRALIAN WAR MEMORIAL (Map ref: 15 H4)
One of the world's biggest war museums, the memorial has over four million display items as well as features honouring Australia's war victims

NATIONAL MUSEUM OF AUSTRALIA (Map ref: 15 B7)
Housed in contemporary surrounds, this collection examines the history of Australia through the themes of land, nation and people

FACT FILE

Population: 321 700

Land area: 2 358 sq km

Percentage of total area of Australia: .09%

Most famous resident: prime minister of the day

Key event: Floriade (garden festival, September–October)

CAPITAL CITY

CANBERRA
(Map ref: 15 C4)

One of the world's few planned cities, Canberra incorporates grand boulevards, a huge ornamental lake and a series of highly visible public buildings which house, among other things, the nation's parliament, its highest court and its most valuable cultural assets. Beyond the city centre, great tracts of native bush provide a frame for the city's well-serviced and eminently livable suburbs. Attractions include the city's political and cultural institutions, the village-like inner-city neighbourhoods, the diplomatic missions, the parks including the Botanic Gardens, and the many lake-based activities on offer including cycling, boating and walking.

VISITOR INFORMATION

Canberra Visitors Centre
330 Northbourne Avenue,
Dickson
(02) 6205 0044
www.visitcanberra.com.au

FACT FILE

Population: 4 822 700

Land area: 227 010 sq km

Percentage of total area of Australia: 3%

Famous historic figure: Ned Kelly (1855–1880)

Key event: Melbourne Cup (November)

CAPITAL CITY

MELBOURNE
(Map ref: 19 C6)

Melbourne is a multicultural metropolis with a distinctly European feel. It has some of Australia's best cultural institutions, extraordinary historic and modern architecture, elegant public gardens, world-class sporting and cultural events, and the best shopping and dining opportunities this side of the equator. Trademark attractions include the Queen Victoria Market, Federation Square, the Exhibition Building and neighbouring Melbourne Museum, the Melbourne Cricket Ground, and the city's many inner city 'villages' such as St Kilda and Fitzroy.

VISITOR INFORMATION

Melbourne Visitors Centre
Federation Square
Cnr Flinders St and St Kilda Rd
(03) 9658 9658

Tourism Victoria
13 2842
www.visitvictoria.com.au

VICTORIA

Victoria is a compact state, but diverse in terms of landscape, culture and population. It is a wonderful touring destination, with most areas just a few hours from the capital Melbourne. The state's 1800-kilometre coastline incorporates some of the country's most stunning scenery, while inland attractions include wine and gourmet food-producing regions, alpine landscapes, rainforest, semi-arid deserts and major historic centres. Top activities for visitors include bushwalking, rock climbing, skiing, surfing, wildlife-watching and fishing.

STATE HIGHLIGHTS

PHILLIP ISLAND (Map ref: 21 L13)
The island's nightly parade of little (fairy) penguins is one of the state's top attractions

GREAT OCEAN ROAD (Map ref: 25 N12)
World-class surfing spots, historic wrecks and lighthouses, rainforest walks and up-market holiday towns are to be found along this scenic coastal drive

GOLDFIELDS (Map ref: 25 O3)
This area preserves gold-rush history in its many heritage towns, and recreates the drama of the period at the historic theme park Sovereign Hill

THE GRAMPIANS (Map ref: 24 H2)
An internationally acclaimed rock-climbing destination with great walking and camping opportunities, beautiful bush scenery, and many rock-art sites

YARRA VALLEY (Map ref: 22 E3)
Thirty or so top-class wineries occupy a lovely rural setting just over an hour's drive from Melbourne

Twelve Apostles, Great Ocean Road

SOUTH AUSTRALIA

South Australia offers wide vistas, clears skies, warm weather and great food and wine. Its 3700-kilometre coastline is a mecca for anglers, surfers, divers and wildlife watchers. Its winegrowing areas produce some of Australia's best wine, while its landscape features, including the Flinders Ranges, are famous for their beauty and grandeur the world over. Its elegant capital Adelaide hosts one of the world's great arts festivals. The best touring seasons are spring and autumn, though many enjoy the hot, dry summers, particularly along the coast.

Barossa Valley wine region

STATE HIGHLIGHTS

BAROSSSA VALLEY (Map ref: 36 E4)
Australia's best-known wine region offers cellar-door tastings, scenic landscapes, excellent food, rich history and a rustic atmosphere

KANGAROO ISLAND (Map ref: 38 F12)
This remote Southern Ocean island is home to thousands of sea lions and seals as well as the jaw-dropping Remarkable Rocks

THE NULLARBOR (Map ref: 42 C3)
Wild seas, whales, towering cliffs and desert plains are features of this iconic landscape in the state's far west

ADELAIDE HILLS (Map ref: 36 D10)
Just half an hour from Adelaide, this busy tourist area has bushland, farmland, wineries and historic villages, including the quaint community of Hahndorf

FLINDERS RANGES (Map ref: 41 K8)
This arid, ancient landscape is a major camping and walking destination, offering a taste of the history, culture and landscape of the outback

FACT FILE

Population: 1 514 900

Land area: 978 810 sq km

Percentage of total area of Australia: 12.7%

Wine production: 50% of all wine produced in Australia

Key event: Adelaide Festival of the Arts (February–March, even-numbered years)

CAPITAL CITY

ADELAIDE
(Map ref: 35 F10)
Set along the wide curves of the River Torrens, Adelaide is an attractive city of churches, graceful public buildings, wide streets and generous parklands. It is a small but cosmopolitan centre known for its multicultural restaurants, enviable calendar of events and lively markets, particularly Central Market in the city centre. It has very good cultural institutions, including the Art Gallery of South Australia, and along the coast are peaceful beaches fronting the calm waters of Gulf St Vincent. The city is easy to negotiate and offers good access to popular nearby regions, including the Fleurieu Peninsula, Adelaide Hills and Clare Valley.

VISITOR INFORMATION

South Australian Visitor and Travel Centre
18 King William St, Adelaide
(08) 8303 2220; 1300 655 276
www.southaustralia.com

FACT FILE

Population: 1 906 100

Land area: 2 526 786 sq km

Percentage of total area of Australia: 33%

Number of wildflower species: 11 000

Key event: Perth International Arts Festival

CAPITAL CITY

PERTH

(Map ref: 51 C6)

Perth, closer to cities in Asia than some other Australian capitals, is a modern, independent metropolis. It has a wealth of natural features including a warm, dry climate, sensational surf beaches, a river setting and outlying landscapes of hills and forests, making it one of Australia's most livable cities. Top attractions include the huge inner-city reserve of Kings Park as well as the Swan River, the Perth Zoo and the cultural attractions of Northbridge. Daytrips from Perth include Fremantle, Rottnest, Darling Range and Swan Valley.

VISITOR INFORMATION

Western Australia Visitor Centre
Cnr Forrest Pl. and Wellington St, Perth
(08) 9483 1111; 1300 361 351
www.westernaustralia.net

WESTERN AUSTRALIA

Most of the population of this enormous state is concentrated in the far south near Perth. Here you'll find vineyards, wildflower displays, forest of huge karri trees and a beautiful coastline offering top-class leisure opportunities. The northern but more remote coastline is equally spectacular, where attractions include Ningaloo Reef, the wild dolphins of Monkey Mia, the Pinnacles Desert and the popular resort town of Broome. Long distances separate towns in most areas of the state. Drivers should familiarise themselves with conditions before setting out, and avoid travelling at the height of summer.

The Pinnacles, Nambung National Park

STATE HIGHLIGHTS

ROTTNEST ISLAND (Map ref: 54 B4)
This tiny island of sandy coves, heritage sites and shipwrecks retains a peaceful holiday atmosphere, despite playing host to 500 000 visitors a year

MONKEY MIA AND NINGALOO REEF (Map ref: 55 B10)
Monkey Mia, part of World Heritage-listed Shark Bay, is home to around 400 dolphins. Ningaloo Reef, further north, is a major diving destination

MARGARET RIVER AND THE SOUTH-WEST (Map ref: 53 C10)
This region features many well-known wineries as well as some great opportunities for fishing, diving and surfing along the Limestone Coast

BROOME AND THE KIMBERLEY (Map ref: 60 G9, 61 L6)
Broome claims a balmy winter climate and one of the world's most beautiful beaches, while inland, ancient rock domes and rock art enrich the ancient landscape

FREMANTLE (Map ref: 52 B5)
'Freo', just 19 kilometres south-west of Perth, is a historic maritime settlement with great restaurants and cafes, heritage buildings and impressive museums

NORTHERN TERRITORY

The remote Northern Territory is Australia's last frontier. Its 'Top End' reaches far into the tropics while its southern extremities occupy the continent's desert heart. It is known the world over for some truly unique sights, including Uluru, and the Aboriginal rock art of Kakadu. Visitors to the Territory tend to base themselves around the two main centres 1500 kilometres apart: the capital Darwin in the north, and the desert township of Alice Springs at the heart of the Red Centre. The best time to travel is May to October.

TERRITORY HIGHLIGHTS

ULURU (Map ref: 70 E12)
This famous monolith with a circumference of 9 kilometres, rises dramatically from the flat, red desert plains and is richly inscribed with meaning

LITCHFIELD NATIONAL PARK (Map ref: 64 C8)
Two hours from Darwin, this popular park has waterfalls, gorges, giant termite mounds and great places to walk and camp

ALICE SPRINGS (Map ref: 71 J8)
A lively and well-serviced desert centre, with great cultural attractions and access to the stunning MacDonnell Ranges

KAKADU NATIONAL PARK (Map ref: 65 O2)
This park protects around 5000 sites of one of the world's oldest rock-art collections as well as landscapes of huge ecological importance

TERRITORY WILDLIFE PARK (Map ref: 64 D4)
This award-winning park near Darwin is a showcase for the flora and fauna of northern Australia

Kata Tjuta, Uluru–Kata Tjuta National Park

FACT FILE

Population: 200 000

Land area: 1 335 742 sq km

Percentage of total area of Australia: 17.5%

Aboriginal land as percentage of territory: 40%

Key event: Mindil Beach Sunset Market (Thursday evenings, May–October)

CAPITAL CITY

DARWIN
(Map ref: 63 E8)

This city of the far north fuses modern architecture and civic order with the tropical chaos of a wet/dry weather system, abundant foliage growth and constant incursions from native creatures. Despite its small size, it has excellent facilities for locals and visitors, not least of which is its range of great ethnic restaurants. Other attractions include the waterfront leisure precinct, the historic structures that survived both the Japanese bombers of WWII and Cyclone Tracy, the museums and galleries, and the Mindil Beach Sunset Market, where the riotous and eclectic spirit of the territory appears at its best.

VISITOR INFORMATION

Tourism Top End
Cnr Mitchell and Knuckey sts, Darwin
(08) 8936 2499; 1300 138 886
www.tourismtopend.com.au

Northern Territory Tourist Commission
13 3068
www.ntholidays.com.au

FACT FILE

Population: 3 635 100

Land area: 1 723 936 sq km

Percentage of total area of Australia: 22.5%

Number of World Heritage areas: 5

Key event: Birdsville Races (September)

CAPITAL CITY

BRISBANE

(Map ref: 73 E7)

This sunny city straddles the curves of the Brisbane River. It is a pleasant mix of old and new, with its gold-hued colonial buildings sitting comfortably among the gleaming high-rise structures of recent years. Central attractions include the major leisure and cultural precinct of South Bank and the lively inner-city neighbourhoods such as Fortitude Valley and Toowong. Outlying attractions include the subtropical Mount Coot-tha Botanic Gardens as well as Brisbane Forest Park, the Lone Pine Koala Sanctuary, the islands of Moreton Bay and the coastal community of Redcliffe.

VISITOR INFORMATION

Brisbane Visitor Information Centre
Queen St Mall
(07) 3006 6290

Tourism Queensland
13 8833
www.queensland-holidays.com.au

QUEENSLAND

Queensland is a major holiday destination for both interstate and overseas travellers. A series of resort communities, offering beautiful beaches and world-class facilities, are to be found along the coast. Offshore lies the brilliant underwater landscape of the Great Barrier Reef. Hinterland areas protect World Heritage forests, while inland, great tracts of farm and grazing land dominate, even in the far reaches of the state's vast outback. The far north is frontier country: a mostly pristine wonderland of ancient forests and remote coastline.

STATE HIGHLIGHTS

GOLD COAST (Map ref: 75 H11)
With 35 beautiful beaches, major resorts, theme parks and every kind of activity on offer, this is Australia's biggest, busiest holiday playground

GREAT BARRIER REEF (Map ref: 79 M3)
The world's largest reef has brilliant coral seascapes, a vast population of sea creatures and around 900 islands, 22 of which cater for visitors

CAIRNS (Map ref: 81 N6)
The tropical city of Cairns provides access to the reef as well as to World Heritage rainforest, Aboriginal rock art and the remote coastal towns of the far north

Palm Cove, north of Cairns

FRASER ISLAND
(Map ref: 77 Q3)
A World Heritage island with massive dunes, lakes and rainforest; nearby Hervey Bay plays host to 400 humpback whales each spring

LAMINGTON NATIONAL PARK
(Map ref: 77 P11)
Not far from Brisbane, this popular park preserves a wonderland of rainforests and volcanic ridges, and is great for walkers and campers

TASMANIA

Australia's only island state offers some extraordinary attractions including World Heritage-protected wilderness, fine examples of the nation's earliest colonial history and a burgeoning wine and gourmet food industry. The state's small size and quiet roads make it a great place for an extended driving holiday; many visitors find they can comfortably cover the major attractions in around ten days. The island also attracts adventure travellers from around the world with its superb bushwalking and white-water rafting opportunities.

Cradle Mountain–Lake St Clair National Park

STATE HIGHLIGHTS

PORT ARTHUR HISTORIC SITE (Map ref: 91 N10)
This remarkable site preserves the ruins of what was once an extensive convict complex, established in 1830

CRADLE MOUNTAIN–LAKE ST CLAIR (Map ref: 92 F1)
These two iconic World Heritage features sit at either end of the eight-day Overland Track, regarded as one of the world's great bushwalks

WINEGLASS BAY (Map ref: 93 Q4)
This tranquil bay surrounded by wilderness is the scenic centerpiece of the beautiful east coast

STRAHAN AND THE FRANKLIN (Map ref: 92 D3)
The west coast fishing village of Strahan leads to the Franklin River, one of the state's great wilderness experiences and a mecca for whitewater rafters

TASMANIAN WINE ROUTE (Map ref: 95 L8)
World-class cool-climate wines are to be found at boutique wineries along the Tamar River, near the historic city of Launceston

FACT FILE

Population: 470 000

Land area: 68 401 sq km

Percentage of total area of Australia: .9%

Number of islands: 1000

Key event: Ten Days on the Island (March–April)

CAPITAL CITY

HOBART
(Map ref: 89 E8)

The tiny capital of Hobart is Australia's prettiest and most historic city. Whole precincts, including the village-like suburb of Battery Point and the lively Constitution Dock, retain their original 19th-century feel and appearance. The suburbs spread out on either side of the broad Derwent River estuary, and rise up the lower slopes of the magnificently forested Mount Wellington, the summit of which affords spectacular views on a clear day. The city's key attraction is the Salamanca Market, a lively arts and crafts and fresh food market held each Saturday in Salamanca Place. The most prominent arts institution is the Tasmanian Museum and Art Gallery.

VISITOR INFORMATION

Tasmanian Travel and Information Centre
Cnr Elizabeth and Davey sts, Hobart
(03) 6230 8233
www.discovertasmania.com.au

PLANNING YOUR TRIP

Careful forward planning will help you have the best possible holiday, particularly if you intend to travel through remote areas, in places subject to weather extremes, during school holidays or to popular tourist areas that are likely to be booked out far in advance.

See pages viii to xv for details of visitor information organisations and inside back cover for other useful contacts

Travel information

Try to gather as much information as possible before leaving home. Overseas visitors should contact the Australian Tourist Commission or the Australian embassy in their own country. Each state and territory has its own tourist information service offering travel advice as well as bookings for accommodation and tours. Information is available via phone, the Internet and over the counter.

When to travel

With a few exceptions, you can travel to most areas of Australia year-round. Avoid the tropical north between November and April when the wet season brings with it high humidity, torrential downpours and tropical storms. Avoid the desert and other outback areas during summer when daytime temperatures hover in the forties. In winter the temperature in the Australian Alps dips below freezing, but few complain as long as it snows. Tasmania, southern Victoria and Canberra are chilly in winter, but many travellers find they enjoy the seasonal variety.

Peak seasons

Australia's busiest holiday periods are the summer school break (late December to end of January), the Easter break (late March or April) and school holiday periods in June and September. The alpine resorts are heavily booked during the ski season which runs from June to September. The high season in Queensland runs from April to September with some variance depending on the area. Sporting events and major festivals put pressure on accommodation and transport in cities and towns throughout the year and travellers should make a point of checking what's on where and when.

Student and youth travellers

Students under the age of 26 should equip themselves with an International Student Identity Card (ISIC), which can be used to obtain student discounts for many products and services throughout Australia; apply at travel agencies specialising in student travel (for

TRAVELLERS FROM OVERSEAS

Visitors to Australia must have a passport that is valid for longer than the intended period of stay. In addition, all visitors must have a visa. Visitor visas are available for three- or six-month periods and are generally issued as ETAs (Electronic Transfer Authority). They can be obtained through the website of the Department of Immigration and Multicultural Affairs (DIMIA) or from your travel agent. If you wish to extend your stay, contact DIMIA before your visa expires; extensions are generally granted on the condition that the length of your stay does not exceed 12 months.

Australia has diplomatic missions in countries around the world offering information on entry requirements, customs and general issues of concern to travellers. A list of missions is available from the Department of Foreign Affairs. Embassies and high commissions are located in Canberra.

TRAVEL TIP

ELECTRICAL APPLIANCES

You may need to purchase an adaptor to use your electrical appliances in Australia. Australia's electrical current is 240–250 volts AC and plugs have either two or three pins. Some hotels provide hairdryers as well as 110-volt sockets for shavers but others do not. Adaptors can be purchased in electrical and hardware stores throughout the country.

Floriade garden festival, Canberra

example, STA Travel in Australia). There are a number of organisations in Australia providing travel services for young travellers as well as reliable backpacker accommodation. These include the Australian YHA, the YMCA of Australia (hostels/hotels in Perth, Brisbane and Darwin), the YWCA of Australia (hostels/hotels in Sydney and Melbourne) and VIP Backpackers.

Staying in touch

Make your communication arrangements ahead of travelling. Mobile phone use is widespread in Australia, however the phone networks do not cover many rural and remote areas. Outback travellers should consider hiring a satellite phone. Internet cafes are popular in the cities and in many rural towns as well. Sending and receiving email via a portable email address (try Hotmail or Yahoo!) is a good, cheap way of staying in touch with family and friends. You can use an Australian post office as a mailing address; the envelope needs to be marked 'Post Restante' and include your name, and the location and postcode of the relevant office.

Parks and permits

National parks in some states charge a small entry fee. This can be paid on site or in advance at park information centres. If you intend to camp in popular areas, contact park authorities well in advance of your trip as sites are often booked early. There are areas of Aboriginal land right across Australia, with a particularly high concentration in Queensland and the Northern Territory. In many cases Aboriginal communities ask that visitors apply for a permit to visit these areas. Some communities issue passes on the spot, others ask visitors to apply in advance. Contact the relevant visitor information centre for further details.

KEY AUSTRALIAN EVENTS

JANUARY

Australia Day celebrations (25 January, national)

Australian Open (tennis, Melbourne)

Country Music Festival (Tamworth, NSW)

Sydney Festival (arts)

FEBRUARY

Gay and Lesbian Mardi Gras (Sydney)

FEBRUARY–MARCH

Adelaide Festival of the Arts (even-numbered years)

Perth International Arts Festival

Womadelaide (world music, Adelaide)

MARCH

Australian Formula One Grand Prix (Melbourne)

MARCH–APRIL

Ten Days on the Island (arts, Tasmania)

APRIL

Anzac Day marches (25 April, national)

Melbourne International Comedy Festival

SEPTEMBER

AFL Grand Final (football, Melbourne)

Festival of Darwin (arts)

Kings Park Wildflower Festival (Perth)

NRL Grand Final (football, Sydney)

SEPTEMBER–OCTOBER

Floriade (garden festival, Canberra)

OCTOBER

Energex Brisbane Festival (arts)

Gold Coast Indy 300 (motor-racing)

Melbourne Festival (arts)

NOVEMBER

Melbourne Cup (horse race)

Driving along the Great Ocean Road, Victoria

CAR HIRE

Rental cars are widely available throughout Australia. Prominent car-hire companies have outlets at airports, in city centres and other high volume tourist areas. Smaller companies are less accessible but offer cheaper rates. Always check the conditions of hire carefully, particularly with regards to insurance. Most companies impose a high insurance excess (around $1500) to be paid by the driver in the event of an accident. A daily payment of around $20 will reduce this to under $300. Many car-hire companies will not cover standard vehicles for off-road travel. Contact details:

Avis ∅13 6333 www.avis.com

Budget ∅1300 362 848 www.budget.com.au

Europcar ∅13 1390 www.deltaeuropcar.com.au

Hertz ∅13 3039 www.hertz.com

Thrify ∅1300 367 227 www.thrify.com.au

TRAVELLING BY CAR

Driving long distances is a fact of life in a country the size of Australia. Forward planning and the observance of some basic tips on comfort and rules of safety will ensure you have the best possible trip.

Checking your car

Get your mechanic to do a full service and safety check on your vehicle ahead of travelling. Then, just before you set out, do the visual POWER check (petrol, oils, water, electrics and rubbers) recommended by Australia's motoring organisations.

Roadside assist

For a small annual fee, state-based motoring organisations provide roadside service anywhere in Australia (drivers from other states are covered by reciprocal arrangements between organisations). Various levels of cover are available; enquire about the different features to find out what level of cover will work best for you. Contact details:

New South Wales (NRMA) ∅13 2132 www.nrma.com.au
Australian Capital Territory (NRMA) ∅13 2132 www.nrma.com.au
Victoria (RACV) ∅13 1955 www.racv.com.au
South Australia (RAA) ∅(08) 8202 4600 www.raa.net
Western Australia (RAC) ∅13 1704 www.rac.com.au
Northern Territory (AANT) ∅(08) 8981 3837 www.aant.com.au
Queensland (RACQ) ∅13 1950 www.racq.com.au
Tasmania (RACT) ∅(03) 6232 6300 www.ract.com.au

Road rules

Uniform national road rules apply in Australia but some rules vary to suit local conditions. A number of outback roads in the Northern Territory have no speed limit. In Melbourne, to ensure the smooth and safe running of trams, vehicles turning right must first pull to the left and not queue across tram tracks, not overtake a tram on its right, and stop behind a tram when it has stopped to allow passengers on or off. For further information contact your state-based motoring organisation or the National Road Transport Commission (NRTC), phone (03) 9321 8444, website www.nrtc.gov.au

Courtesy

It is important to do your bit towards keeping the roads safe. Focus on your driving, not the mistakes and behaviour of others. Don't gesture to other drivers or use your horn to indicate annoyance. Allow other drivers to merge, enter traffic from side streets and change lanes easily. Be particularly aware of pedestrians, cyclists and motorcyclists.

Safe driving

For a safe trip observe the following tips:

- Always leave a two-second gap between your car and the vehicle ahead of you, regardless of speed
- Keep left unless overtaking
- Indicate 30 metres before turning or changing lanes
- Stop behind the line at lights and stop signs
- Drive defensively: underestimate the skills and concentration of other drivers
- Avoid fatigue: do not drive when you would normally sleep, take a break every two hours, limit driving to a maximum of ten hours per day and watch for fatigue symptoms such as daydreaming, sore eyes and aches and pains
- Make seat, belt and rear-view mirror adjustments before heading off
- Concentrate on the task at hand: do not use your phone, light cigarettes, have animated discussions or fiddle with stereo equipment as you drive

Accident

In all states and territories of Australia, any accident in which someone is injured must be reported to police at once or within 24 hours. It is advisable to report any accident that involves substantial property damage in order to avoid and/or simplify legal and insurance problems down the track. Exchange names, addresses and insurance details with other parties involved in an accident, but do not discuss details or admit liability. Wait until you are thinking clearly again before making a statement to police.

Towing

When towing you need to ensure your rig (car, van and towing apparatus) complies with national regulations. You should also make a point of familiarising yourself with reversing, avoiding trailer sway and allowing for the added length of the vehicle. For further information contact the NRTC or your state motoring organisation. Caravan dealers and fitters and suppliers of towing equipment are also a good source of information.

TRAVEL TIP

PACKING THE CAR

For safety in the event of an accident, limit the items carried in the passenger compartment to necessities. If you are travelling in a sedan, secure the heavier items in the boot. Dispose of litter as soon as possible, particularly glass bottles and cans.

Towing your accommodation requires extra care

TRAVELLING BY AIR, TRAIN, COACH AND BOAT

Australia has a good, integrated transport system for those who choose to travel without a car, or who wish to use other forms of transport to supplement car travel.

See pages viii to xv for details of visitor information organisations and inside back cover for other useful contacts

International air travel

Most international visitors to Australia arrive by air, with around 50 international carriers servicing the country. Australia has several international arrival and departure points, with the busiest being Sydney and Melbourne. Many travellers flying from Europe opt for a stopover, often in Asia, to avoid the discomfort of the long-haul flight. Prior to landing in Australia passengers are asked to fill in customs documents. It is important to answer the questions as honestly as possible; Australia has strict customs regulations and failure to make a full declaration can result in heavy fines.

Domestic air travel and fly/drive

Australia's two domestic airlines, Qantas and Virgin, offer a range of discounted fares that are advertised regularly in newspapers. The best way to get a cheap flight is to book early (more than three weeks in advance) via the internet. Check conditions carefully; there is often little or no flexibility with heavily discounted fares. Fly/drive packages are a good way to focus on areas of interest and eliminate many hours of driving; check details with your travel agent.

Rail and motor-rail

Rail travel is a popular holiday experience in Australia, particular on routes that traverse remote regions such as the Indian *Pacific* (Sydney–Perth), the *Ghan* (Adelaide–Alice Springs) and the *Queenslander* (Brisbane–Cairns). Darwin and Hobart are the only capital cities not serviced by rail. Queensland, Victoria and New South Wales have a good range of country services. Motor-rail (travelling with your car on the train) is widely available and is a great way of getting a bit of a break from driving.

Coach

For travellers on a budget and without time constraints, coach travel makes for a safe, cheap and hassle-free way of getting around. Big companies such as Greyhound Pioneer and McCafferty's offer a range of travel passes that allow passengers to disembark from and rejoin services at different places around the country.

BY BOAT

Boat trips can be a holiday in themselves as well as a means of getting from one place to another. Consider hiring a houseboat on the Hawkesbury River or Lake Eildon, taking a paddlewheeler cruise of the Murray, or even chartering your own yacht in the Whitsundays. Contact the relevant state visitor centre for further information. Ferries service a number of islands off the mainland including the island state of Tasmania. The *Spirit of Tasmania I* and *II* make daily voyages across Bass Strait between Melbourne and Devonport.

Spirit of Tasmania, *passenger and car ferry between Melbourne and Devonport*

ACCOMMODATION

Australia's accommodation options include everything from caravan parks and motels to cattle stations, houseboats, luxury resorts and intimate bed and breakfasts. Australia has no official ratings system, however various guides, including those produced by state motoring bodies, rate accommodation outlets according to their own criteria.

See pages viii to xv for details of visitor information organisations and inside back cover for other useful contacts

Resorts, hotels, motels

Major accommodation chains operate motels, apartments and resorts around Australia. These organisations have central booking services and generally make for a reliable choice. Small boutique hotels and specialist resorts (such as eco resorts) are becoming increasingly popular for their individual style and service; keep an eye out for reviews in travel and lifestyle magazines.

Holiday houses and apartments

Holiday houses and apartments make good sense for families. Most apartments are part of large accommodation chains, while houses and cottages tend to be privately owned, and managed through the local visitor information and/or real estate agent. In many cases, you can view properties and make bookings on the internet.

Caravan parks

Caravan parks are a good, cheap accommodation option. In addition to offering sites for travelling vans, most caravan parks offer on-site caravans and cabins (you may need to bring your own linen) as well as areas for tents. Well-run parks with good facilities tend to book up well in advance so you need to plan ahead.

Camping in national parks

Most national parks have campsites, though facilities vary greatly. In some parks, campsites are allocated on a first-come, first-served basis; in others, bookings need to be made weeks or even months in advance.

Bed and breakfast and farmstay accommodation

With both these options you are essentially a paying guest in someone's house, cottage, barn or homestead. Although not for everyone, many people find this sort of accommodation a way of avoiding the impersonality and sameness of hotels and motels.

KID FRIENDLY

If you have children, make sure you mention them when booking accommodation. In the interests of their childfree patrons, a number of places discourage or ban children. There are other places, however, that actively welcome children with facilities that range from cots and high chairs to all-day kids clubs and babysitting services.

Caravan parks are a good, cheap accommodation option

BACKPACKER ACCOMMODATION

Backpacker accommodation is provided at budget rates in communal surrounds. Although aimed at the youth market, this kind of accommodation is also suitable for budget-conscious families and older travellers. There are a number of organisations in Australia that run hostels in various locations. See *Planning your trip* page xvi.

HEALTH AND SAFETY

Australia is a relatively safe holiday destination, however travellers should ensure they are well aware of local environmental hazards as well as issues to do with personal security.

See inside back cover for useful health and safety contacts

Sun and surf

To avoid heatstroke and sun damage, stay in the shade between 11 am and 3 pm, wear protective clothing, including a hat, and apply sunblock regularly. Swimmers should never swim alone or at unpatrolled beaches. Do not allow children to enter the water until you are confident conditions are safe.

Floods and bushfire

Keep well informed of prevailing conditions, particularly in remote areas. Flash floods can occur without warning. Only camp in riverbeds or close to the edges of creeks or streams if you know it's safe. Avoid bushfire-prone regions on days of critical fire danger (total fire bans); if you must travel, carry woollen blankets as a shield against fire and bottles of water to keep hydrated if trapped.

Property and personal protection

Keep yourself and your property safe while on holiday by following these simple measures:

- Do not hitchhike or pick up hitchhikers
- If you are flagged down, assess the situation before leaving the safety of your car
- Make sure you are fully insured
- Keep your vehicle locked at all times
- Do not leave valuables such as phones, bags and cameras in your car
- Use a money belt
- If staying in a motel/hotel do not leave valuables in the room
- Take care when withdrawing money at ATMs

First aid

If you are planning to travel through remote areas, consider signing up for first aid training ahead of your trip. Administering aid in the event of an accident or other medical emergency can often help save lives. St John Ambulance conducts courses in branches all around Australia and also sells a range of first-aid kits.

DANGEROUS CREATURES

The following creatures are dangerous; avoid contact and obey warning signs.

Box jellyfish
Found in tropical waters from October to May

Blue-ringed octopus
Common in rock pools around Australia

Sharks
Prevalent throughout Australian waters

Saltwater crocodiles
Found in estuaries and rivers in northern Australia

Spiders and snakes
Found across Australia; check bedding, clothes and shoes in high-risk areas

Obey warning signs for your own safety

EPIRBS

EPIRBs (Emergency Position Indicator Radio Beacons) are used by bushwalkers, sailors and drivers in remote locations. If you activate an EPIRB (and this should only be done in extreme emergencies), you send a signal that allows rescue authorities to pinpoint your exact location. EPIRBs are cheap (around $200) and very portable.

MONEY MATTERS

Worrying about money can take the pleasure out of a holiday. Put your finances in order before you leave home, particularly if you are planning a long trip. Work out a budget, plan your cash flow and make arrangements for bills to be paid in your absence.

Budgets

A holiday budget should include costs for accommodation, food, transport and entertainment. Making advance bookings will help you estimate some costs, particularly accommodation costs. Fuel costs vary quite a bit and are likely to be higher in remote areas. Keep some money aside for emergencies.

Paying bills

If you are planning a long trip it's a good idea to make advance arrangements for bill paying. Arrange with your bank to have regular bills (insurance, mortgage, subscriptions) paid by direct debit from your account. Other bills can be paid using a credit/EFT card and the phone or internet. Australia Post outlets accept cash, cheque or card payments for bills on behalf of a large number of organisations.

Banking

Many towns no longer have a single bank, let alone branches of different banks. You will need to plan ahead for over-the-counter transactions. Apart from depositing cheques, most bank services can now be accessed by ATMs and the phone or internet (unlike banks, internet cafes can now be found everywhere). Australia Post, through its service Giropost, acts as an agent for a number of banks and credit unions; services offered include cheque deposits, withdrawals and transfers.

Cash, card or cheque

For reasons of security and convenience, cards are the preferred method of payment for larger transactions these days. A credit card linked to other accounts will allow you to replenish cash, pay for purchases using credit or EFTPOS and pay household bills as you travel. But cash still has its uses. Many small businesses (markets, cafes, roadside stalls) are strictly cash-only. Other businesses impose a minimum card transaction amount of between $10 and $20. Retailers rarely accept cheques these days. It's also a good idea to carry an extra card not linked to your main account. This will give you access to funds in the event that you have to cancel your primary card. The use of travellers cheques by overseas visitors is also still common.

CURRENCY

The local currency is the Australian dollar, which is divided into 100 cents. There is no limit to the amount of foreign or Australian currency that can be brought in or out of the country, but amounts of $10 000 or more must be declared to customs. At the time of going to press, the Australian dollar was buying US$ 0.66, € 0.56, £ 0.40 and ¥ 0.78. Exchange rates can be checked daily on the Reserve Bank of Australia website www.rba.gov.au

Australian currency

LOST CARDS

If your card is lost or stolen, notify your bank immediately. Most banks have 24-hour lost card service, so there is no need to wait for the resumption of regular banking hours. Overseas visitors should contact the relevant card organisation direct. See inside back cover for contact details.

New South Wales

Location Map

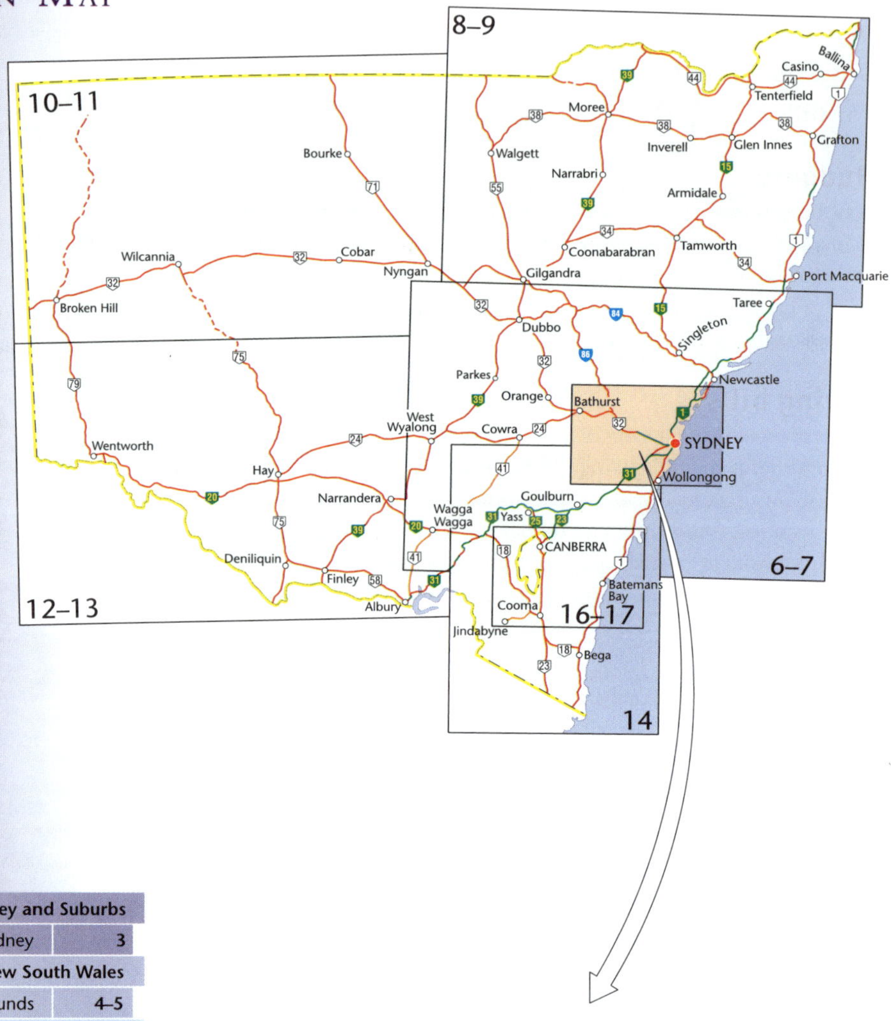

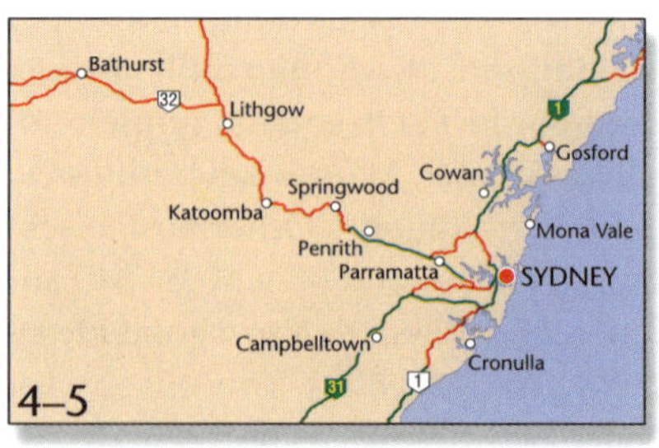

0 0.25 0.5 0.75 1 km
Accommodation
ANA Hotel Sydney 1 D5
Four Points Sheraton 2 C8
Hilton Sydney 3 E9
Hotel Intercontinental Sydney 4 F5
Novotel Sydney on Darling Harbour 5 B9
Park Hyatt Sydney 6 E2
Parkroyal at Darling Harbour 7 C9
The Regent Sydney 8 E5
Renaissance Sydney Hotel 9 E5
Sydney Central YHA 10 D12
The Westin Sydney 11 E7
The York Apartment Hotel 12 D6
Note: Only a sample range of accommodation is listed; inclusion is not necessarily a recommendation.
General Information
Cadmans Cottage (NPWS Info. Centre) 13 E4
Central Railway Station 14 D13
City Central Police Station 15 D10
Coach Tour Departures 16 E3
General Post Office 17 E7
Interstate & Country Coach Terminal 18 E12
Motoring Organisation (NRMA) 19 D7
Qantas Travel Centre 20 E6
Sydney Ferries 21 F4
Sydney Visitor Centre 22 E3
Places of Interest
Art Gallery of New South Wales 23 H7
Australian Museum 24 F9
Australian National Maritime Museum 25 B8
Campbell's Storehouse 26 E3
Chinatown 27 D11
Chinese Garden 28 C10
Government House 29 G4
Hyde Park Barracks Museum 30 F8
IMAX Theatre 31 C9
Justice & Police Museum 32 F5
Museum of Contemporary Art 33 E4
Museum of Sydney 34 F5
Parliament of NSW 35 F7
Powerhouse Museum 36 B11
Queen Victoria Building 37 D8
Royal Botanic Gardens 38 H6
St Mary's Cathedral 39 F8
Star City (casino, hotel & theatres) 40 A7
State Library of NSW 41 F6
Susannah Place 42 D4
Sydney Aquarium 43 C8
Sydney Harbour Bridge 44 F1
Sydney Observatory 45 D4
Sydney Opera House 46 G3
Sydney Tower 47 E8
Sydney Town Hall 48 D9
Victoria Barracks 49 I13
TO NORTH SYDNEY
SYDNEY HARBOUR
PORT JACKSON
Walsh Bay
Dawes Point
Millers Point
The Rocks
Sydney Cove
Farm Cove
Woolloomooloo Bay
ROYAL BOTANIC GARDENS
The Domain
SYDNEY
Darling Harbour
Cockle Bay
Pyrmont
Woolloomooloo
Potts Point
Kings Cross
Darlinghurst
Hyde Park
Ultimo
Haymarket
Paddington
Broadway
Surry Hills
TO PENRITH
TO WATSONS BAY
TO BONDI
TO AIRPORT

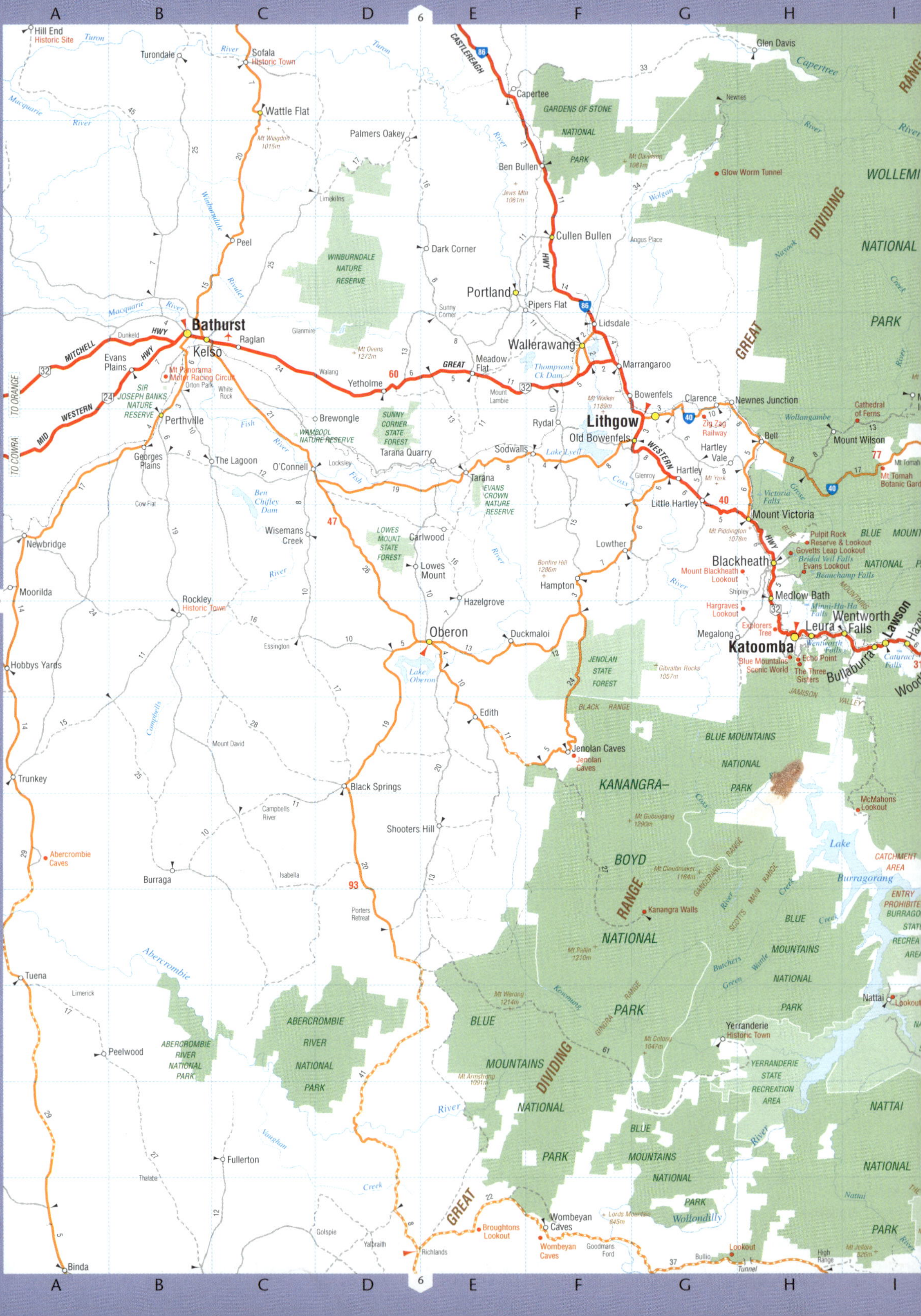

A B C D E F G H I
1 2 3 4 5 6 7 8 9 10 11 12 13
Hill End
Historic Site
Turondale
Sofala
Historic Town
Wattle Flat
Mt Wiagdon 1015m
Palmers Oakey
Capertee
GARDENS OF STONE
NATIONAL
PARK
Glen Davis
Capertree
Newnes
Glow Worm Tunnel
WOLLEMI
NATIONAL
PARK
DIVIDING
GREAT
RANGE
Ben Bullen
Mt Davidson 1081m
Jews Mtn 1061m
Limekilns
Peel
Dark Corner
Cullen Bullen
Angus Place
WINBURNDALE
NATURE
RESERVE
Portland
Pipers Flat
Lidsdale
Bathurst
Kelso
Raglan
Dunkeld
Glanmire
Mt Ovens 1272m
Sunny Corner
Wallerawang
Marrangaroo
Thompsons Ck Dam
MITCHELL HWY
Evans Plains
Mt Panorama
Motor Racing Circuit
Orton Park
White Rock
Walang
Yetholme
GREAT
Meadow Flat
Mount Lambie
Bowenfels
Clarence
Newnes Junction
Cathedral of Ferns
TO ORANGE
SIR JOSEPH BANKS NATURE RESERVE
Perthville
MID WESTERN
Brewongle
SUNNY CORNER STATE FOREST
WAMBOOL NATURE RESERVE
Rydal
Mt Walker 1189m
Lithgow
Zig Zag Railway
Wollangambe
Mount Wilson
Old Bowenfels
Bell
TO COWRA
Georges Plains
The Lagoon
O'Connell
Locksley
Tarana Quarry
Sodwalls
Lake Lyell
Hartley Vale
Mt Tomah
Mt Tomah Botanic Gardens
Tarana
WESTERN
Hartley
Glenroy
Mt York
Victoria Falls
Cow Flat
Ben Chifley Dam
EVANS CROWN NATURE RESERVE
Little Hartley
Grose
Mount Victoria
Wisemans Creek
LOWES MOUNT STATE FOREST
Carlwood
Mt Piddington 1078m
Pulpit Rock Reserve & Lookout
BLUE MOUNTAINS
Newbridge
Lowther
Govetts Leap Lookout
Bridal Veil Falls
Evans Lookout
Beauchamp Falls
Lowes Mount
Bonfire Hill 1286m
Blackheath
Mount Blackheath Lookout
NATIONAL
Moorilda
Hampton
Shipley
Rockley
Historic Town
Hazelgrove
Medlow Bath
Minni-Ha-Ha Falls
Hargraves Lookout
Wentworth Falls
Lawson
Explorers Tree
Leura
Megalong
Hobbys Yards
Essington
Oberon
Duckmaloi
Katoomba
Echo Point
Blue Mountains Scenic World
The Three Sisters
Bullaburra
Cataract Falls
Lake Oberon
JENOLAN STATE FOREST
Gibraltar Rocks 1057m
JAMISON VALLEY
Campbells
Edith
BLACK RANGE
BLUE MOUNTAINS NATIONAL PARK
Mount David
Jenolan Caves
Trunkey
Black Springs
KANANGRA–
Campbells River
Shooters Hill
Mt Gubougang 1290m
Cox
McMahons Lookout
Lake
Abercrombie Caves
BOYD
Mt Cloudmaker 1164m
GANGERANG RANGE
CATCHMENT AREA
Burraga
Isabella
Burragorang
ENTRY PROHIBITED
Porters Retreat
RANGE
Kanangra Walls
SCOTTS MAIN RANGE
BLUE
Tuena
Abercrombie
Mt Paling 1210m
NATIONAL
MOUNTAINS
Butchers
Wattle
Green
NATIONAL
Limerick
Mt Werong 1214m
Kowmung
GINGRA RANGE
PARK
PARK
Nattai
Lookout
ABERCROMBIE RIVER NATIONAL PARK
ABERCROMBIE RIVER NATIONAL PARK
BLUE
Yerranderie
Historic Town
Peelwood
MOUNTAINS
Mt Colong 1047m
YERRANDERIE STATE RECREATION AREA
DIVIDING
Mt Armstrong 1091m
River
NATIONAL
BLUE
NATTAI
PARK
MOUNTAINS
NATIONAL
Fullerton
Vaughan
NATIONAL
Thalaba
PARK
Creek
GREAT
Wombeyan Caves
Lords Mountain 845m
Nattai
Wollondilly
PARK
Broughtons Lookout
Wombeyan Caves
Goodmans Ford
Golspie
Yalbraith
Richlands
Bullio
Lookout
Tunnel
High Range
Mt Jellore 826m
Binda
River
Macquarie
Turon
Winburndale
Rivulet
Fish
Wolgan
Capertree
Coxs

0 5 10 15 20 25 30 km
J K L M N O P Q R
1 2 3 4 5 6 7 8 9 10 11 12 13
TO NEWCASTLE
Morisset
Brightwaters
Sunshine
Gwandalan
Nords Wharf
Catherine Hill Bay
Mannering Park
Wyee
Lake Munmorah
MUNMORAH STATE RECREATION AREA
Doyalson
BUDGEWOI
TOUKLEY
NORAVILLE
NORAH HEAD
Mandalong
Dooralong
Jilliby
Ravensdale
Cedar Brush
Kulnura
Yarramalong
WYONG
TUGGERAH
GOROKAN
Tuggerah Lake
Wyong Creek
Palmdale
Palm Grove
Somersby
Fowlers Lookout
OURIMBAH
LONG JETTY
THE ENTRANCE NORTH
THE ENTRANCE
TOOWOON BAY
WYRRABALONG NATIONAL PARK
BATEAU BAY
FORRESTERS BEACH
TUMBI UMBI
NARARA
LISAROW
MATCHAM
WAMBERAL
GOSFORD
ERINA
TERRIGAL
The Skillion
POINT CLARE
KINCUMBER
AVOCA BEACH
MACMASTERS BEACH
BOUDDI NATIONAL PARK
WOY WOY
ETTALONG
UMINA
KILLCARE
WAGSTAFFE
Brisbane Water
BRISBANE WATER NATIONAL PARK
Patonga
Warrah Lookout
Broken Bay
Mooney Mooney
Brooklyn
Central Mangrove
Peats Ridge
Mangrove Mountain
Upper Mangrove Creek
Mangrove Creek
Ten Mile Hollow
Lower Mangrove
Glenworth Valley
Calga
Mount White
Australian Reptile Park & Wildlife Sanctuary
Old Sydney Town
Spencer
Gunderman
Laughtondale
Wisemans Ferry
Webbs Creek
St Albans
DHARUG NATIONAL PARK
MARRAMARRA NATIONAL PARK
MUOGAMARRA NATURE RESERVE
YENGO NATIONAL PARK
PARR STATE RECREATION AREA
PUTTY RD
Colo Heights
Central Colo
Upper Colo
Colo
Leets Vale
Maroota
Sackville North
Blaxlands Ridge
East Kurrajong
Comleroy Road
Kurrajong Heights
Bellbird Hill Lookout
Kurrajong
Glossodia
Kurmond
Ebenezer
Cattai
Bowen Mountain
North Richmond
Freemans Reach
Wilberforce
Richmond
Agnes Banks
Clarendon
Pitt Town
Maraylya
Windsor
McGraths Hill
Londonderry
Vineyard
Glenorie
Galston
Cowan
BEROWRA
KU-RING-GAI CHASE NATIONAL PARK
Kenthurst
Annangrove
Windsor Downs
RIVERSTONE
Rouse Hill Estate
SCHOFIELDS
Marsden Park
QUAKERS HILL
GLENHAVEN
CASTLE HILL
HORNSBY
ST IVES
PYMBLE
TERREY HILLS
FRENCHS FOREST
PALM BEACH
WHALE BEACH
AVALON
NEWPORT
MONA VALE
ELANORA HEIGHTS
NARRABEEN
COLLAROY
DEE WHY
MANLY
BALGOWLAH
SYDNEY HARBOUR NP
MOSMAN
WATSONS BAY
DOVER HEIGHTS
CHATSWOOD
LANE COVE
NORTH SYDNEY
BALMAIN
SYDNEY
For more detail on Central Sydney see page 3
PADDINGTON
BONDI
COOGEE
KINGSFORD
MAROUBRA
BOTANY
SYDNEY AIRPORT
MARRICKVILLE
LA PEROUSE
KURNELL
BOTANY BAY NATIONAL PARK
CRONULLA
Bate Bay
SYLVANIA
MIRANDA
SUTHERLAND
BLAKEHURST
BRIGHTON LE SANDS
HURSTVILLE
PEAKHURST
BEXLEY
REVESBY
BANKSTOWN
MILPERRA
BELFIELD
STRATHFIELD
HOMEBUSH BAY
GLADESVILLE
RYDE
PARRAMATTA
MERRYLANDS
FAIRFIELD
CABRAMATTA
LIVERPOOL
BLACKTOWN
ROOTY HILL
Featherdale Wildlife Park
MOUNT DRUITT
ST MARYS
KINGSWOOD
PENRITH
EASTERN CREEK
Wonderland Sydney
HORSLEY PARK
Prospect Reservoir
CECIL PARK
Erskine Park
Mulgoa
Wallacia
Luddenham
Badgerys Creek
Austral
Rossmore
Bringelly
LEPPINGTON
Catherine Field
Oran Park (Raceway)
MACQUARIE FIELDS
MINTO
MILITARY RESERVE
LEUMEAH
CAMPBELLTOWN
NARELLAN
Cobbitty
Theresa Park
Brownlow Hill
CAMDEN
GRASMERE
Glenmore
The Oaks
Mount Hunter
Menangle Park
Menangle
Cawdor
Mowbray Park
Picton
Maldon
Douglas Park
Appin
Wilton
Tahmoor
Bargo
Yanderra
Hilltop
Yerrinbool
Wedderburn
HEATHCOTE
Waterfall
Maianbar
Bundeena
ROYAL NATIONAL PARK
Audley
Wattamolla
Garie Beach
Helensburgh
Otford
Stanwell Tops
Lawrence Hargrave Memorial & Lookout
Stanwell Park
Coalcliff
Clifton
Scarborough
Wombarra
Coledale
Sublime Point Lookout
Austinmer
Thirroul
BULLI
CORRIMAL
TO SHELLHARBOUR
Woronora Reservoir
Nepean Reservoir
Avon Reservoir
Cordeaux Reservoir
Lake Cataract
Appin Falls
DHARAWAL STATE RECREATION AREA
DHARAWAL NATURE RESERVE
BENTS BASIN SRA
Springwood
Winmalee
Valley Heights
Warrimoo
Martins Lookout
Blaxland
Glenbrook
Silverdale
Hawkesbury Heights
Hawkesbury Lookout
Hawkesbury Museum
Vale of Avoca Lookout
SOUTH
PACIFIC
OCEAN
CENTRAL COAST
N

Nevertire
Buddabaddah
Trangie
Gin Gin
Narromine
Dubbo
Eumungerie
Mendooran
Balladdran
Merrygoen
Coolah
Dunedoo
Cassilis
Cobbora
Mogriguy
Brocklehurst
Elong Elong
Ballimore
Birriwa
Uarbry
Ulan
Gulgong
Wongarbon
Geurie
Tottenham
Albert
Tullamore
Fifield
Trundle
Tomingley
Peak Hill
Bulgandramine
Yeoval
Wellington
Mudgee
Rylstone
Kandos
Cumnock
Alectown
Condobolin
Ootha
Bogan Gate
Parkes
Molong
Manildra
Orange
Bathurst
Forbes
Bedgerebong
Jemalong
Eugowra
Cudal
Canowindra
Blayney
Millthorpe
Carcoar
Lithgow
Portland
Wallerawang
Oberon
Ungarie
Girral
Grenfell
Cowra
Woodstock
Lyndhurst
Trunkey
West Wyalong
Wyalong
Barmedman
Quandialla
Bimbi
Young
Boorowa
Crookwell
Taralga
Temora
Stockinbingal
Harden
Murrumburrah
Cootamundra
Goulburn
Marulan
Grong Grong
Coolamon
Ganmain
Junee
Yass
Gunning
Murrumbateman
Coolac
Gundagai
Wagga Wagga
Tumut
Tarcutta
Adelong
Batlow
Canberra
Queanbeyan
Bungendore
Braidwood
ACT
Kosciuszko National Park
The Rock
Henty
Yerong Creek
Forest Hill
Tumbarumba
Captains Flat

0 20 40 60 80 100 km
J K L M N O P Q R
1 2 3 4 5 6 7 8 9 10 11 12 13
SOUTH
PACIFIC
OCEAN
TASMAN
SEA
CENTRAL
COAST
ILLAWARRA
For more detail on Sydney & Surrounds see pages 4–5
Taree
Harrington
Wingham
Old Bar
Gloucester
Forster–Tuncurry
BOOTI BOOTI NATIONAL PARK
Bulahdelah
Smiths Lake
Seal Rocks
MYALL LAKES NATIONAL PARK
Tea Gardens
Hawks Nest
Shoal Bay
Nelson Bay
Anna Bay
TOMAREE NATIONAL PARK
Dungog
Stroud
Scone
Aberdeen
Muswellbrook
Denman
Singleton
Branxton
MAITLAND
Cessnock
Raymond Terrace
NEWCASTLE
CHARLESTOWN
Swansea
Morisset
Wyee
Lake Munmorah
TOUKLEY
WYONG
THE ENTRANCE
GOSFORD
TERRIGAL
KINCUMBER
UMINA
WOLLEMI NATIONAL PARK
YENGO NATIONAL PARK
BARRINGTON TOPS NATIONAL PARK
Windsor
Richmond
Springwood
Blaxland
Glenbrook
PENRITH
PARRAMATTA
MANLY
SYDNEY
HOMEBUSH
LIVERPOOL
CAMPBELLTOWN
CAMDEN
Picton
Appin
Helensburgh
Stanwell Park
WOLLONGONG
PORT KEMBLA
SHELLHARBOUR
Kiama
Gerringong
Berry
Bomaderry
Nowra
Shoalhaven Heads
Culburra
Callala Bay
Huskisson
Vincentia
Sanctuary Point
Sussex Inlet
Mittagong
Bowral
Moss Vale
Bundanoon
Robertson
Milton
Ulladulla
Burrill Lake
Tabourie Lake
Bawley Point
Kioloa

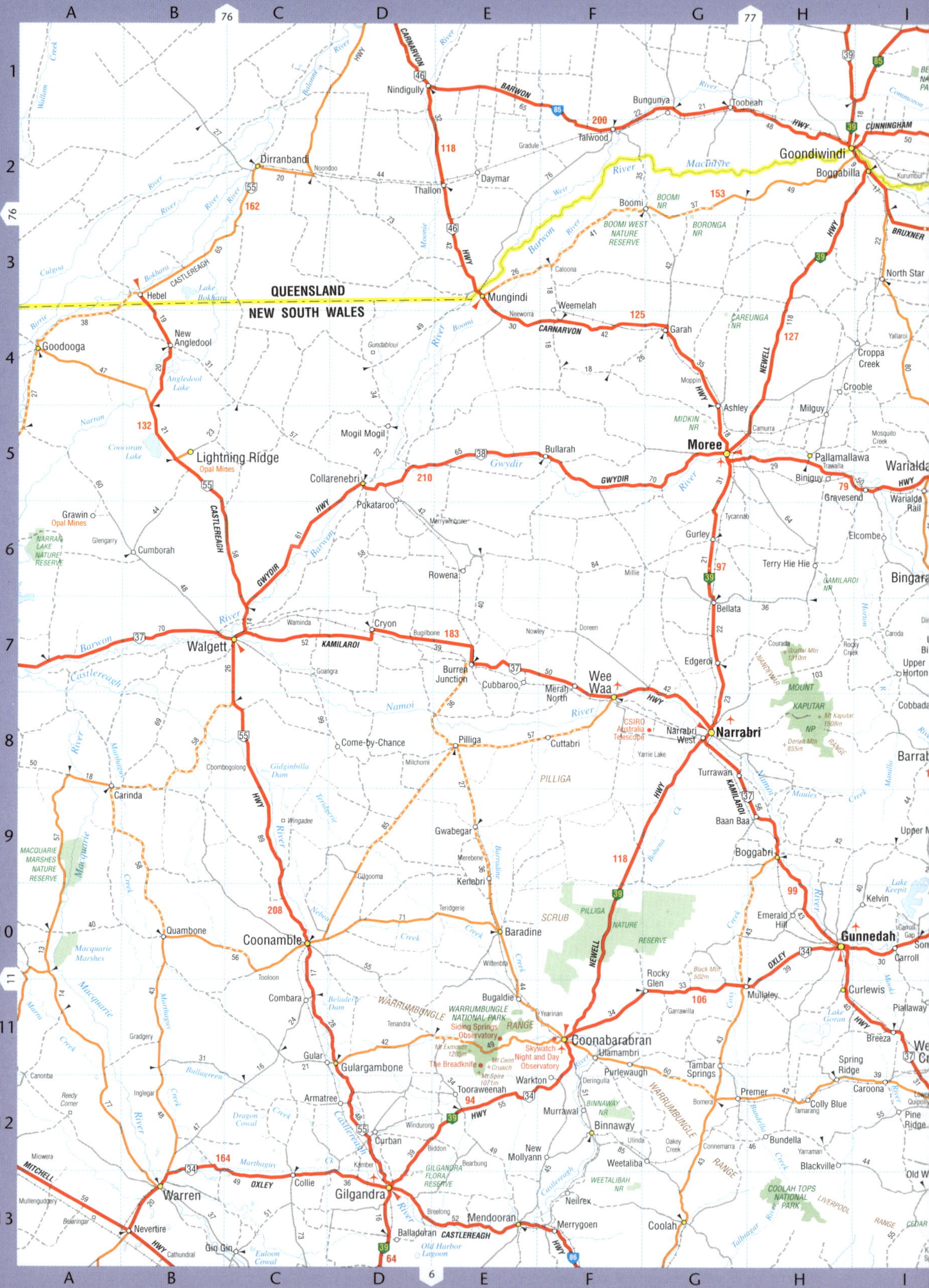
QUEENSLAND
NEW SOUTH WALES
Dirranbandi
Nindigully
Bungunya
Toobeah
Talwood
Goondiwindi
Boggabilla
Thallon
Daymar
Boomi
Hebel
Mungindi
Weemelah
Garah
New Angledool
Goodooga
North Star
Croppa Creek
Ashley
Moree
Lightning Ridge
Opal Mines
Bullarah
Collarenebri
Pokataroo
Pallamallawa
Warialda
Gravesend
Grawin
Cumborah
Rowena
Gurley
Terry Hie Hie
Bingara
Bellata
Walgett
Cryon
Burren Junction
Wee Waa
Edgeroi
Narrabri
Narrabri West
Pilliga
Cuttabri
Come-by-Chance
Carinda
Gwabegar
Baan Baa
Boggabri
Kenebri
Baradine
Coonamble
Quambone
Gunnedah
Curlewis
Coonabarabran
Mullaley
Rocky Glen
Gulargambone
Tambar Springs
Warrumbungle National Park
Siding Springs Observatory
Binnaway
Mendooran
Coolah
Gilgandra
Warren
Nevertire
Collie
Curban
Coolah Tops National Park
Mount Kaputar NP
Pilliga Nature Reserve
Macquarie Marshes Nature Reserve
Castlereagh Hwy
Kamilaroi Hwy
Gwydir Hwy
Newell Hwy
Oxley Hwy
Carnarvon Hwy
Barwon Hwy
Cunningham Hwy
Mitchell Hwy

0 20 40 60 80 100 km
J K L M N O P Q R
1 2 3 4 5 6 7 8 9 10 11 12 13
77
7
COOLANGATTA
TWEED HEADS
Fingal
Banora Point
Chinderah
Terranora
Kingscliff
Tumbulgum
Cudgen
Murwillumbah
Condong
Bogangar
Hastings Point
Pottsville
Mooball
Burringbar
Crabbes Creek
Billinudgel
New Brighton
Ocean Shores
Brunswick Heads
Mullumbimby
Tyagarah
Cape Byron
Byron Bay
Newrybar
Suffolk Park
Knockrow
Lennox Head
Nimbin
Dunoon
Bangalow
Clunes
The Channon
Modanville
Goolmangar
Bexhill
Eltham
Alphadale
Wollongbar
Lismore
Alstonville
Ballina
Meerschaum Vale
Empire Vale
Tatham
Coraki
Wardell
Broadwater
BROADWATER NP
Woodburn
New Italy
Evans Head
Tabbimoble
BUNDJALUNG NATIONAL PARK
Iluka
Yamba
Angourie
Wooloweyah Estuary
YURAYGIR NATIONAL PARK
Brooms Head
Harwood
Chatsworth
Maclean
Lawrence
Tyndale
Ulmarra
Tucabia
Grafton
Junction Hill
Copmanhurst
Seelands
Eatonsville
Pillar Valley
Minnie Water
Lake Hiawatha
Wooli
North Solitary Island
Red Rock
Corindi Beach
Arrawarra
Mullaway
Woolgoolga
Sandy Beach
Emerald Beach
Moonee Beach
Korora
Coffs Harbour
MUTTONBIRD ISLAND NR
Boambee
Sawtell
Bonville
BONGIL BONGIL NATIONAL PARK
Mylestom
Raleigh
Urunga
Valla Beach
Hyland Park
Nambucca Heads
Scotts Head
Warrell Creek
Stuarts Point
Trial Bay Gaol
South West Rocks
Jerseyville
HAT HEAD NP
Kinchela
Smithtown
Gladstone
Hat Head
Kempsey
Crescent Head
Kundabung
LIMEBURNERS CREEK NR
Point Plomer
Port Macquarie
LAKE INNES NATURE RESERVE
Wauchope
Lake Cathie
Bonny Hills
North Haven
Dunbogan
Laurieton
CROWDY BAY NATIONAL PARK
Crowdy Head
Harrington
Taree
Purfleet
Coopernook
Moorland
Lansdowne
Johns River
Kendall
Kew
Herons Creek
Telegraph Point
Pembroke
Beechwood
Long Flat
Ellenborough
Byabarra
Bagnoo
Comboyne
Elands
Ellenborough Falls
Bobin
Killabakh
Marlee
Wingham
Tinonee
Burrell Creek
Mount George
Kimbriki
Bundook
Macksville
Bowraville
Taylors Arm
Bellbrook
Eungai Creek
Willawarrin
Frederickton
Green Hill
Bellingen
Dorrigo
DORRIGO NATIONAL PARK
Hernani
Ebor
Ebor Falls
Point Lookout
NEW ENGLAND NATIONAL PARK
CATHEDRAL ROCK NP
Wollomombi
Wollomombi Falls
Hillgrove
Armidale
Uralla
Dangars Falls
Kentucky
Walcha
Walcha Road
Woolbrook
Bendemeer
Moonbi
Kootingal
Tamworth
Attunga
Moore Creek
Nemingha
Dungowan
Woolomin
Niangala
Nundle
Wallabadah
Ardglen
Blandford
Ellerston
Moonan Flat
Tomalla
Nowendoc
Mount Seaview
Yarrowitch
Brackendale
Tia
Tia Falls
Apsley Falls
OXLEY WILD RIVERS NATIONAL PARK
WERRIKIMBE NATIONAL PARK
WILLI WILLI NATIONAL PARK
KUMBATINE NP
Kangaroo Flat
Moona Plains
Lower Creek
Comara
Guyra
Black Mountain
Llangothlin
Ben Lomond
Glencoe
Glen Innes
Deepwater
Dundee
Emmaville
Wellingrove
Inverell
Elsmore
Gilgai
Stannifer
Tingha
Bundarra
Delungra
Ashford
Bukkulla
Graman
Texas
Bonshaw
Mingoola
Inglewood
Karara
Warwick
Yangan
Killarney
Tannymorel
Queen Mary Falls
Legume
Woodenbong
Urbenville
Mulli Mulli
Tooloom
TOOLOOM NP
Old Bonalbo
Bonalbo
Mummulgum
Casino
Tabulam
Drake
Tenterfield
Liston
Stanthorpe
Applethorpe
The Summit
Thulimbah
Cottonvale
Dalveen
Braeside
Pozieres
Amiens
Severnlea
Glen Aplin
Ballandean
Wallangarra
GIRRAWEEN NP
SUNDOWN NP
BOONOO BOONOO NATIONAL PARK
BALD ROCK NP
Boonoo Boonoo Falls
Kyogle
Wiangaree
Cawongla
Rukenvale
Toonumbar
Ettrick
Fairy Hill
Bentley
Georgica
Rathdowney
Maroon
Kyogle
Mallanganee
MALLANGANEE NP
Coombell
Rappville
Camira Creek
Whiporie
Lawrence Road
Baryulgil
Jackadgery
Coutts Crossing
Waterview Heights
Power Station
Nymboida
Glenreagh
Coramba
Ulong
Lowanna
Dundurrabin
Nana Glen
Safety Beach
Corindi
WASHPOOL NATIONAL PARK
GIBRALTAR RANGE NP
NYMBOIDA NATIONAL PARK
GUY FAWKES RIVER NATIONAL PARK
MANN RIVER NATURE RESERVE
Red Range
Mole River
Torrington
Stannum
Bolivia
QUEENSLAND
NEW SOUTH WALES
GREAT DIVIDING RANGE
NEW ENGLAND
SOUTH PACIFIC OCEAN
Kingstown
Yarrowyck
Thunderbolt's Cave
Balancing Rock Formations
KINGS PLAINS NATIONAL PARK
MOUNT YARROWYCK NR
SEVEN SISTERS
THE BASIN NATURE RESERVE
IRONBARK NATURE RESERVE
LINTON NR
WARRABAH NP
WATSONS CREEK NR
BEN HALLS GAP NP
WOKO NATIONAL PARK
MUMMEL GULF NATIONAL PARK
Copeton Dam
Pindari Dam
Glen Lyon Dam
Coolmunda Reservoir
Leslie Dam
Chaffey Reservoir
COTTAN-BIMBANG NP
TAPIN TOPS NP
CAMELS HUMP NR
BORDER RANGES NP
MT WARNING NP
NIGHTCAP NP
MT BARNEY NP
MAIN RANGE NATIONAL PARK
LAMINGTON NP
Springbrook
Chillingham
Tyalgum
Uki
The Risk
RICHMOND RANGE NP
BUNGAWALBIN NP
FORTIS CREEK NP
BANYABBA NR
CHAELUNDI NP
HORTONS CREEK NR
NYMBOI-BINDERAY NP
CASCADE NP
BINDARRI NP
BELLINGER RIVER NP
DUNGGIR NP
GWYDIR HWY
NEW ENGLAND HWY
PACIFIC HWY
OXLEY HWY
WATERFALL WAY
THUNDERBOLTS WAY
N

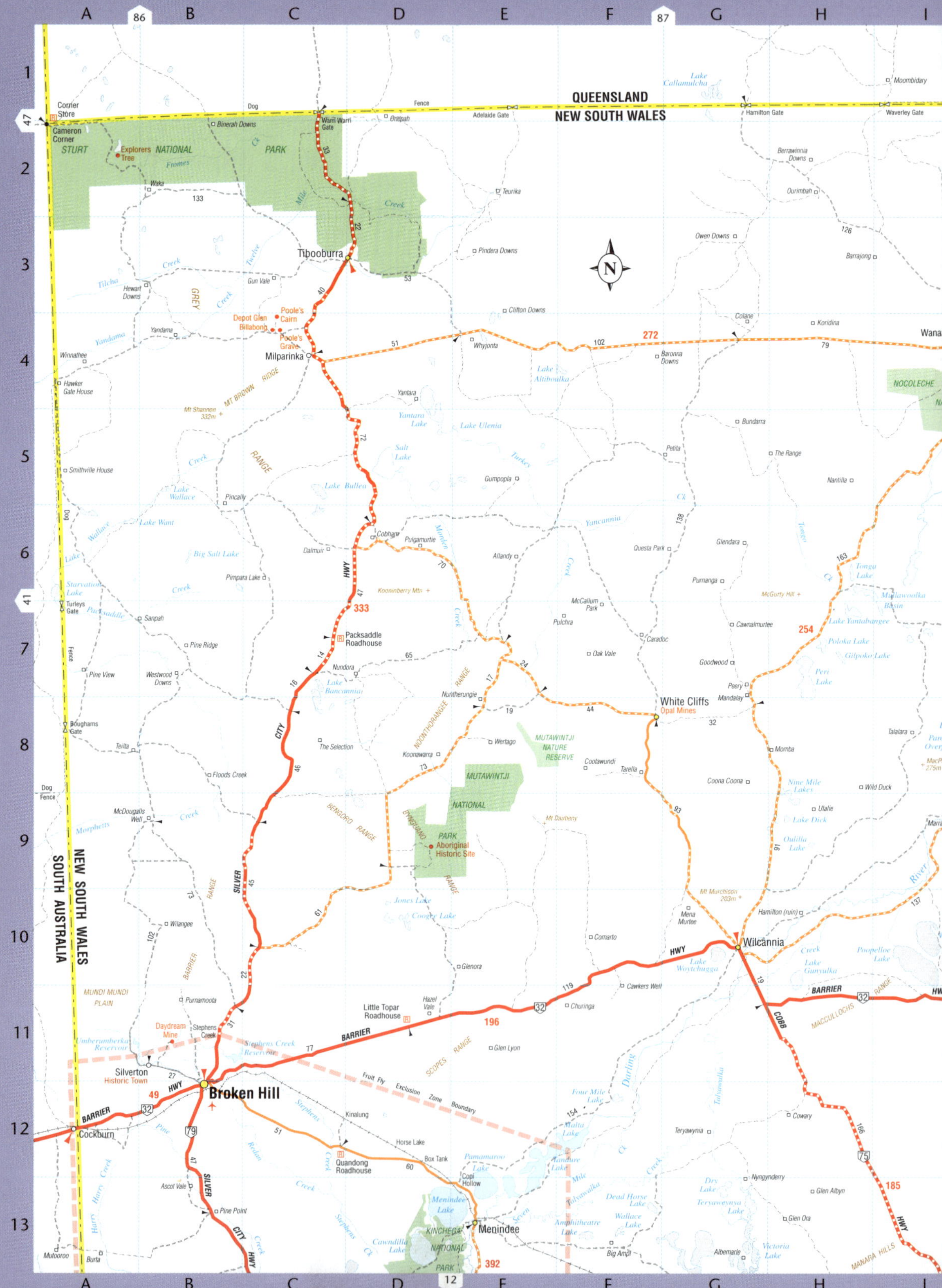
QUEENSLAND
NEW SOUTH WALES
SOUTH AUSTRALIA
Cameron Corner
Corner Store
STURT NATIONAL PARK
Explorers Tree
Waka
Binerah Downs
Warri Warri Gate
Dog Fence
Adelaide Gate
Hamilton Gate
Waverley Gate
Moombidary
Lake Callamulcha
Berrawinnia Downs
Ourimbah
Teurika
Owen Downs
Barrajong
Pindera Downs
Tibooburra
Hewart Downs
Gun Vale
Depot Glen Billabong
Poole's Cairn
Poole's Grave
Yandama
Winnathee
Milparinka
Clifton Downs
Colane
Koridina
Whyjonta
272
Baronna Downs
Wanaaring
NOCOLECHE
Hawker Gate House
MT BROWN RIDGE
Mt Shannon 332m
Yantara
Yantara Lake
Lake Ulenia
Lake Altiboulka
Bundarra
The Range
Smithville House
RANGE
Salt Lake
Petita
Gumpopla
Nantilla
Lake Bullea
Lake Wallace
Pincally
Lake Want
Yancannia
Cobham
Pulgamurtie
Dalmuir
Allandy
Questa Park
Glendara
Big Salt Lake
Pimpara Lake
Tonga Lake
Starvation Lake
Kooninberry Mtn
333
Purnanga
McGurty Hill
Mullawoolka Basin
Turleys Gate
Sanpah
Pulchra
McCallum Park
Cawnalmurtee
254
Lake Yantabangee
Caradoc
Packsaddle Roadhouse
Pine Ridge
Oak Vale
Poloka Lake
Gilpoko Lake
Nundora
Goodwood
Pine View
Westwood Downs
Lake Bancannia
Nuntherungie
Peri Lake
Peery
Mandalay
White Cliffs
Opal Mines
Boughams Gate
NOONTHORANGEE RANGE
Wertago
MUTAWINTJI NATURE RESERVE
Cootawundi
Tarella
Momba
Talalara
Teilta
The Selection
Koonawarra
Coona Coona
Wild Duck
Floods Creek
MUTAWINTJI NATIONAL PARK
Nine Mile Lakes
Dog Fence
McDougalls Well
BENGORO RANGE
Mt Daubeny
Ulalie
Lake Dick
Morphetts
Aboriginal Historic Site
Oulilla Lake
Mt Murchison 203m
Jones Lake
Coogee Lake
Hamilton (ruin)
Mena Murtee
Wilangee
Comarto
Wilcannia
Glenora
Lake Woytchugga
Poopelloe Lake
Lake Gunyulka
MUNDI MUNDI PLAIN
Purnamoota
Cawkers Well
BARRIER
Churinga
Little Topar Roadhouse
Hazel Vale
196
MACCULLOCHS RANGE
Daydream Mine
Stephens Creek
Stephens Creek Reservoir
Umberumberka Reservoir
Glen Lyon
SCOPES RANGE
Silverton Historic Town
Fruit Fly Exclusion Zone Boundary
Broken Hill
Four Mile Lake
Darling
Coway
Cockburn
Kinalung
Horse Lake
Malta Lake
Teryawynia
Quandong Roadhouse
Box Tank
Pamamaroo Lake
Tandure Lake
Copi Hollow
Nyngynderry
Glen Albyn
185
Ascot Vale
Menindee Lake
Dead Horse Lake
Dry Lake
Teryaweynya Lake
Glen Ora
Pine Point
KINCHEGA NATIONAL PARK
Menindee
Wallace Lake
Amphitheatre Lake
Cawndilla Lake
Victoria Lake
Big Ampi
Albemarle
MANARA HILLS
Mutooroo
Burta
392
SILVER CITY HWY
BARRIER HWY
COBB HWY
A B C D E F G H I
1 2 3 4 5 6 7 8 9 10 11 12 13

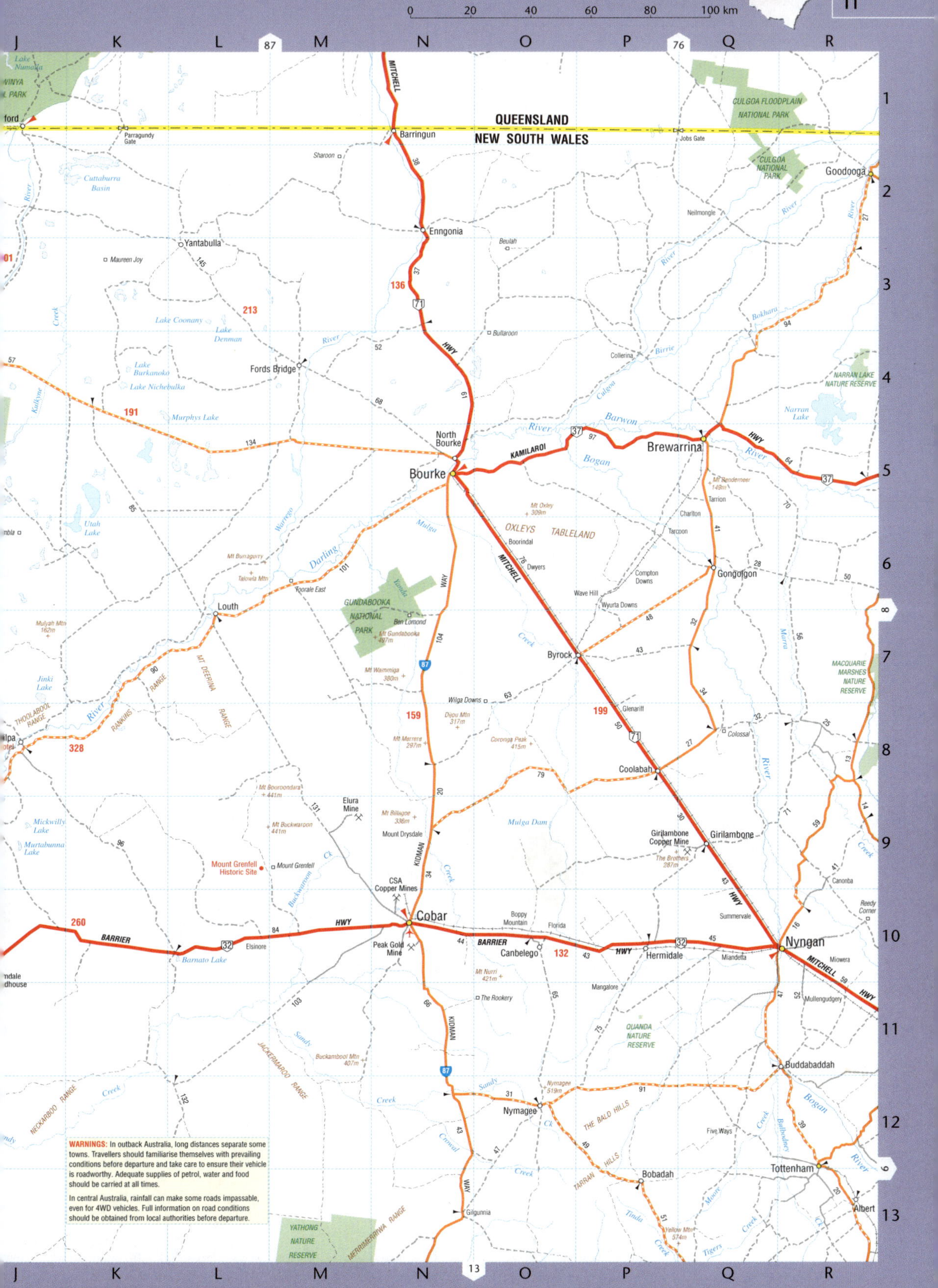
0 20 40 60 80 100 km
QUEENSLAND
NEW SOUTH WALES
Barringun
Parragundy Gate
Jobs Gate
CULGOA FLOODPLAIN NATIONAL PARK
CULGOA NATIONAL PARK
Goodooga
Sharoon
Cuttaburra Basin
Neilmongle
Enngonia
Yantabulla
Maureen Joy
Beulah
Lake Coonany
Lake Denman
Bullaroon
Collerina
Fords Bridge
Lake Burkanoko
Lake Nichebulka
Murphys Lake
NARRAN LAKE NATURE RESERVE
Narran Lake
North Bourke
Bourke
KAMILAROI
Brewarrina
Barwon River
Bogan
Mt Bendemeer 149m
Tarrion
Charlton
Tarcoon
Mt Oxley 309m
OXLEYS TABLELAND
Boorindal
Dwyers
Utah Lake
Darling
Mt Burragorry
Talowia Mtn
Toorale East
GUNDABOOKA NATIONAL PARK
Ben Lomond
Mt Gundabooka 497m
Louth
Compton Downs
Wave Hill
Wyurta Downs
Gongolgon
Mulyah Mtn 162m
Byrock
MACQUARIE MARSHES NATURE RESERVE
Jinki Lake
MT DEERINA RANGE
RANKINS RANGE
THOOLABOOL RANGE
Mt Wammiga 380m
Wilga Downs
Glenariff
Dijou Mtn 317m
Mt Merrere 297m
Coronga Peak 415m
Colossal
Coolabah
Mt Booroondara 441m
Mt Buckwaroon 441m
Elura Mine
Mt Billagoe 336m
Mount Drysdale
Mulga Dam
Mickwilly Lake
Murtabunna Lake
Girilambone Copper Mine
Girilambone
The Brothers 287m
Mount Grenfell Historic Site
Mount Grenfell
CSA Copper Mines
Cobar
Canonba
Reedy Corner
Summervale
Boppy Mountain
Florida
BARRIER HWY
KIDMAN WAY
MITCHELL HWY
Elsinore
Barnato Lake
Peak Gold Mine
Canbelego
Hermidale
Miandetta
Nyngan
Miowera
Mt Nurri 421m
The Rookery
Mangalore
Mullengudgery
QUANDA NATURE RESERVE
JACKERMAROO RANGE
Buckambool Mtn 407m
Buddabaddah
NECKARBOO RANGE
Nymagee 519m
Nymagee
THE BALD HILLS
Five Ways
TARRAN HILLS
Bobadah
Tottenham
Albert
Gilgunnia
YATHONG NATURE RESERVE
MERRIMERRIWA RANGE
Yellow Mtn 574m
WARNINGS: In outback Australia, long distances separate some towns. Travellers should familiarise themselves with prevailing conditions before departure and take care to ensure their vehicle is roadworthy. Adequate supplies of petrol, water and food should be carried at all times.
In central Australia, rainfall can make some roads impassable, even for 4WD vehicles. Full information on road conditions should be obtained from local authorities before departure.

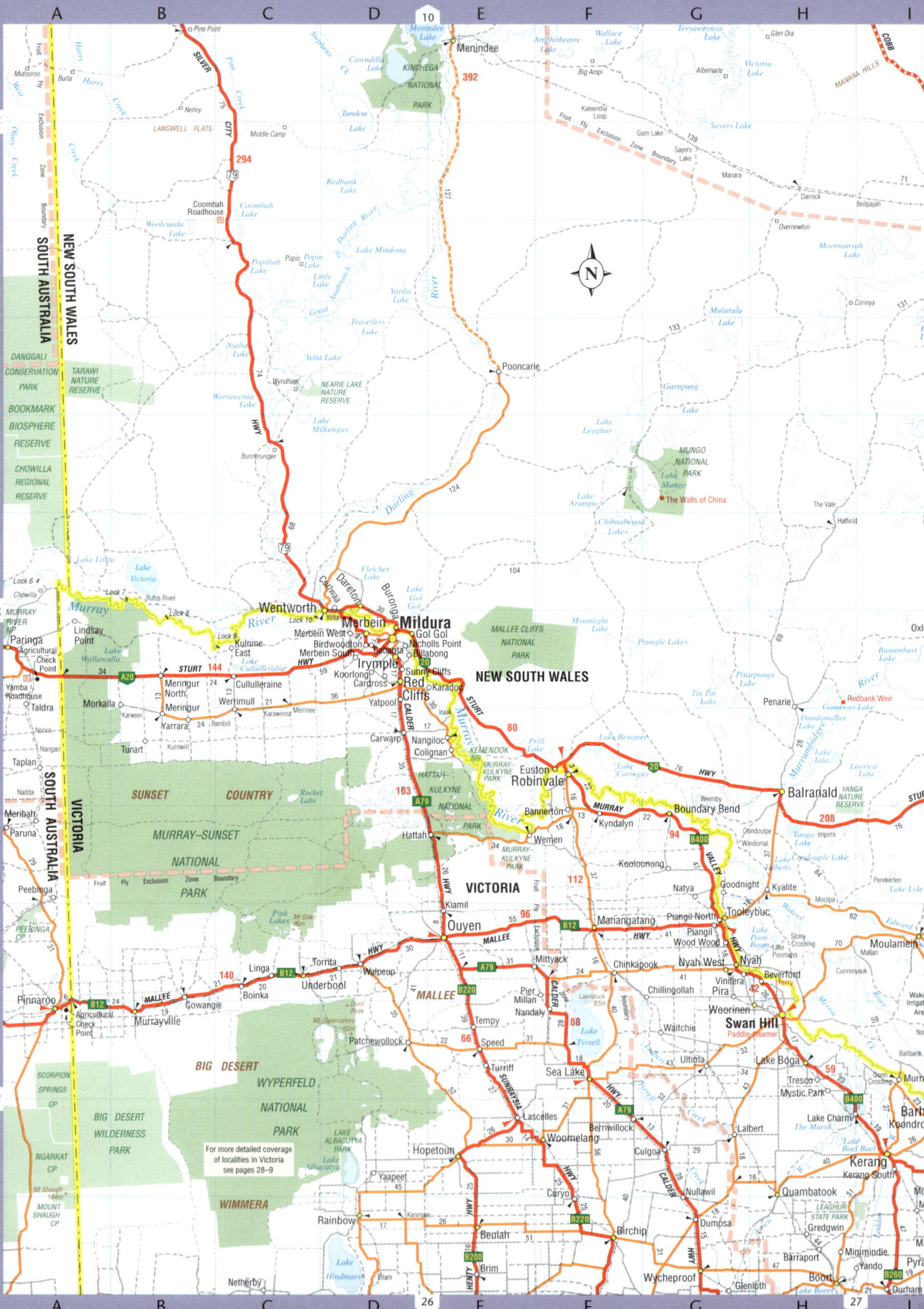

For more detailed coverage of localities in Victoria see pages 28–9

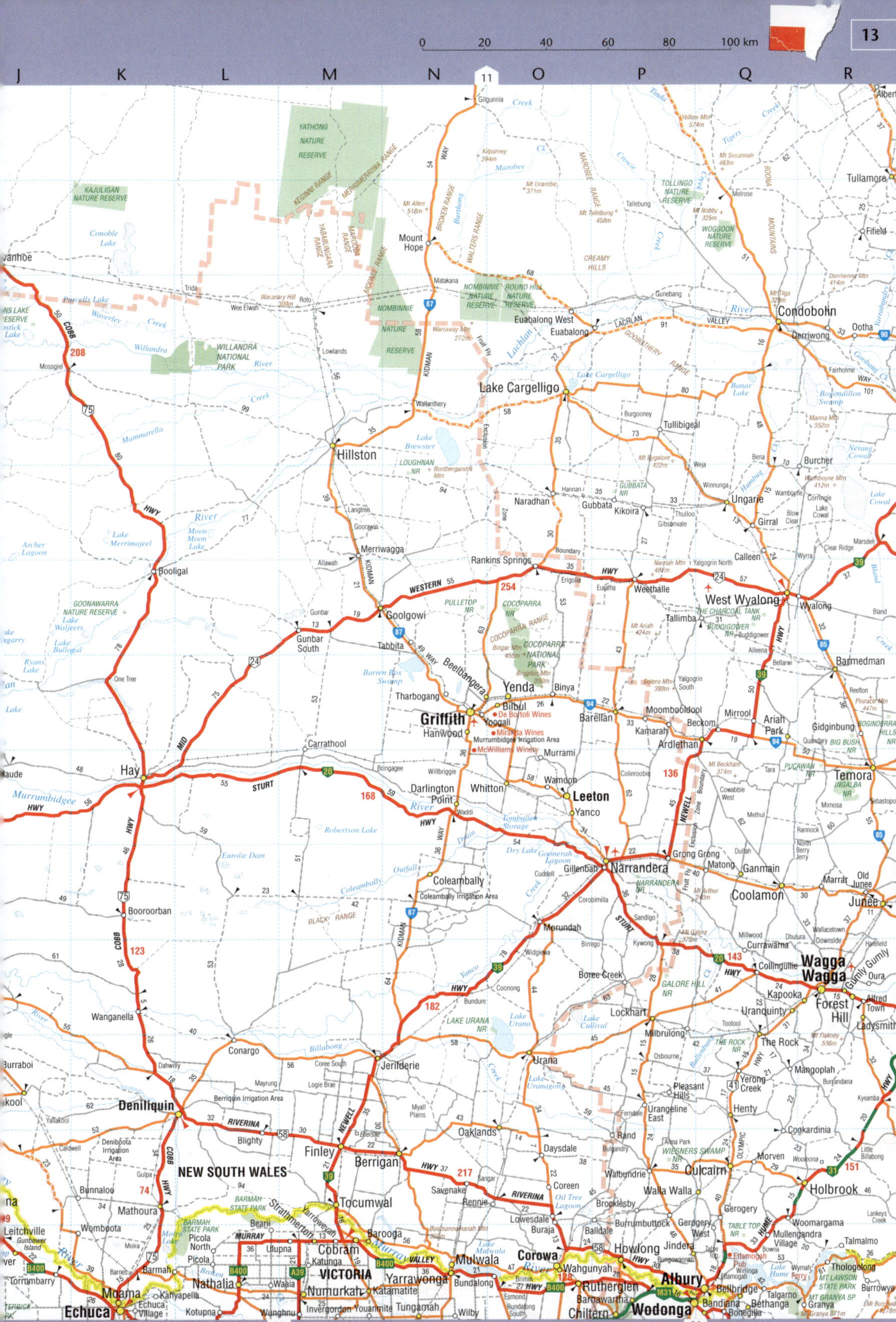
0 20 40 60 80 100 km
J K L M N O P Q R
1 2 3 4 5 6 7 8 9 10 11 12 13
11
30
31
Gilgunnia
Albert
Tullamore
Fifield
Condobolin
Derriwong
Ootha
Melrose
Tallebung
Mount Hope
Ivanhoe
Trida
Wee Elwah
Roto
Matakana
Euabalong West
Euabalong
Gunebang
Mossgiel
Lowlands
Wallanthery
Lake Cargelligo
Burgooney
Tullibigeal
Hillston
Langtree
Goorawin
Merriwagga
Allawah
Naradhan
Hannan
Gubbata
Kikoira
Ungarie
Girral
Burcher
Weja
Bena
Winnunga
Thulloo
Gibsonvale
Wamboyne
Corringle
Lake Cowal
Blow Clear
Clear Ridge
Marsden
Calleen
Wyrra
Booligal
Boundary
Rankins Springs
Erigolia
Euratha
Weethalle
Yalgogrin North
West Wyalong
Wyalong
Bland
Tallimba
Buddigower
Alleena
Gunbar
Goolgowi
Gunbar South
Tabbita
Bellarwi
Barmedman
One Tree
Beelbangera
Yenda
Binya
Yalgogrin South
Reefton
Tharbogang
Griffith
Bilbul
Yoogali
Hanwood
Barellan
Moombooldool
Kamarah
Beckom
Ardlethan
Mirrool
Ariah Park
Gidginbung
Quandary
Temora
Carrathool
Murrami
Hay
Maude
Bringagee
Willbriggie
Darlington Point
Whitton
Wamoon
Leeton
Yanco
Waddi
Colinroobie
Cowabbie West
Methul
Mimosa
Sebastopol
Tara
Rannock
North Berry Jerry
Narrandera
Gillenbah
Grong Grong
Matong
Ganmain
Coolamon
Marrar
Old Junee
Junee
Coleambally
Cuddell
Corobimilla
Sandigo
Booroorban
Morundah
Birrego
Kywong
Millwood
Currawarna
Dhulura
Wallacetown
Downside
Harefield
Collingullie
Wagga Wagga
Gumly Gumly
Oura
Widgiewa
Boree Creek
Kapooka
Uranquinty
Forest Hill
Alfred Town
Ladysmith
Coonong
Bundure
Wanganella
Lockhart
Milbrulong
Tootool
The Rock
Conargo
Dahwilly
Jerilderie
Coree South
Urana
Osborne
Mangoplah
Burrandana
Mayrung
Logie Brae
Pleasant Hills
Yerong Creek
Kyeamba
Deniliquin
Berriquin Irrigation Area
Myall Plains
Urangeline East
Henty
Yallakool
Blighty
Oaklands
Ferndale
Cookardinia
Caldwell
Deniboota Irrigation Area
Finley
Berrigan
Daysdale
Bulgandry
Alma Park
Culcairn
Morven
Little Billabong
Gulpa
NEW SOUTH WALES
Sangar
Walbundrie
Walla Walla
Woomahgarma
Holbrook
Bunnaloo
Tocumwal
Savernake
Rennie
Coreen
Brocklesby
Gerogery
Mathoura
Wombooota
Lowesdale
Buraja
Balldale
Burrumbuttock
Gerogery West
Woomargama
Mullengandra Village
Lankeys Creek
Talmalmo
Leitchville
Moira
Picola North
Picola
Bearii
Strathmerton
Barooga
Cobram
Ulupna
Katunga
Mulwala
Corowa
Wahgunyah
Howlong
Jindera
Table Top
Bowna
Thologolong
Torrumbarry
Barnes
Barmah
Nathalia
Waaia
VICTORIA
Yarrawonga
Bundalong
Brimin
Rutherglen
Albury
Wirlinga
Ettamogah
Bellbridge
Talgarno
Burrowye
Moama
Kanyapella
Numurkah
Katamatite
Esmond
Barnawartha
Bethanga
Granya
Echuca
Echuca Village
Kotupna
Wunghnu
Invergordon
Youanmite
Tungamah
Wilby
Chiltern
Wodonga
Bandiana
Bonegilla
Murrumbidgee
Lachlan River
Murray River
Willandra Creek
Mammarella
Conoble Lake
Purcells Lake
Waverley Creek
Lake Merrimajeel
Archer Lagoon
Lake Waljeers
Lake Bullogal
Ryans Lake
Lake Brewster
Barren Box Swamp
Robertson Lake
Eurolie Dam
Tombullen Storage
Dry Lake
Gooenah Lagoon
Lake Urana
Lake Cullival
Lake Uranagong
Oil Tree Lagoon
Lake Mulwala
Lake Hume
Billabong
Banar Lake
Bogandillon Swamp
Nerang Cowal
YATHONG NATURE RESERVE
KAJULIGAN NATURE RESERVE
NOMBINNIE NATURE RESERVE
NOMBINNIE NATURE RESERVE
ROUND HILL NATURE RESERVE
TOLLINGO NATURE RESERVE
WOGGOON NATURE RESERVE
WILLANDRA NATIONAL PARK
GOONAWARRA NATURE RESERVE
LOUGHNAN NR
GUBBATA NR
PULLETOP NR
COCOPARRA NR
COCOPARRA NATIONAL PARK
THE CHARCOAL TANK NR
BUDDIGOWER NR
BOGINDERRA HILLS NR
BIG BUSH NR
PUCAWAN NR
INGALBA NR
NARRANDERA NR
GALORE HILL NR
LAKE URANA NR
THE ROCK NR
WIESNERS SWAMP NR
TABLE TOP NR
BARMAH STATE PARK
MT LAWSON STATE PARK
MT GRANYA SP
KEGINNI RANGE
MERRIMERRIWA RANGE
YABABUNGARA RANGE
BROKEN RANGE
WALTERS RANGE
MAROBEE RANGE
BOONA MOUNTAINS
CREAMY HILLS
GOOBOTHERY RANGE
COCOPARRA RANGE
BLACK RANGE
Mt Allen 518m
Kilparney 294m
Mt Urambie 371m
Mt Tallebung 458m
Mt Nobby 325m
Yellow Mtn 574m
Mt Sussannah 483m
Warraway Hill 309m
Warraway Mtn 272m
Mt Bygalore 422m
Mt Ariah 424m
Bingar Mtn 455m
Brogden Mtn 399m
Bolero Mtn 399m
Mt Beckham 374m
Pinnacle Mtn 447m
Mt Arthur 240m
Mt Galore 379m
Mt Flakney 536m
Derriwong Mtn 414m
Mt Tilga 328m
Manna Mtn 552m
Wamboyne Mtn 412m
Narriah Mtn 487m
De Bortoli Wines
Miranda Wines
McWilliams Winery
Murrumbidgee Irrigation Area
Coleambally Irrigation Area
Ettamogah Pub
Wymah Ferry
COBB HWY
KIDMAN WAY
LACHLAN VALLEY WAY
WESTERN HWY
MID WESTERN HWY
STURT HWY
NEWELL HWY
OLYMPIC HWY
HUME HWY
RIVERINA HWY
MURRAY VALLEY HWY
Fruit Fly Exclusion Zone
208 254 168 136 143 123 182 74 217 128 151

0 20 40 60 80 100 km
A B C D E F G H I
1 2 3 4 5 6 7 8 9 10 11 12 13
Grenfell
Young
Temora
Cootamundra
Junee
Harden
Murrumburrah
Boorowa
Yass
Gundagai
Tumut
Goulburn
Crookwell
Marulan
Mittagong
Bowral
Moss Vale
Bundanoon
Picton
Warragamba
Silverdale
Berry
Nowra
Bomaderry
Huskisson
Vincentia
Sanctuary Pt
Sussex Inlet
Ulladulla
Milton
Burrill Lake
CANBERRA
Queanbeyan
ACT
Murrumbateman
Bungendore
Braidwood
Captains Flat
Batemans Bay
Moruya
Narooma
Bermagui
Bega
Tathra
Merimbula
Pambula
Eden
Bombala
Cooma
Berridale
Jindabyne
Thredbo
Khancoban
Corryong
Tumbarumba
Batlow
Talbingo
Adaminaby
Cabramurra
Delegate
Cann River
Mallacoota
Genoa
Omeo
Swifts Creek
Tambo Crossing
Buchan
Forest Hill
Tarcutta
Adelong
Coolac
Jugiong
NEW SOUTH WALES
VICTORIA
KOSCIUSZKO NATIONAL PARK
NAMADGI NATIONAL PARK
DEUA NATIONAL PARK
WADBILLIGA NATIONAL PARK
MORTON NATIONAL PARK
ALPINE NATIONAL PARK
SNOWY RIVER NATIONAL PARK
ERRINUNDRA NATIONAL PARK
BEN BOYD NATIONAL PARK
CROAJINGOLONG NATIONAL PARK
EAST GIPPSLAND
SOUTH PACIFIC OCEAN
TASMAN SEA
HUME HWY
FEDERAL HWY
MONARO HWY
PRINCES HWY
SNOWY MOUNTAINS HWY
Lake Eucumbene
Lake Jindabyne
Lake George
Mt Kosciuszko 2228m
Cape Howe
Green Cape
For more detail on Canberra & Surrounds see pages 16–17
6
13
32
33

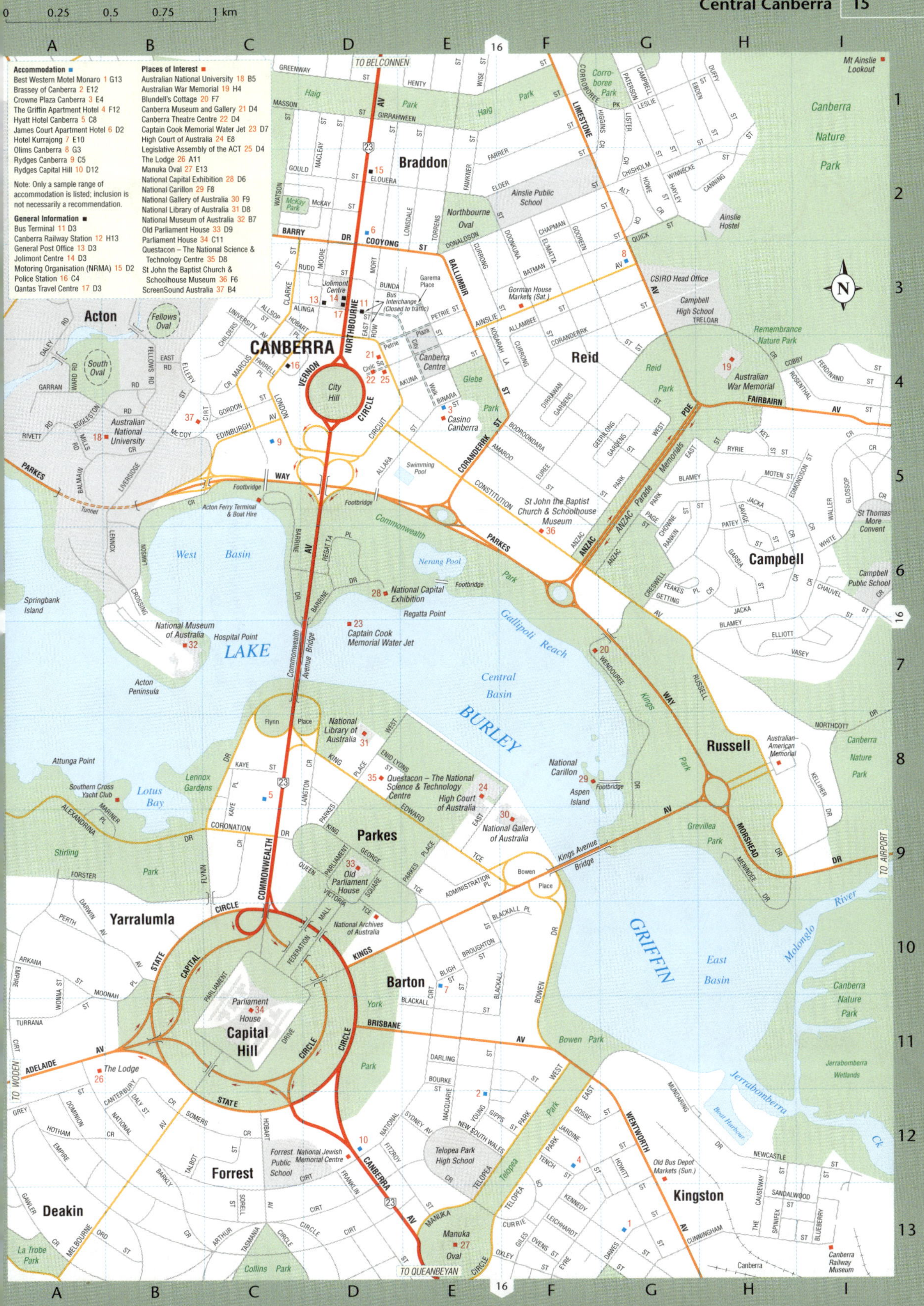
0 0.25 0.5 0.75 1 km
Accommodation
Best Western Motel Monaro 1 G13
Brassey of Canberra 2 E12
Crowne Plaza Canberra 3 E4
The Griffin Apartment Hotel 4 F12
Hyatt Hotel Canberra 5 C8
James Court Apartment Hotel 6 D2
Hotel Kurrajong 7 E10
Olims Canberra 8 G3
Rydges Canberra 9 C5
Rydges Capital Hill 10 D12
Note: Only a sample range of accommodation is listed; inclusion is not necessarily a recommendation.
General Information
Bus Terminal 11 D3
Canberra Railway Station 12 H13
General Post Office 13 D3
Jolimont Centre 14 D3
Motoring Organisation (NRMA) 15 D2
Police Station 16 C4
Qantas Travel Centre 17 D3
Places of Interest
Australian National University 18 B5
Australian War Memorial 19 H4
Blundell's Cottage 20 F7
Canberra Museum and Gallery 21 D4
Canberra Theatre Centre 22 D4
Captain Cook Memorial Water Jet 23 D7
High Court of Australia 24 E8
Legislative Assembly of the ACT 25 D4
The Lodge 26 A11
Manuka Oval 27 E13
National Capital Exhibition 28 D6
National Carillon 29 F8
National Gallery of Australia 30 F9
National Library of Australia 31 D8
National Museum of Australia 32 B7
Old Parliament House 33 D9
Parliament House 34 C11
Questacon – The National Science & Technology Centre 35 D8
St John the Baptist Church & Schoolhouse Museum 36 F6
ScreenSound Australia 37 B4
TO BELCONNEN
Braddon
CANBERRA
City Hill
Acton
Reid
Campbell
Russell
Parkes
Barton
Yarralumla
Capital Hill
Forrest
Deakin
Kingston
Canberra Nature Park
Mt Ainslie Lookout
LAKE BURLEY GRIFFIN
West Basin
Central Basin
East Basin
Gallipoli Reach
Commonwealth Park
Kings Park
Stirling Park
York Park
Bowen Park
Collins Park
Glebe Park
Telopea Park
Haig Park
Grevillea Park
Lennox Gardens
Lotus Bay
Springbank Island
Acton Peninsula
Aspen Island
Regatta Point
Hospital Point
Attunga Point
Commonwealth Avenue Bridge
Kings Avenue Bridge
Molonglo River
Jerrabomberra Wetlands
TO QUEANBEYAN
TO WODEN
TO AIRPORT
Remembrance Nature Park
Canberra Centre
Casino Canberra
National Archives of Australia
Australian-American Memorial
CSIRO Head Office
Campbell High School
Ainslie Public School
Telopea Park High School
Forrest Public School
National Jewish Memorial Centre
St Thomas More Convent
Campbell Public School
Old Bus Depot Markets (Sun.)
Gorman House Markets (Sat.)
Canberra Railway Museum
Ainslie Hostel
Northbourne Oval
Manuka Oval
Fellows Oval
South Oval
Southern Cross Yacht Club
Acton Ferry Terminal & Boat Hire
Nerang Pool
Swimming Pool
Bus Interchange (Closed to traffic)
Garema Place
Jolimont Centre
A B C D E F G H I
1 2 3 4 5 6 7 8 9 10 11 12 13
16

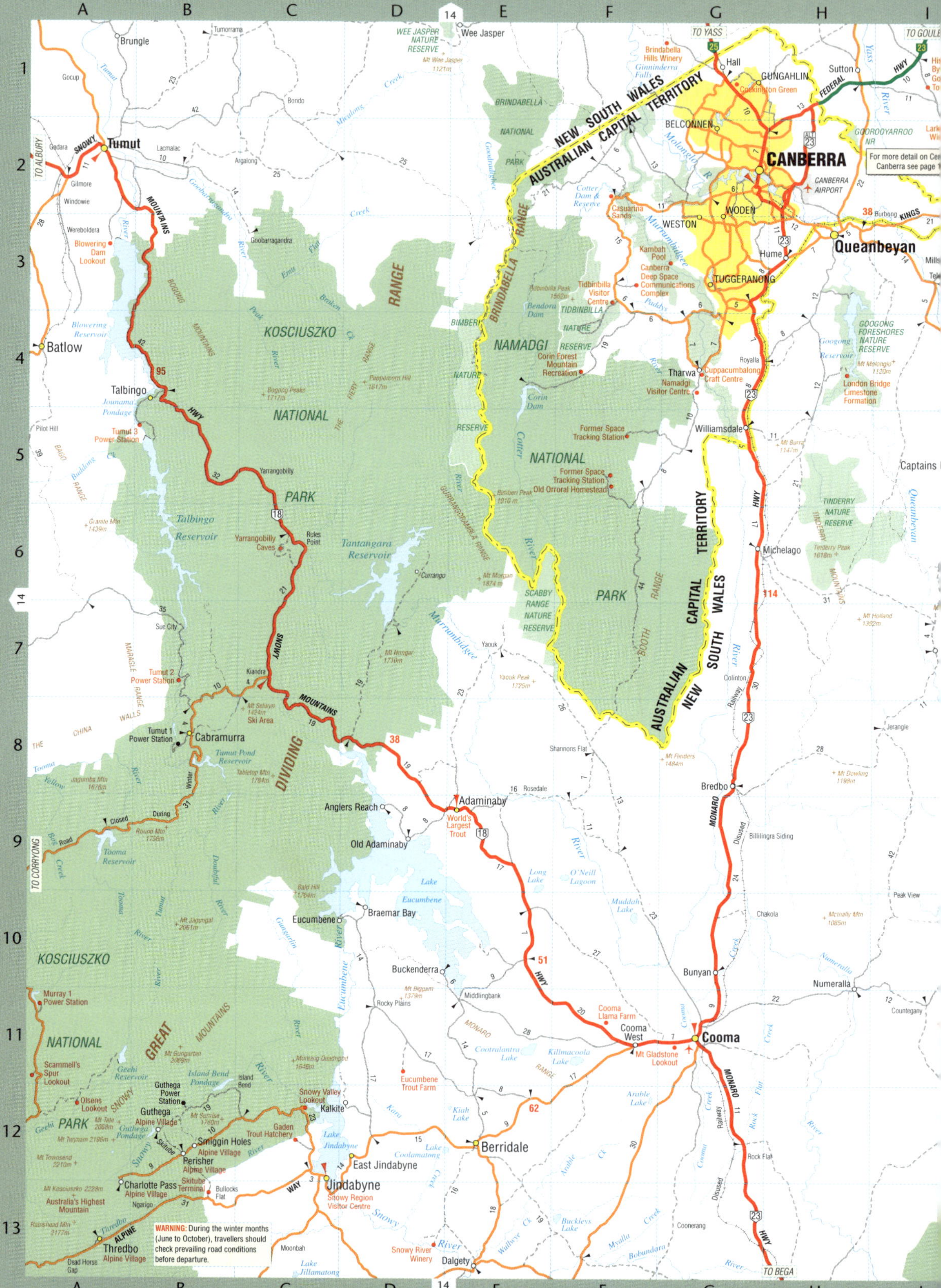

CANBERRA
Queanbeyan
Tumut
Batlow
Talbingo
Cabramurra
Adaminaby
Old Adaminaby
Anglers Reach
Eucumbene
Braemar Bay
Buckenderra
Cooma
Cooma West
Berridale
Jindabyne
East Jindabyne
Dalgety
Thredbo Alpine Village
Perisher Alpine Village
Smiggin Holes Alpine Village
Guthega Alpine Village
Charlotte Pass Alpine Village
Bredbo
Bunyan
Michelago
Williamsdale
Tharwa
Hume
Hall
Sutton
Numeralla
Wee Jasper
Brungle
Kiandra
Yarrangobilly
Rules Point
GUNGAHLIN
BELCONNEN
WESTON
WODEN
TUGGERANONG
CANBERRA AIRPORT
KOSCIUSZKO NATIONAL PARK
NAMADGI NATIONAL PARK
BRINDABELLA NATIONAL PARK
BIMBERI NATURE RESERVE
SCABBY RANGE NATURE RESERVE
TIDBINBILLA NATURE RESERVE
TINDERRY NATURE RESERVE
GOOGONG FORESHORES NATURE RESERVE
WEE JASPER NATURE RESERVE
AUSTRALIAN CAPITAL TERRITORY
NEW SOUTH WALES
Lake Eucumbene
Lake Jindabyne
Talbingo Reservoir
Tantangara Reservoir
Blowering Reservoir
Tooma Reservoir
Tumut Pond Reservoir
Googong Reservoir
Murrumbidgee River
Snowy River
SNOWY MOUNTAINS HWY
MONARO HWY
FEDERAL HWY
KINGS HWY
ALPINE WAY
GREAT DIVIDING RANGE
Yarrangobilly Caves
Mt Selwyn Ski Area
World's Largest Trout
Cooma Llama Farm
Mt Gladstone Lookout
Snowy Region Visitor Centre
Snowy River Winery
Eucumbene Trout Farm
Gaden Trout Hatchery
Skitube Terminal
Canberra Deep Space Communications Complex
Tidbinbilla Visitor Centre
Corin Forest Mountain Recreation
Cuppacumbalong Craft Centre
Namadgi Visitor Centre
Old Orroral Homestead
Former Space Tracking Station
Brindabella Hills Winery
Cockington Green
Mt Kosciuszko 2228m Australia's Highest Mountain
Murray 1 Power Station
Tumut 1 Power Station
Tumut 2 Power Station
Tumut 3 Power Station
Guthega Power Station
London Bridge Limestone Formation
TO YASS
TO GOULBURN
TO ALBURY
TO CORRYONG
TO BEGA
For more detail on Canberra see page 1
WARNING: During the winter months (June to October), travellers should check prevailing road conditions before departure.

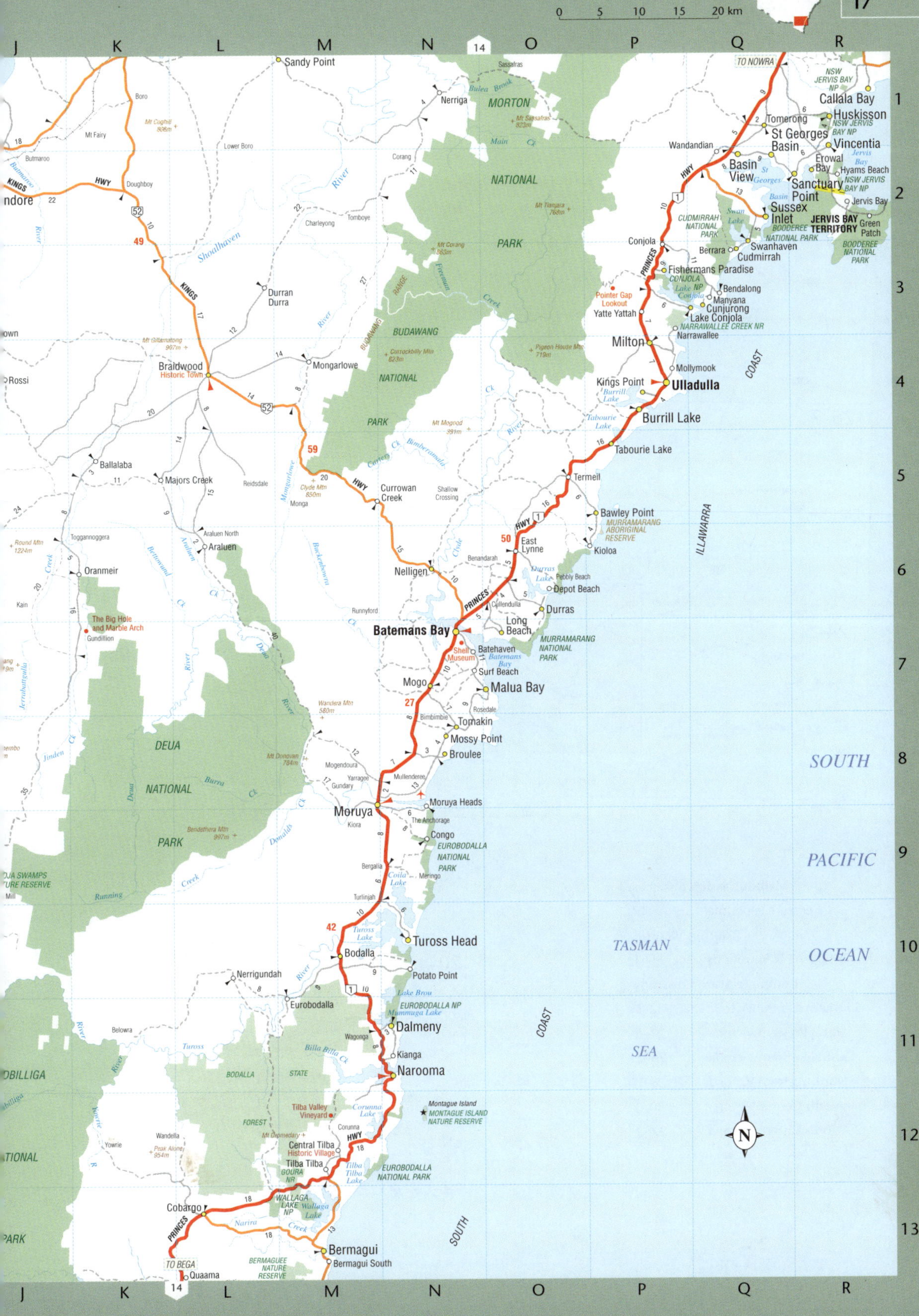
0 5 10 15 20 km
J K L M N O P Q R
14
1 2 3 4 5 6 7 8 9 10 11 12 13
TO NOWRA
TO BEGA
Sandy Point
Sassafras
Bulea Brook
Nerriga
MORTON
Mt Sassafras 823m
Main Ck
NATIONAL
PARK
Mt Tianjara 768m
Boro
Mt Coghill 806m
Mt Fairy
Lower Boro
Corang
Butmaroo
Doughboy
KINGS HWY
ndore
Charleyong
Tomboye
River
Shoalhaven
Mt Corang 863m
Freeman Ck
Creek
RANGE
BUDAWANG
BUDAWANG
NATIONAL
PARK
Durran Durra
Mt Gillamatong 907m
Currockbilly Mtn 823m
Pigeon House Mtn 719m
Braidwood
Historic Town
Mongarlowe
Rossi
Mt Mogrod 391m
Bimberamala
Cabbage Ck
Ballalaba
Majors Creek
Reidsdale
Clyde Mtn 850m
Monga
Mongarlowe
Currowan Creek
Shallow Crossing
Round Mtn 1224m
Toggannoggera
Araluen North
Araluen
Oranmeir
Kain
Nelligen
Benandarah
Runnyford
The Big Hole and Marble Arch
Gundillion
Deua River
Wandera Mtn 580m
DEUA
NATIONAL
PARK
Jinden Ck
Mt Donovan 784m
Burra Ck
Mogendoura
Yarragee
Gundary
Bendethera Mtn 997m
Donalds Ck
Running Creek
Mill
Kiora
Moruya
Mullenderee
Moruya Heads
The Anchorage
Congo
EUROBODALLA NATIONAL PARK
Bergalia
Coila Lake
Meringo
Turlinjah
Tuross Lake
Tuross Head
Bodalla
Potato Point
Nerrigundah
Eurobodalla
Lake Brou
EUROBODALLA NP
Mummuga Lake
Dalmeny
Belowra
Wagonga
Kianga
Narooma
Billa Billa Ck
BODALLA STATE FOREST
Tilba Valley Vineyard
Corunna Lake
Corunna
Mt Dromedary
Montague Island
MONTAGUE ISLAND NATURE RESERVE
Central Tilba Historic Village
Tilba Tilba
GOURA NR
Tilba Tilba Lake
EUROBODALLA NATIONAL PARK
Wandella
Yowrie
Peak Alone 954m
WALLAGA LAKE NP
Wallaga Lake
Cobargo
Narira Creek
Bermagui
Bermagui South
BERMAGUEE NATURE RESERVE
Quaama
PRINCES HWY
Batemans Bay
Shell Museum
Batehaven
Batemans Bay
Surf Beach
Mogo
Malua Bay
Rosedale
Bimbimbie
Tomakin
Mossy Point
Broulee
Cullendulla
Long Beach
Durras
Durras Lake
Pebbly Beach
Depot Beach
MURRAMARANG NATIONAL PARK
East Lynne
Kioloa
Bawley Point
MURRAMARANG ABORIGINAL RESERVE
Termeil
Tabourie Lake
Burrill Lake
Kings Point
Ulladulla
Mollymook
Milton
Narrawallee
NARRAWALLEE CREEK NR
Lake Conjola
Cunjurong
Manyana
Bendalong
CONJOLA NP
Conjola Lake
Fishermans Paradise
Pointer Gap Lookout
Yatte Yattah
Conjola
Berrara
Cudmirrah
Swanhaven
CUDMIRRAH NATIONAL PARK
Swan Lake
Sussex Inlet
Basin View
St Georges Basin
Tomerong
Wandandian
Sanctuary Point
Erowal Bay
Vincentia
Hyams Beach
Huskisson
Callala Bay
NSW JERVIS BAY NP
JERVIS BAY TERRITORY
BOODEREE NATIONAL PARK
Jervis Bay
Green Patch
COAST
ILLAWARRA
SOUTH PACIFIC OCEAN
TASMAN SEA
COAST
SOUTH
N

Victoria

Location Map

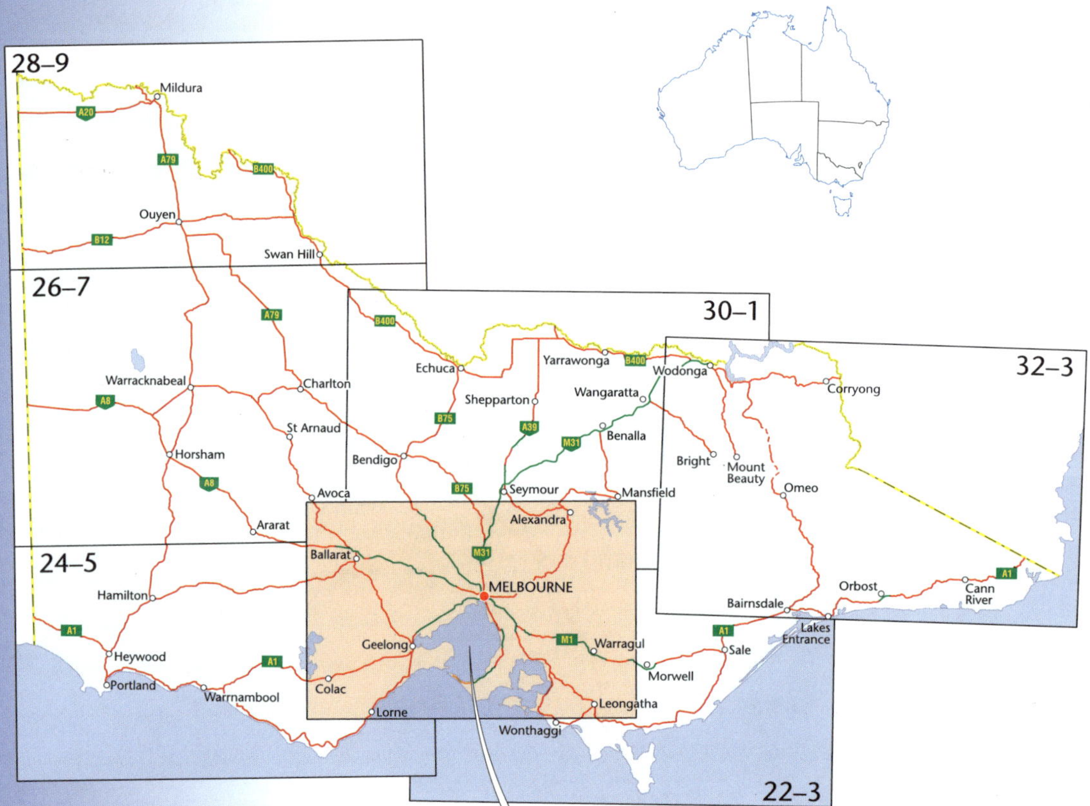

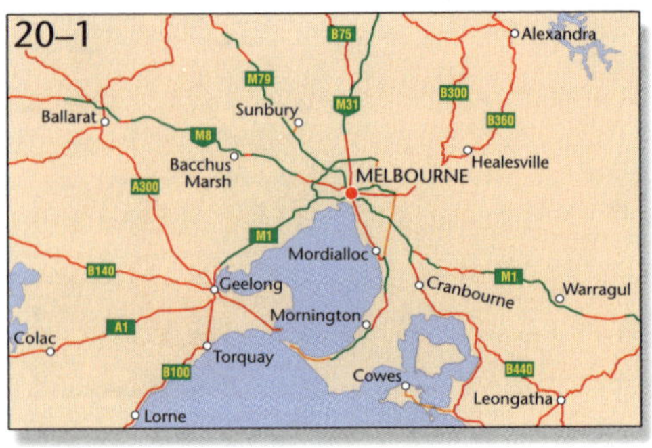

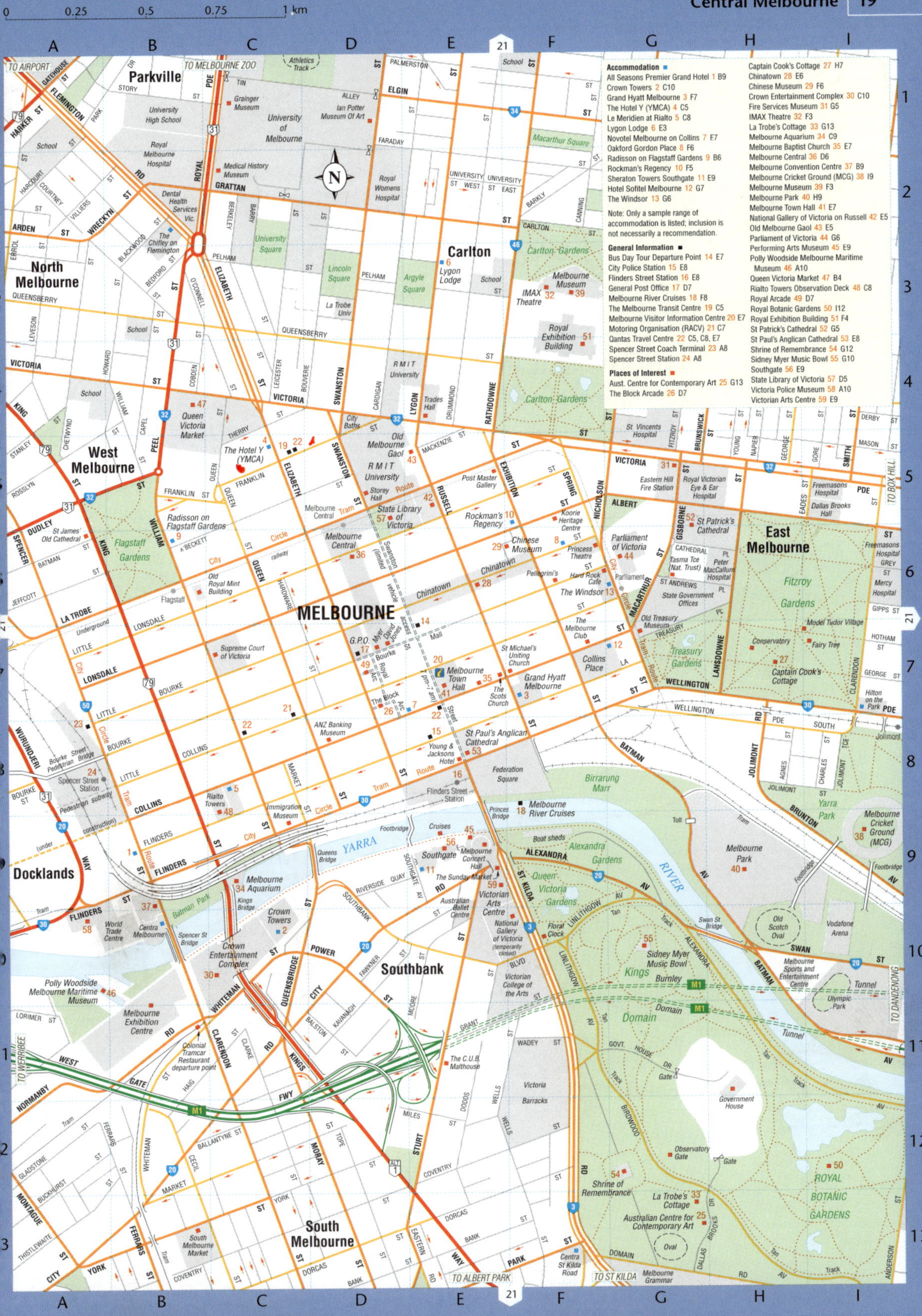
0 0.25 0.5 0.75 1 km
Accommodation
All Seasons Premier Grand Hotel 1 B9
Crown Towers 2 C10
Grand Hyatt Melbourne 3 F7
The Hotel Y (YMCA) 4 C5
Le Meridien at Rialto 5 C8
Lygon Lodge 6 E3
Novotel Melbourne on Collins 7 E7
Oakford Gordon Place 8 F6
Radisson on Flagstaff Gardens 9 B6
Rockman's Regency 10 F5
Sheraton Towers Southgate 11 E9
Hotel Sofitel Melbourne 12 G7
The Windsor 13 G6
Note: Only a sample range of accommodation is listed; inclusion is not necessarily a recommendation.
General Information
Bus Day Tour Departure Point 14 E7
City Police Station 15 E8
Flinders Street Station 16 E8
General Post Office 17 D7
Melbourne River Cruises 18 F8
The Melbourne Transit Centre 19 C5
Melbourne Visitor Information Centre 20 E7
Motoring Organisation (RACV) 21 C7
Qantas Travel Centre 22 C5, C8, E7
Spencer Street Coach Terminal 23 A8
Spencer Street Station 24 A8
Places of Interest
Aust. Centre for Contemporary Art 25 G13
The Block Arcade 26 D7
Captain Cook's Cottage 27 H7
Chinatown 28 E6
Chinese Museum 29 F6
Crown Entertainment Complex 30 C10
Fire Services Museum 31 G5
IMAX Theatre 32 F3
La Trobe's Cottage 33 G13
Melbourne Aquarium 34 C9
Melbourne Baptist Church 35 E7
Melbourne Central 36 D6
Melbourne Convention Centre 37 B9
Melbourne Cricket Ground (MCG) 38 I9
Melbourne Museum 39 F3
Melbourne Park 40 H9
Melbourne Town Hall 41 E7
National Gallery of Victoria on Russell 42 E5
Old Melbourne Gaol 43 E5
Parliament of Victoria 44 G6
Performing Arts Museum 45 E9
Polly Woodside Melbourne Maritime Museum 46 A10
Queen Victoria Market 47 B4
Rialto Towers Observation Deck 48 C8
Royal Arcade 49 D7
Royal Botanic Gardens 50 I12
Royal Exhibition Building 51 F4
St Patrick's Cathedral 52 G5
St Paul's Anglican Cathedral 53 E8
Shrine of Remembrance 54 G12
Sidney Myer Music Bowl 55 G10
Southgate 56 E9
State Library of Victoria 57 D5
Victoria Police Museum 58 A10
Victorian Arts Centre 59 E9
Parkville
Carlton
North Melbourne
West Melbourne
MELBOURNE
East Melbourne
Docklands
Southbank
South Melbourne
University of Melbourne
Carlton Gardens
Flagstaff Gardens
Fitzroy Gardens
Treasury Gardens
Kings Domain
Royal Botanic Gardens
Alexandra Gardens
Queen Victoria Gardens
Birrarung Marr
Yarra Park
Yarra River

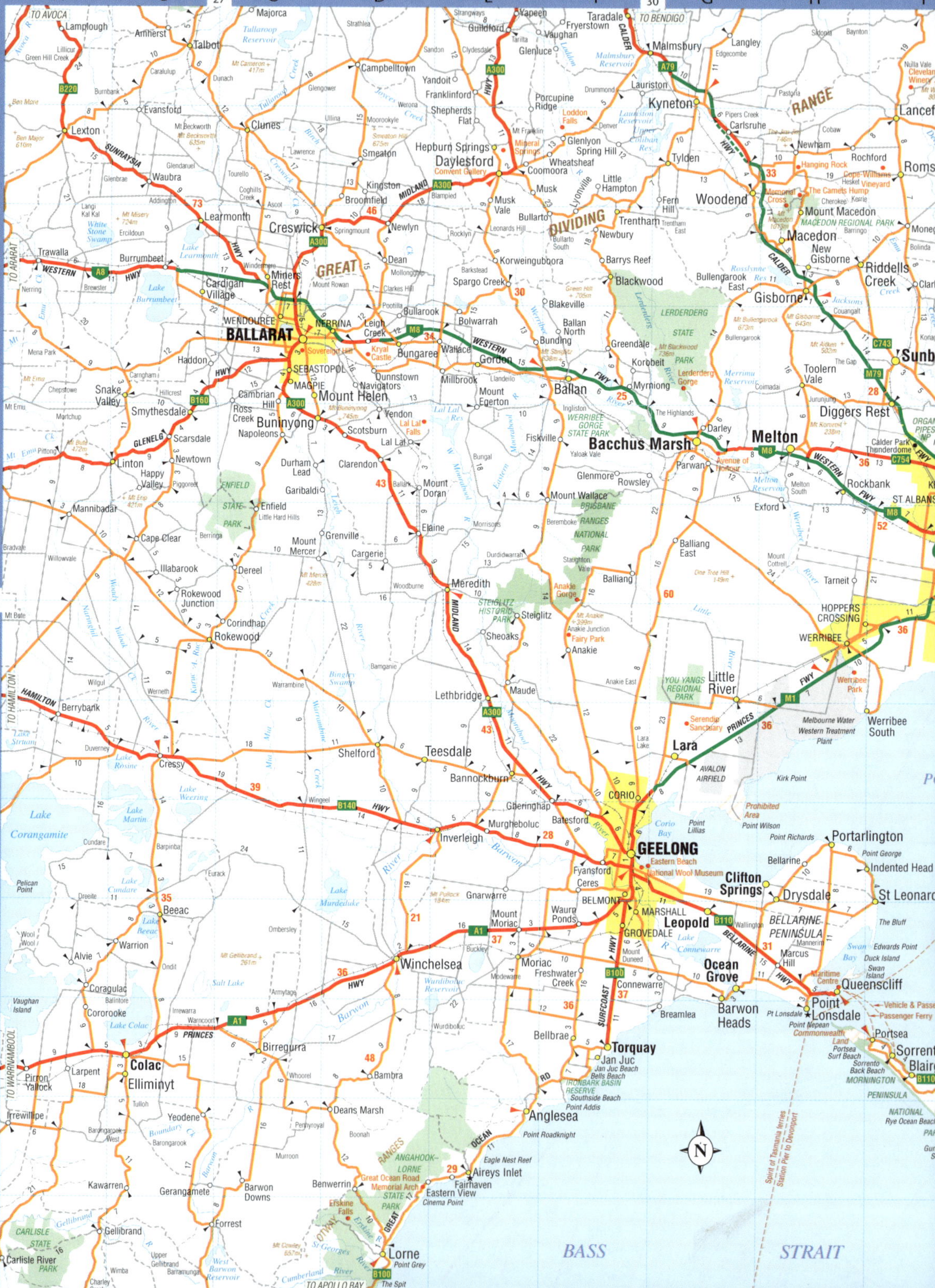
TO AVOCA
Lamplough
Amherst
Talbot
Majorca
Tullaroop Reservoir
Yapeen
Guildford
Fryerstown
Taradale
TO BENDIGO
Malmsbury
Langley
Vaughan
Glenluce
Malmsbury Reservoir
Clydesdale
Campbelltown
Yandoit
Franklinford
Lauriston
Kyneton
Porcupine Ridge
Loddon Falls
Shepherds Flat
Carlsruhe
RANGE
Lancefield
Evansford
Lexton
Clunes
Smeaton
Hepburn Springs
Daylesford
Convent Gallery
Mineral Springs
Glenlyon
Spring Hill
Tylden
Newham
Rochford
Romsey
Hanging Rock
Waubra
Kingston
Coomoora
Wheatshead
Musk
Little Hampton
Woodend
Memorial Cross
The Camels Hump
Mount Macedon
MACEDON REGIONAL PARK
Learmonth
Creswick
Broomfield
Newlyn
Musk Vale
Bullarto
DIVIDING
Trentham
Macedon
White Stone Swamp
Lake Learmonth
Springmount
Dean
New Gisborne
Riddells Creek
Trawalla
TO ARARAT
WESTERN HWY
Burrumbeet
Miners Rest
GREAT
Korweinguboora
Barrys Reef
Blackwood
Cardigan Village
Lake Burrumbeet
Spargo Creek
Bullengarook East
Gisborne
Bullarook
Blakeville
LERDERDERG STATE PARK
WENDOUREE
BALLARAT
NERRINA
Leigh Creek
Bolwarrah
Ballan North
Sovereign Hill
Kryal Castle
Bungaree
Wallace
Gordon
Bunding
Greendale
Korobeit
Lerderderg Gorge
Toolern Vale
Sunbury
Haddon
SEBASTOPOL
MAGPIE
Dunnstown
Navigators
Millbrook
Mount Egerton
Ballan
Myrniong
Merrimu Reservoir
Diggers Rest
Snake Valley
Smythesdale
Cambrian Hill
Mount Helen
Ross Creek
Buninyong
Napoleons
Yendon
Lal Lal Falls
Scotsburn
Lal Lal
WERRIBEE GORGE STATE PARK
Fiskville
Bacchus Marsh
Darley
Melton
Scarsdale
Newtown
Linton
Happy Valley
Durham Lead
Clarendon
Mount Doran
Glenmore
Rowsley
Parwan
Avenue of Honour
Melton Reservoir
Rockbank
Calder Park Thunderdome
ST ALBANS
Mannibadar
ENFIELD STATE PARK
Enfield
Little Hard Hills
Garibaldi
Elaine
Mount Wallace
BRISBANE RANGES NATIONAL PARK
Exford
Cape Clear
Grenville
Mount Mercer
Cargerie
Balliang East
Illabarook
Dereel
Meredith
Balliang
Tarneit
Rokewood Junction
STEIGLITZ HISTORIC PARK
Anakie Gorge
Steiglitz
HOPPERS CROSSING
Corindhap
Rokewood
Sheoaks
Fairy Park
Anakie
WERRIBEE
Werribee Park
Maude
YOU YANGS REGIONAL PARK
Little River
HAMILTON
Berrybank
Lethbridge
Serendip Sanctuary
PRINCES
Melbourne Water Western Treatment Plant
Werribee South
Shelford
Teesdale
Lara
Cressy
AVALON AIRFIELD
Bannockburn
Lake Rosine
Lake Weering
Lake Martin
Gheringhap
CORIO
Batesford
Corio Bay
Lake Corangamite
Inverleigh
Murgheboluc
GEELONG
Eastern Beach
National Wool Museum
Portarlington
Indented Head
Fyansford
Ceres
Clifton Springs
Drysdale
St Leonards
Lake Cundare
Beeac
Lake Beeac
Gnarwarre
Mount Moriac
Waurn Ponds
BELMONT
MARSHALL
Leopold
GROVEDALE
BELLARINE PENINSULA
Lake Murdeduke
Warrion
Alvie
Winchelsea
Moriac
Freshwater Creek
Ocean Grove
Marcus Hill
Coragulac
Cororooke
Lake Colac
Wurdiboluc Reservoir
Connewarre
Barwon Heads
Queenscliff
Point Lonsdale
Colac
Elliminyt
Birregurra
Bellbrae
Torquay
Jan Juc
Portsea
Sorrento
Blairgowrie
Pirron Yallock
Larpent
TO WARRNAMBOOL
Bambra
Yeodene
Deans Marsh
Anglesea
Irrewillipe
Eagle Nest Reef
Airleys Inlet
Fairhaven
Eastern View
Kawarren
Gerangamete
Barwon Downs
Benwerrin
ANGAHOOK-LORNE STATE PARK
Forrest
Gellibrand
Erskine Falls
CARLISLE STATE PARK
Carlisle River
Lorne
BASS
STRAIT
TO APOLLO BAY
Spirit of Tasmania ferries Station Pier to Devonport

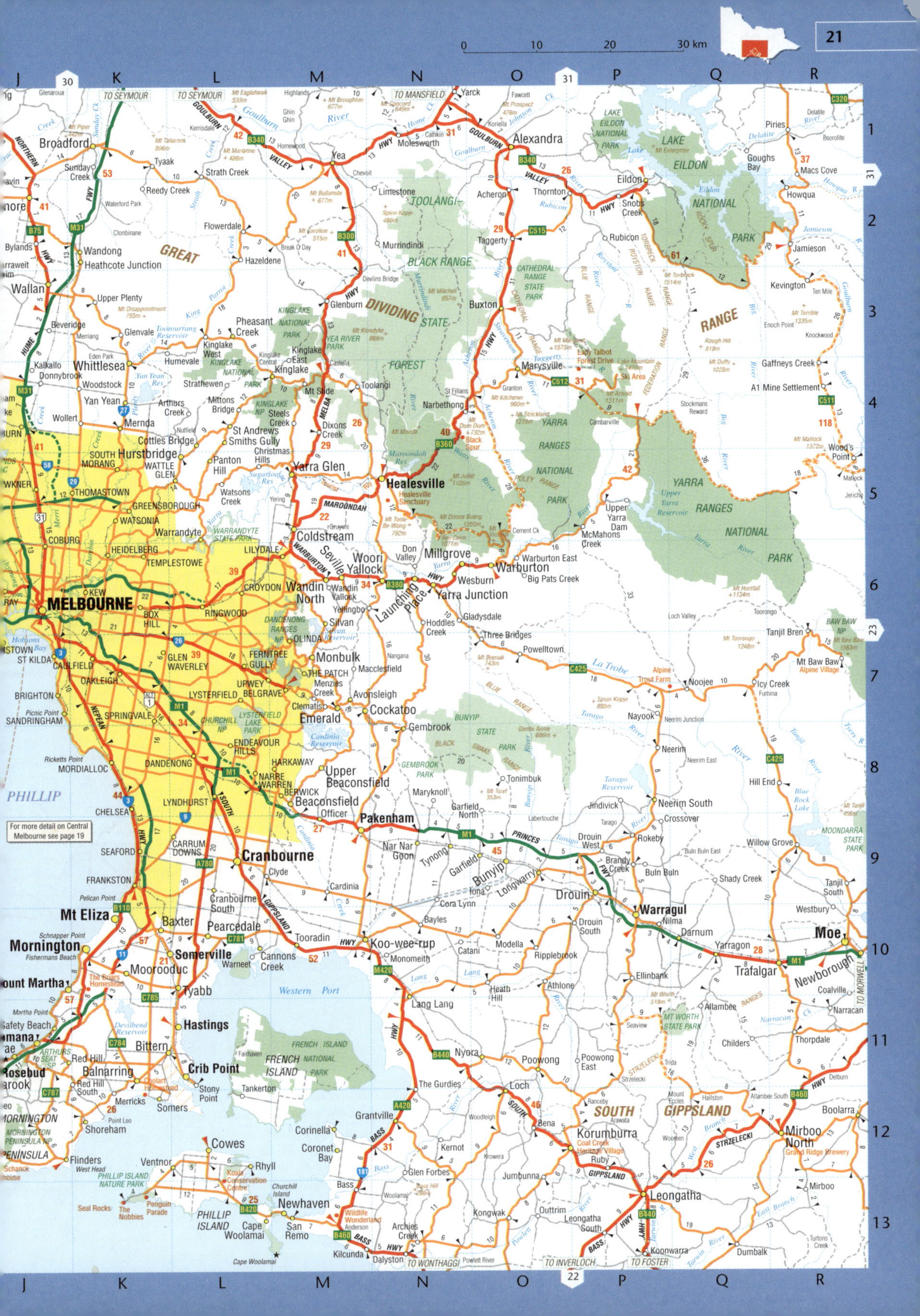
0 10 20 30 km
J K L M N O P Q R
1 2 3 4 5 6 7 8 9 10 11 12 13
30
31
23
22
TO SEYMOUR
TO MANSFIELD
TO WONTHAGGI
TO INVERLOCH
TO FOSTER
TO MORWELL
Broadford
Sunday Creek
Tyaak
Reedy Creek
Strath Creek
Flowerdale
Hazeldene
Wandong
Heathcote Junction
Wallan
Upper Plenty
Beveridge
Glenvale
Whittlesea
Humevale
Kalkallo
Donnybrook
Woodstock
Yan Yean
Wollert
Mernda
Arthurs Creek
Strathewen
Kinglake West
Kinglake
Kinglake East
Pheasant Creek
Mittons Bridge
Steels Creek
St Andrews
Smiths Gully
Christmas Hills
Cottles Bridge
Hurstbridge
SOUTH MORANG
WATTLE GLEN
Panton Hill
Watsons Creek
THOMASTOWN
GREENSBOROUGH
WATSONIA
COBURG
HEIDELBERG
TEMPLESTOWE
Warrandyte
WARRANDYTE STATE PARK
LILYDALE
CROYDON
RINGWOOD
KEW
MELBOURNE
BOX HILL
GLEN WAVERLEY
FERNTREE GULLY
DANDENONG RANGES NP
OLINDA
Monbulk
Silvan
ST KILDA
CAULFIELD
OAKLEIGH
BRIGHTON
SANDRINGHAM
SPRINGVALE
UPWEY
BELGRAVE
LYSTERFIELD
THE PATCH
Menzies Creek
Clematis
Emerald
Avonsleigh
Cockatoo
Gembrook
ENDEAVOUR HILLS
DANDENONG
MORDIALLOC
HARKAWAY
NARRE WARREN
BERWICK
Upper Beaconsfield
Beaconsfield
Officer
Pakenham
LYNDHURST
CHELSEA
CARRUM DOWNS
SEAFORD
FRANKSTON
Cranbourne
Clyde
Cranbourne South
Cardinia
Mt Eliza
Baxter
Pearcedale
Mornington
Somerville
Mooroodue
Tyabb
Hastings
Tooradin
Koo-wee-rup
Monomeith
Cannons Creek
Western Port
Bittern
Crib Point
Red Hill
Balnarring
Rosebud
Merricks
Somers
Stony Point
Shoreham
Flinders
FRENCH ISLAND NATIONAL PARK
Tankerton
Cowes
Rhyll
Ventnor
PHILLIP ISLAND
San Remo
Newhaven
Cape Woolamai
Corinella
Coronet Bay
Grantville
Bass
Glen Forbes
Kilcunda
Dalyston
Archies Creek
Kernot
The Gurdies
Lang Lang
Nyora
Loch
Poowong
Poowong East
Bena
Korumburra
Jumbunna
Kongwak
Outtrim
Leongatha
Leongatha South
Koonwarra
Ruby
Mirboo North
Mirboo
Dumbalk
Boolarra
SOUTH GIPPSLAND
Yea
Molesworth
Yarck
Alexandra
Acheron
Thornton
Eildon
Snobs Creek
Taggerty
Rubicon
Murrindindi
Limestone
Glenburn
Buxton
TOOLANGI–BLACK RANGE
GREAT DIVIDING RANGE
STATE FOREST
CATHEDRAL RANGE STATE PARK
Toolangi
Marysville
Narbethong
Dixons Creek
Yarra Glen
Healesville
Coldstream
Seville
Woori Yallock
Wandin North
Don Valley
Millgrove
Warburton
Warburton East
Wesburn
Yarra Junction
Launching Place
Gladysdale
Hoddles Creek
Three Bridges
Powelltown
YARRA RANGES NATIONAL PARK
Upper Yarra Dam
McMahons Creek
LAKE EILDON NATIONAL PARK
Goughs Bay
Macs Cove
Howqua
Jamieson
Kevington
Gaffneys Creek
A1 Mine Settlement
Wood's Point
Noojee
Icy Creek
Tanjil Bren
Mt Baw Baw
Nayook
Neerim
Neerim South
Crossover
Jindivick
Rokeby
Drouin West
Brandy Creek
Buln Buln
Drouin
Warragul
Nilma
Darnum
Yarragon
Trafalgar
Moe
Newborough
Westbury
Tanjil South
Willow Grove
Shady Creek
Hill End
BUNYIP STATE PARK
Tonimbuk
Maryknoll
Garfield North
Nar Nar Goon
Tynong
Garfield
Bunyip
Longwarry
Iona
Cora Lynn
Bayles
Catani
Modella
Ripplebrook
Heath Hill
Athlone
Drouin South
Ellinbank
Allambee
Childers
Thorpdale
Narracan
Coalville
MT WORTH STATE PARK
MOONDARRA STATE PARK
PRINCES
M1
M31
C425
B340
B300
B360
B380
B440
A420
B420
B460
C515
C512
C511
C320
C781
C785
C784
C787
B110
A780
B75
HUME
HWY
FWY
For more detail on Central Melbourne see page 19
PHILLIP

A
B
C
D
E
F
G
H
I
30
31
25
1
2
3
4
5
6
7
8
9
10
11
12
13
Tylden
Newham
Hanging Rock
Rochford
Romsey
Woodend
Memorial Cross
Mount Macedon
MACEDON REGIONAL PARK
Macedon
Monegeetta
Riddells Creek
New Gisborne
Gisborne
Clarkefield
Bullengarook East
LERDERDERG STATE PARK
Lerderderg Gorge
Sunbury
Toolern Vale
Diggers Rest
Bacchus Marsh
Melton
Parwan
Rowsley
Exford
Rockbank
Balliang East
Tarneit
WERRIBEE
Little River
Werribee South
Lara
CORIO
GEELONG
Portarlington
Bellarine
Indented Head
Clifton Springs
Drysdale
St Leonards
MARSHALL
Leopold
BELLARINE PENINSULA
Marcus Hill
Ocean Grove
Queenscliff
Point Lonsdale
Barwon Heads
Breamlea
Point Nepean
Portsea
Sorrento
MORNINGTON PENINSULA NATIONAL PARK
Rye
Rosebud
Dromana
Safety Beach
ARTHURS SEAT SP
Red Hill
Balnarring
MORNINGTON PENINSULA
Shoreham
Flinders
Cape Schanck
Mount Martha
Mornington
Somers
Bittern
Crib Point
Stony Point
Hastings
Tyabb
Somerville
Baxter
Pearcedale
FRANKSTON
Cranbourne South
Cranbourne
Tooradin
Cardinia
Warneet
Western Port
FRENCH ISLAND NATIONAL PARK
FRENCH ISLAND
Tankerton
Cowes
Ventnor
Rhyll
The Nobbies
Penguin Parade
PHILLIP ISLAND
Newhaven
Cape Woolamai
San Remo
Corinella
Coronet Bay
Grantville
Bass
Kilcunda
Dalyston
Wonthaggi
State Coal Mine
Dudley
Cape Paterson
Inverloch
Venus Bay
BUNURONG MARINE AND COASTAL PARK
Anderson Inlet
Tarwin Lower
Waratah Bay
Walkerville
Walkerville South
Cape Liptrap
Fish Creek
Meeniyan
Stony Creek
Buffalo
Leongatha
Leongatha South
Koonwarra
Korumburra
Kongwak
Outtrim
Jumbunna
Archies Creek
Glen Forbes
Kernot
The Gurdies
Loch
Nyora
Bena
Poowong
Lang Lang
Heath Hill
Athlone
Koo-wee-rup
Modella
Ripplebrook
Drouin
Drouin South
Warragul
Nilma
Darnum
Yarragon
Trafalgar
Ellinbank
Allambee
Bayles
Cora Lynn
Longwarry
Bunyip
Garfield
Tynong
Nar Nar Goon
Pakenham
Beaconsfield
Upper Beaconsfield
BERWICK
Cockatoo
Gembrook
Tonimbuk
BUNYIP STATE PARK
Avonsleigh
Macclesfield
Monbulk
OLINDA
BELGRAVE
Emerald
Silvan
Wandin North
Seville
Woori Yallock
Launching Place
Hoddles Creek
Three Bridges
Gladysdale
Powelltown
Yarra Junction
Millgrove
Warburton
Warburton East
Coldstream
Yarra Glen
Healesville
LILYDALE
RINGWOOD
BOX HILL
MELBOURNE
FOOTSCRAY
COBURG
KEILOR
ALTONA
BRIGHTON
OAKLEIGH
DANDENONG
LYNDHURST
THOMASTOWN
CRAIGIEBURN
Bulla
Yuroke
Mickleham
Kalkallo
Donnybrook
Woodstock
Yan Yean
Wollert
Mernda
Hurstbridge
Cottles Bridge
Smiths Gully
Panton Hill
St Andrews
Whittlesea
Kinglake
Kinglake West
Pheasant Creek
KINGLAKE NATIONAL PARK
Glenburn
Toolangi
Dixons Creek
Steels Creek
Flowerdale
Hazeldene
Wandong
Heathcote Junction
Wallan
Upper Plenty
Beveridge
Glenvale
Darraweit Guim
Bylands
Murrindindi
Taggerty
Rubicon
Buxton
Marysville
Narbethong
Black Spur
YARRA RANGES NATIONAL PARK
McMahons Creek
LAKE EILDON NP
Noojee
Icy Creek
Neerim
Neerim South
Jindivick
Rokeby
Crossover
Drouin West
Brandy Creek
Buln Buln
Shady Creek
PORT PHILLIP
BASS STRAIT
For more detail on Melbourne & Surrounds see pages 20–1
Spirit of Tasmania ferries Station Pier to Devonport

0 10 20 30 40 50 km
ALPINE NATIONAL PARK
AVON WILDERNESS PARK
MITCHELL RIVER NATIONAL PARK
BAW BAW NATIONAL PARK
HOLEY PLAINS STATE PARK
TARRA-BULGA NATIONAL PARK
MORWELL NATIONAL PARK
THE LAKES NATIONAL PARK
GIPPSLAND LAKES COASTAL PARK
GIPPSLAND LAKES
EAST GIPPSLAND
GIPPSLAND
NOORAMUNGA MARINE AND COASTAL RESERVE
WILSONS PROMONTORY MARINE PARK
WILSONS PROMONTORY NATIONAL PARK
WILSONS PROMONTORY
WILSONS PROMONTORY RESERVE
TASMAN SEA
Corner Inlet
Ninety Mile Beach
Lake Wellington
Lake Victoria
Lake King
Lake Coleman
Lake Glenmaggie
Swifts Creek
Ensay North
Ensay
Tambo Crossing
Bruthen
Wiseleigh
Clifton Creek
Bullumwaal
Dargo
Waterford
Castleburn
Licola
Culloden
Briagolong
Coongulla
Boisdale
Glenmaggie
Heyfield
Maffra
Newry
Tinamba
Stratford
Airly
Fernbank
Munro
Lindenow
Lindenow South
Woodglen
Walpa
Calulu
Wy Yung
Hillside
Lucknow
East Bairnsdale
Bairnsdale
Aboriginal Museum
Nicholson
Johnsonville
Swan Reach
Metung
Kalimna
Lakes Entrance
Nungurner
Eagle Point
Paynesville
Meerlieu
Loch Sport
Seacombe
Sale
Cobains
Fulham
Kilmany
Kilmany South
Longford
Dutson
Paradise Beach
Golden Beach
Rosedale
Traralgon
Morwell
Newborough
Yallourn North
Tyers
Glengarry
Toongabbie
Cowwarr
Denison
Seaton
Walhalla
Rawson
Erica
Moondarra
Aberfeldy
Wood's Point
Parkers Corner
Churchill
Traralgon South
Callignee
Gormandale
Loy Yang Power Station
Jeeralang North
Carrajung
Carrajung South
Blackwarry
Balook
Jumbuk
Budgeree
Won Wron
Devon North
Yarram
Woodside
Woodside Beach
McLoughlins Beach
Alberton
Alberton West
Gelliondale
Tarraville
Manns Beach
Port Albert
Langsborough
Hedley
Welshpool
Port Welshpool
Toora
Port Franklin
Seaspray
Binginwarri
Tidal River
Entrance Point
South East Point
PRINCES HWY
SOUTH GIPPSLAND HWY
HYLAND HWY
GREAT ALPINE RD
A1
B500
B440
C482

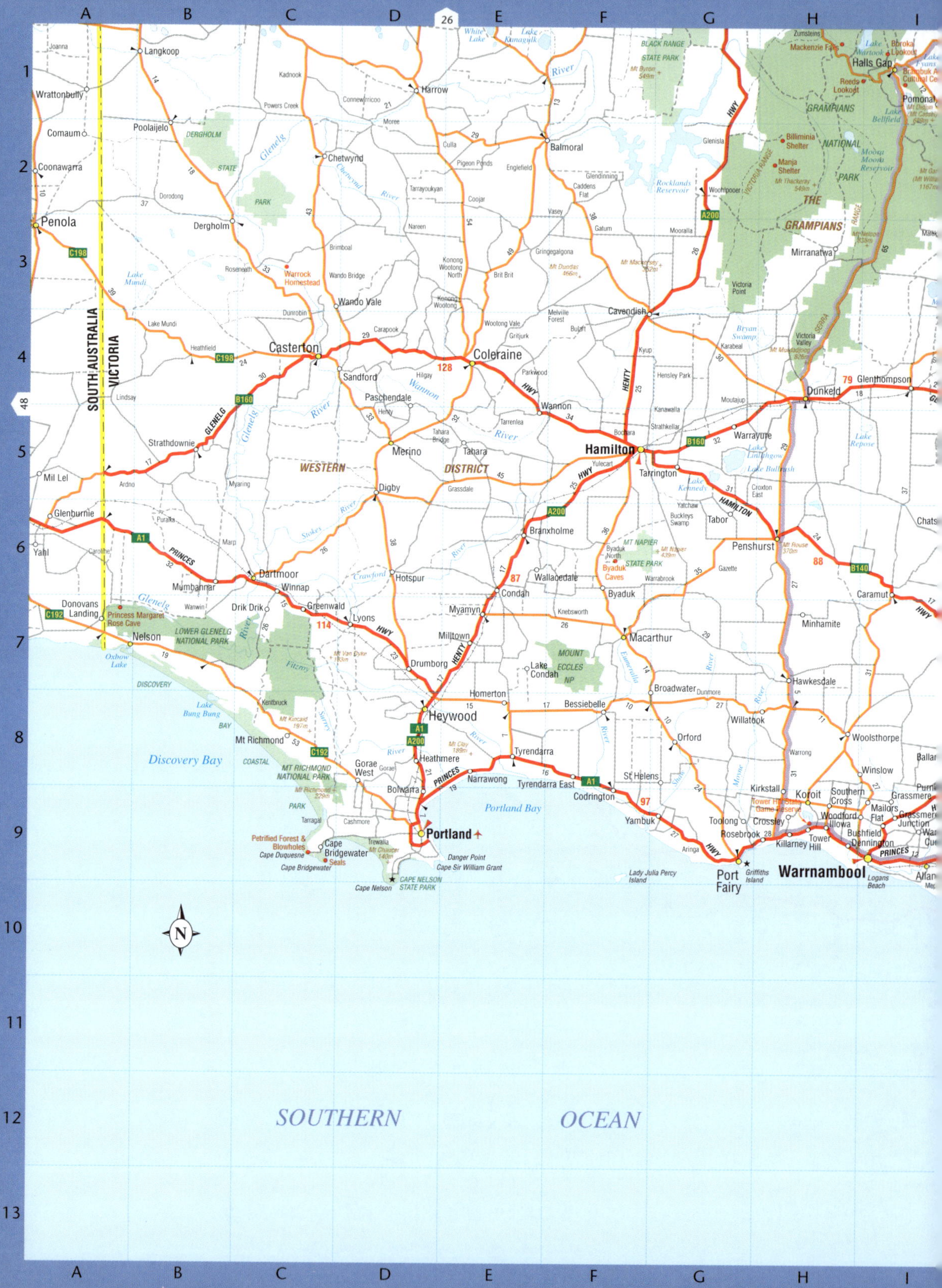

SOUTH AUSTRALIA
VICTORIA
Penola
Wrattonbully
Comaum
Coonawarra
Joanna
Langkoop
Poolaijelo
DERGHOLM STATE PARK
Dergholm
Dorodong
Roseneath
Warrock Homestead
Lake Mundi
Heathfield
Casterton
Sandford
Lindsay
Strathdownie
GLENELG
Mil Lel
Ardno
Glenburnie
Yahl
Caroline
Puralka
Myaring
Marp
Mumbannar
Dartmoor
Winnap
Drik Drik
Wanwin
Donovans Landing
Princess Margaret Rose Cave
LOWER GLENELG NATIONAL PARK
Nelson
Oxbow Lake
DISCOVERY BAY
Lake Bung Bung
Discovery Bay
Kentbruck
Mt Richmond
COASTAL
MT RICHMOND NATIONAL PARK
PARK
Tarragal
Cashmore
Petrified Forest & Blowholes
Cape Duquesne
Cape Bridgewater
Seals
Cape Nelson
CAPE NELSON STATE PARK
Danger Point
Cape Sir William Grant
Portland
Portland Bay
Bolwarra
Gorae West
Gorae
Heathmere
Narrawong
PRINCES
Greenwald
Lyons
Drumborg
Milltown
Myamyn
Condah
Heywood
Homerton
Hotspur
Digby
Merino
Tahara
Tahara Bridge
Henty
Paschendale
Sandford
Hilgay
Coleraine
Wannon
Tarrenlea
WESTERN
DISTRICT
Grassdale
Harrow
Kadnook
Powers Creek
Connewirricoo
Moree
Chetwynd
Culla
Pigeon Ponds
Englefield
Tarrayoukyan
Coojar
Nareen
Brimboal
Wando Bridge
Wando Vale
Dunrobin
Carapook
Konong Wootong North
Konong Wootong
Brit Brit
Wootong Vale
Gritjurk
Balmoral
White Lake
Lake Kanagulk
Glendinning
Caddens Flat
Vasey
Gatum
Gringegalgona
Mt Dundas 466m
Melville Forest
Bulart
Parkwood
Cavendish
Kyup
Rocklands Reservoir
Mooralla
Glenisla
Woohlpooer
BLACK RANGE STATE PARK
Mt Byron 549m
Hamilton
Bochara
Strathkellar
Kanawalla
Hensley Park
Yulecart
Tarrington
Lake Kennedy
Yatchaw
Buckleys Swamp
Tabor
Croxton East
Warrayure
Lake Linlithgow
Lake Bullrush
Moutajup
Karabeal
Bryan Swamp
Branxholme
Wallacedale
MT NAPIER STATE PARK
Mt Napier 439m
Byaduk North
Byaduk Caves
Byaduk
Warrabrook
Knebsworth
Macarthur
MOUNT ECCLES NP
Lake Condah
Broadwater
Dunmore
Bessiebelle
Tyrendarra
Tyrendarra East
Codrington
St Helens
Yambuk
Orford
Willatook
Lady Julia Percy Island
Port Fairy
Griffiths Island
Rosebrook
Toolong
Crossley
Killarney
Kirkstall
Koroit
Tower Hill State Game Reserve
Tower Hill
Southern Cross
Woodford
Illowa
Warrnambool
Logans Beach
Bushfield
Dennington
Mailors Flat
Grassmere
Winslow
Warrong
Woolsthorpe
Hawkesdale
Minhamite
Caramut
Penshurst
Mt Rouse 370m
Gazette
Dunkeld
Glenthompson
Victoria Valley
Victoria Point
Mirranatwa
GRAMPIANS NATIONAL PARK
THE GRAMPIANS
VICTORIA RANGE
SERRA
Billiminia Shelter
Manja Shelter
Mt Thackeray 549m
Reeds Lookout
Halls Gap
Mackenzie Falls
Zumsteins
Boroka Lookout
Pomonal
Lake Bellfield
Lake Wartook
Moora Moora Reservoir
Penshurst
Lake Repose
Chatsworth
Lake Linlithgow
SOUTHERN
OCEAN

0 10 20 30 40 50 km
J K L M N O P Q R
1 2 3 4 5 6 7 8 9 10 11 12 13
27
30
22
Bunjil's Shelter
Great Western
Crowlands
Elmhurst
Amphitheatre
Lamplough
Amherst
Talbot
Daisy Hill
Majorca
Tullaroop Reservoir
Glenlofty
Dunneworthy
Eversley
Ben Nevis 877m
Mt Cameron 417m
Dunach
Strathlea
Loddon
Yapeen
Guildford
Vaughan
Glenluce
Taradale
Barfold
Langley
Malmsbury
Malmsbury Reservoir
Sandon
Campbelltown
Glengower
Yandoit
Porcupine Ridge
Drummond
Lauriston
Kyneton
Carlsruhe
Rhymney Reef
Armstrong
PYRENEES
Mt Lonarch
Evansford
Mt Beckworth 635m
Clunes
Ullina
Hepburn Springs
Loddon Falls
Denver
Upper Coliban Res
Glenlyon
Tylden
Little Hampton
Ararat
LANGI-GHIRAN STATE PARK
Warrak
Mt Buangor 966m
MT BUANGOR STATE PARK
Lexton
SUNRAYSIA
Chute
Glendaruel
Waubra
Lawrence
Smeaton
Broomfield
Kingston
Allendale
MIDLAND
Daylesford
Woodend
Mt Ararat 616m
Buangor
WESTERN
Raglan
Waterloo
Langi Kal Kal
Mt Misery 724m
Coghills Creek
Learmonth
Creswick
Newlyn
Rocklyn
Bullarto
Trentham
Newbury
Lang Logan
Middle Creek
Trawalla
Beaufort
Nerring
Brewster
Burrumbeet
Cardigan Village
Miners Rest
Dean
Spargo Creek
Blackwood
Bullengarook East
Mt Moornambool 522m
Shirley
Lake Burrumbeet
Blakeville
Maroona
Rossbridge
Yalla Y Poora
BALLARAT
Sovereign Hill
Nerrina
Leigh Creek
Bullarook
Bolwarrah
Bungaree
Wallace
LERDERDERG STATE PARK
Bunding
Greendale
Calvert
Tatyoon
Stockyard Hill
Lake Goldsmith
Haddon
Dunnstown
Millbrook
Gordon
Ballan
FWY
Myrniong
Lerderderg Gorge
Willaura
Mt Wejort 371m
Snake Valley
Ross Creek
Mt Helen
Navigators
Lal Lal Res
Baid Hill 340m
Slater Lake
Mt Emu
Mortchup
Smythesdale
Buninyong
Yendon
Mt Egerton
WERRIBEE GORGE STATE PARK
Fiskville
Bacchus Marsh
Mininera
Lake Wongan
Scarsdale
Napoleons
Lal Lal
Parwan
Pittong
Mt Bute 472m
Newtown
Scotsburn
Durham Lead
Clarendon
Bungal
Glenmore
Skipton
HWY
Linton
Happy Valley
ENFIELD STATE PARK
Rowsley
Wickliffe
Westmere
Streatham
Carranballac
GLENELG
Piggoreet
Garibaldi
Mount Doran
Lake Bolac
Lake McLaren
Mt Erip 421m
Enfield
Mount Wallace
BRISBANE RANGES NATIONAL PARK
Mannibadar
Mt Widderin 360m
Cape Clear
Berringa
Grenville
Elaine
Durdidwarrah
Balliang East
Lake Bolac
Nerrin Nerrin
Bradvale
Willowvale
Illabarook
Dereel
Mount Mercer
Cargerie
Vite Vite North
Rokewood Junction
Woodburne
Meredith
Anakie Gorge
Balliang
Mt Hamilton 319m
Pura Pura
Mingay
Mt Bute
Corindhap
STEIGLITZ HISTORIC PARK
Steiglitz
Little
Lake Gillies
Lake Evans
Vite Vite
Rokewood
Sheoaks
Anakie
Dundonnell
Lake Logan
Bamganie
Bingley Swamp
Maude
Anakie East
Woorndoo
Derrinallum
Wilgul
Werneth
Warrambine
Lethbridge
Little River
Lismore
HAMILTON
Lake Tooliorook
Berrybank
Mt Elephant 394m
Shelford
Teesdale
Lara
Darlington
Gnarpurt
Duverney
Cressy
Bannockburn
CORIO
Batesford
PRINCES
Lake Gnarpurt
Lake Weering
Wingeel
Mt Shadwell 292m
Lake Martin
Cloven Hills
Murgheboluc
Inverleigh
Mortlake
Barpinba
Lake
GEELONG
Corangamite
Bookar
Lake Bookar
Eurack
Lake Murdeduke
Gnarwarre
Fyansford
Kolora
Glenormiston North
Dreeite
Ceres
Leopold
Lake Colongulac
Kariah
Beeac
Mount Moriac
MARSHALL
Glenormiston
Lake Beeac
Ombersley
Moriac
Waurn Ponds
Lake Connewarre
Noorat
Mt Noorat 313m
Gnotuk
Wool Wool
Warrion
Ocean Grove
Lake Keilambete
Boorcan
Camperdown
Alvie
Salt Lake
Winchelsea
Freshwater Creek
Framlingham
Terang
Coragulac
Modewarre
Breamlea
Barwon Heads
Cororooke
Pomborneit
Warncoort
Birregurra
Bellbrae
Garvoc
Dixie
Cobrico
Koallah
Lake Colac
Cobden
Tandarook
Stoneyford
Colac
Torquay
Panmure
Mumblin
Pirron Yallock
Larpent
Elliminyt
Bambra
Laang
Ecklin South
Swan Marsh
Lake Elingamite
Carpendeit
Jancourt East
Irrewillipe
Yeodene
Deans Marsh
Anglesea
Glenfyne
Barongarook West
Ayrford
Scotts Creek
Barwon Downs
Murroon
ANGAHOOK-LORNE STATE PARK
Fairhaven
Aireys Inlet
Eastern View
Nullawarre
Brucknell
Cowleys Creek
Benwerrin
Nirranda
Timboon
Simpson
Kawarren
Gerangamete
Curdie Vale
Curdies
Forrest
Nirranda South
Paaratte
Gellibrand
CARLISLE STATE PARK
Mt Cowley 657m
Lorne
Newfield
Waarre
Carlisle River
Kennedys Creek
Wimba
Cumberland
Peterborough
GREAT
Port Campbell
London Bridge
The Arch
PORT CAMPBELL
Loch Ard Gorge
The Twelve Apostles
Gibson Steps
OCEAN
RD
Dinmont
Beech Forest
Mt Sabine 583m
RANGES
Separation Creek
Wye River
Chapple Vale
Weeaproinah
Kennett River
Princetown
NATIONAL PARK
MELBA GULLY STATE PARK
Mt Chapple 550m
Lavers Hill
Tanybryn
OTWAY
Cape Patton
Yuulong
Moonlight Head
Point Reginald
Johanna
OTWAY NATIONAL PARK
Glenaire
Hordern Vale
Paradise
Skenes Creek
Apollo Bay
Marengo
Blanket Bay
Cape Otway
BASS STRAIT

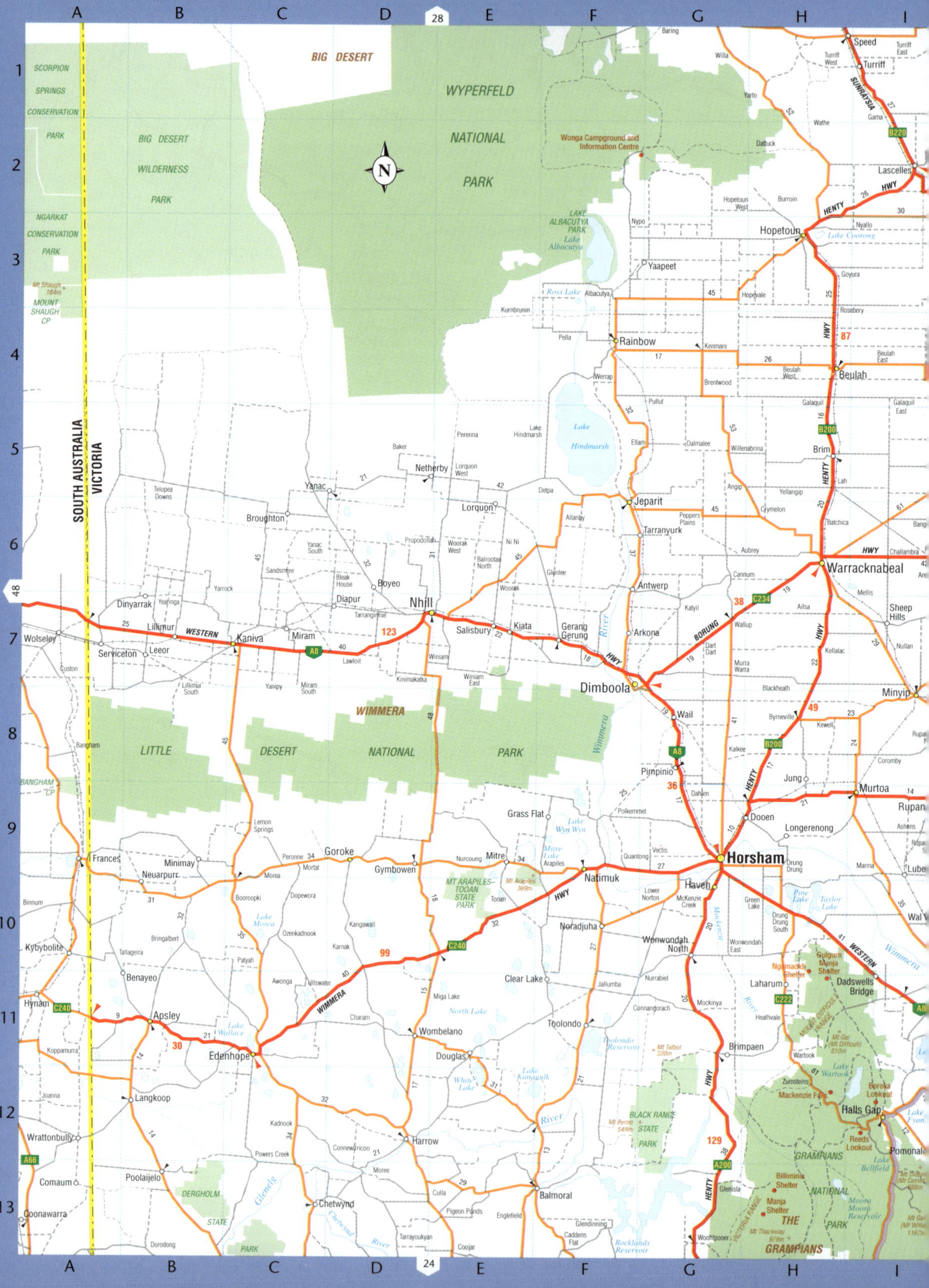
BIG DESERT
WYPERFELD NATIONAL PARK
SCORPION SPRINGS CONSERVATION PARK
BIG DESERT WILDERNESS PARK
NGARKAT CONSERVATION PARK
MOUNT SHAUGH CP
Wonga Campground and Information Centre
LAKE ALBACUTYA PARK
Lake Albacutya
SOUTH AUSTRALIA
VICTORIA
LITTLE DESERT NATIONAL PARK
WIMMERA
BANGHAM CP
MT ARAPILES-TOOAN STATE PARK
BLACK RANGE STATE PARK
DERGHOLM STATE PARK
GRAMPIANS NATIONAL PARK
Lake Hindmarsh
Speed
Turriff
Lascelles
Hopetoun
Yaapeet
Rainbow
Beulah
Brim
Jeparit
Tarranyurk
Warracknabeal
Antwerp
Arkona
Sheep Hills
Dimboola
Wail
Minyip
Pimpinio
Jung
Murtoa
Dooen
Longerenong
Horsham
Haven
Natimuk
Mitre
Gymbowen
Goroke
Grass Flat
Noradjuha
Wonwondah North
Laharum
Dadswells Bridge
Clear Lake
Toolondo
Brimpaen
Halls Gap
Pomonal
Netherby
Yanac
Lorquon
Broughton
Boyeo
Diapur
Nhill
Salisbury
Kiata
Gerang Gerung
Dinyarrak
Lillimur
Kaniva
Miram
Serviceton
Leeor
Wolseley
Frances
Minimay
Neuarpurr
Kybybolite
Benayeo
Hynam
Apsley
Edenhope
Wombelano
Douglas
Langkoop
Wrattonbully
Harrow
Poolaijelo
Comaum
Chetwynd
Balmoral
Coonawarra
WESTERN HWY
BORUNG HWY
HENTY HWY
SUNRAYSIA HWY
WIMMERA HWY
A8
A200
B200
B220
C234
C240
C222
A66

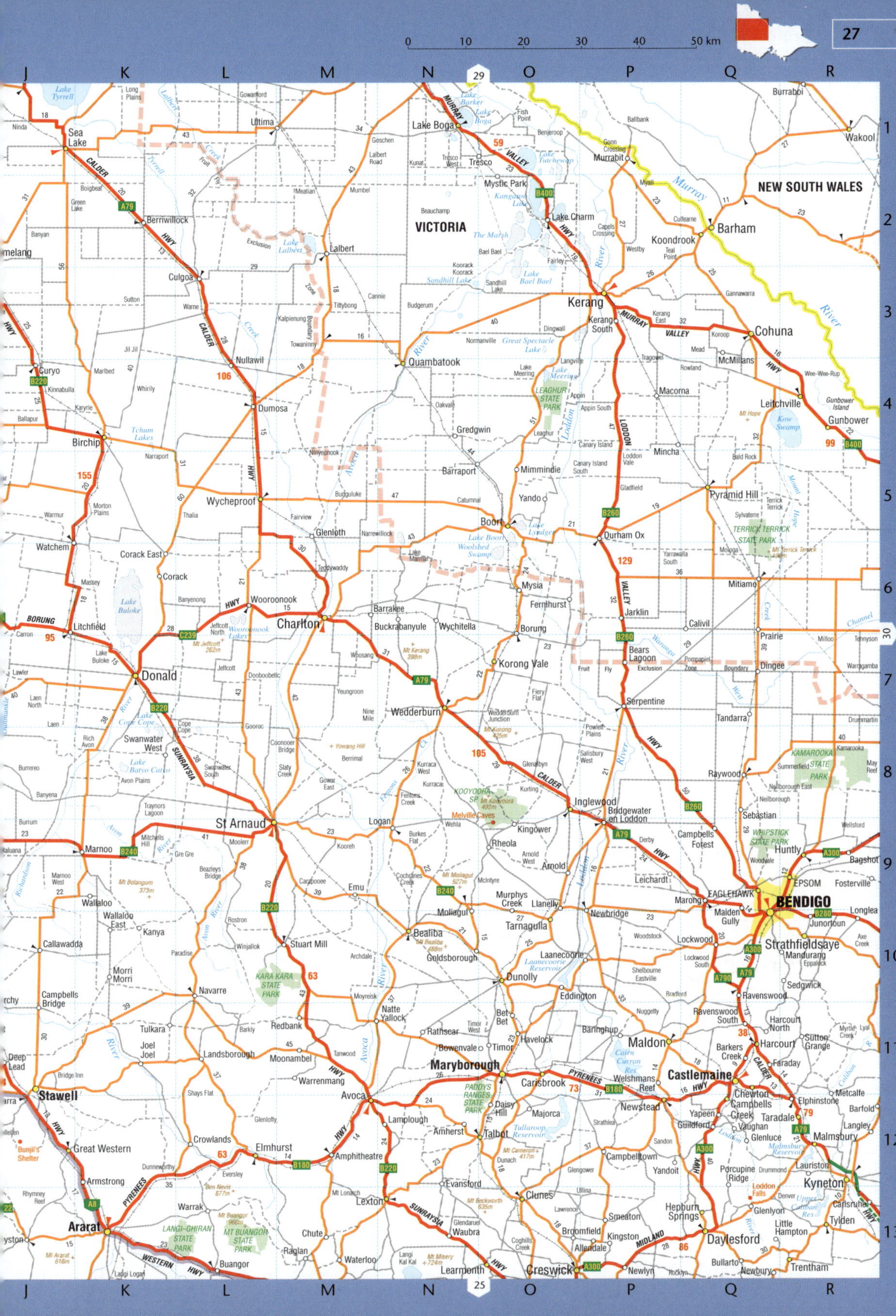
0
10
20
30
40
50 km
J
K
L
M
N
O
P
Q
R
29
25
30
1
2
3
4
5
6
7
8
9
10
11
12
13
VICTORIA
NEW SOUTH WALES
Lake Tyrrell
Sea Lake
Ninda
Long Plains
Gowanford
Ultima
Goschen
Lalbert Road
Lake Boga
Lake Barker
Fish Point
Benjeroop
Burraboi
Ballbank
Wakool
Gonn Crossing
Murrabit
Myall
Murray
Tresco
Tresco West
Kunat
Lake Tutchewop
Mystic Park
Kangaroo Lake
Lake Charm
Beauchamp
Mumbel
Meatian
Boigbeat
Green Lake
Berriwillock
Banyan
Exclusion
Lake Lalbert
Lalbert
The Marsh
Bael Bael
Capels Crossing
Westby
Koondrook
Teal Point
Barham
Cullearne
Culgoa
Sutton
Warne
Kalpienung
Tittybong
Cannie
Budgerum
Kooreh Kooreh
Sandhill Lake
Lake Bael Bael
Fairley
Kerang
Kerang South
Kerang East
Gannawarra
Cohuna
Koroop
Mead
McMillans
Towaninny
Quambatook
Normanville
Great Spectacle Lake
Dingwall
Curyo
Kinnabulla
Jil Jil
Nullawil
Maribed
Whirily
Karyrie
Ballapur
Dumosa
Lake Meering
Langville
LEAGHUR STATE PARK
Appin
Appin South
Tragowel
Rowland
Macorna
Wee-Wee-Rup
Leitchville
Gunbower Island
Gunbower
Kow Swamp
Mt Hope
Birchip
Tchum Lakes
Narraport
Nineyabook
Oakvale
Gredgwin
Leaghur
Canary Island
Canary Island South
Loddon Vale
Mincha
Bald Rock
Barraport
Mimmindie
Gladfield
Pyramid Hill
Terrick Terrick
Sylvaterre
Morton Plains
Warmur
Wycheproof
Thalia
Budgerum
Budgeluke
Catumnal
Yando
Boort
Lake Lyndger
Fairview
Glenloth
Narrewillock
Lake Boort
Woolshed Swamp
Durham Ox
Yarrawalla South
TERRICK TERRICK STATE PARK
Mt Terrick Terrick
Mologa
Watchem
Corack East
Corack
Massey
Teddywaddy
Lake Marmal
Mysia
Fernihurst
Jarklin
Mitiamo
Lake Buloke
Banyenong
Wooroonook
Charlton
Barrakee
Buckrabanyule
Wychitella
Borung
Calivil
Prairie
Milloo
Tennyson
Litchfield
Carron
Jeffcott North
Wooroonook Lakes
Mt Jeffcott 262m
Woosang
Mt Kerang 398m
Korong Vale
Bears Lagoon
Pompapiel
Dingee
Warragamba
Lake Buloke
Lawler
Donald
Jeffcott
Dooboobetic
Fruit
Fly
Exclusion
Zone
Boundary
Laen North
Laen
Yeungroon
Fiery Flat
Serpentine
Tandarra
Drummartin
Lake Cope Cope
Cope Cope
Gooroc
Nine Mile
Wedderburn
Wedderburn Junction
Mt Korong 425m
Powlett Plains
Rich Avon
Swanwater West
Coonooer Bridge
Yowang Hill
Berrimal
Salisbury West
Kamarooka
KAMAROOKA STATE PARK
Summerfield
May Reef
Burrereo
Lake Batyo Catyo
Swanwater South
Slaty Creek
Kurraca West
Kurraca
Glenalbyn
Raywood
Nolborough East
Avon Plains
Banyena
Gowar East
Fentons Creek
KOOYOORA SP
Mt Kooyoora 492m
Kurting
Inglewood
Bridgewater on Loddon
Neilborough
Sebastian
Traynors Lagoon
Burrum
St Arnaud
Logan
Melville Caves
Wehla
Kingower
Derby
Campbells Forest
WHIPSTICK STATE PARK
Wellsford
Mitchells Hill
Marnoo
Moolerr
Gre Gre
Kooreh
Burkes Flat
Rheola
Arnold West
Arnold
Huntly
Bagshot
Woodvale
Beazleys Bridge
Carapooee
Cochranes Creek
Mt Moliagul 527m
McIntyre
Leichardt
EAGLEHAWK
EPSOM
Fosterville
Marnoo West
Mt Bolangum 373m
Emu
Moliagul
Murphys Creek
Tarnagulla
Llanelly
Newbridge
Marong
Maiden Gully
BENDIGO
Longlea
Junortoun
Wallaloo
Wallaloo East
Kanya
Rostron
Bealiba
Mt Bealiba 488m
Goldsborough
Woodstock
Lockwood
Strathfieldsaye
Axe Creek
Callawadda
Paradise
Winjallok
Stuart Mill
Archdale
Laanecoorie
Laanecoorie Reservoir
Shelbourne
Eastville
Lockwood South
Mandurang
Eppalock
Morri Morri
KARA KARA STATE PARK
Dunolly
Sedgwick
Campbells Bridge
Navarre
Moyreisk
Eddington
Bradford
Ravenswood
Natte Yallock
Bet Bet
Nuggetty
Ravenswood South
Tulkara
Barkly
Redbank
Rathscar
Timor West
Baringhup
Harcourt North
Myrtle Creek
Lyal
Joel Joel
Moonambel
Bowenvale
Timor
Havelock
Maldon
Cairn Curran Res
Barkers Creek
Harcourt
Sutton Grange
Deep Lead
Landsborough
Tanwood
Maryborough
Faraday
Bridge Inn
Warrenmang
Carisbrook
Welshmans Reef
Castlemaine
Metcalfe
Stawell
Shays Flat
Avoca
PADDYS RANGES STATE PARK
Daisy Hill
Majorca
Newstead
Chewton
Campbells Creek
Elphinstone
Barfold
Glenlofty
Lamplough
Amherst
Talbot
Tullaroop Reservoir
Strathlea
Yapeen
Guildford
Vaughan
Taradale
Glenluce
Langley
Malmsbury
Malmsbury Reservoir
Bunjil's Shelter
Great Western
Crowlands
Elmhurst
Amphitheatre
Mt Cameron 417m
Dunach
Campbelltown
Sandon
Yandoit
Porcupine Ridge
Drummond
Lauriston
Armstrong
Dunneworthy
Eversley
Ben Nevis 877m
Evansford
Glengower
Ullina
Loddon Falls
Kyneton
Rhymney Reef
Mt Buangor 966m
Mt Lonarch
Lexton
Mt Beckworth 636m
Clunes
Lawrence
Smeaton
Hepburn Springs
Denver
Upper Coliban Res
Carlsruhe
Glenlyon
Tylden
Warrak
LANGI-GHIRAN STATE PARK
MT BUANGOR STATE PARK
Glendaruel
Waubra
Coghills Creek
Broomfield
Kingston
Allendale
Daylesford
Little Hampton
Ararat
Chute
Raglan
Mt Ararat 616m
Langi Logan
Buangor
Waterloo
Langi Kal Kal
Mt Misery 724m
Learmonth
Creswick
Newlyn
Rocklyn
Bullarto
Newbury
Trentham
CALDER HWY
MURRAY VALLEY HWY
LODDON VALLEY HWY
BORUNG HWY
SUNRAYSIA HWY
PYRENEES HWY
WESTERN HWY
MIDLAND HWY
A79
A8
A300
A790
B180
B220
B240
B260
B280
B400
C239

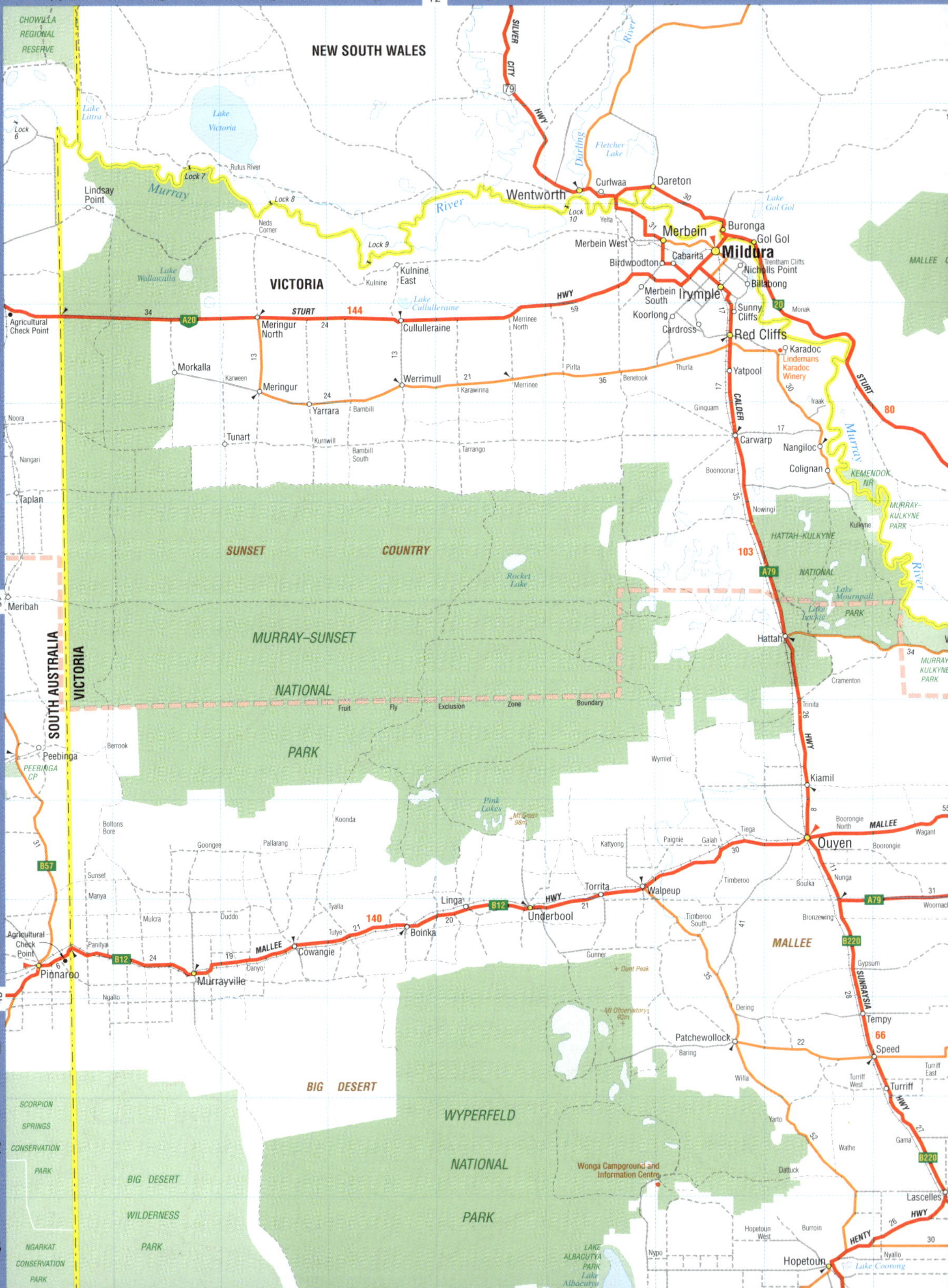
NEW SOUTH WALES
VICTORIA
SOUTH AUSTRALIA
Mildura
Merbein
Irymple
Red Cliffs
Wentworth
Dareton
Curlwaa
Buronga
Gol Gol
Ouyen
Hattah
Kiamil
Walpeup
Underbool
Murrayville
Pinnaroo
Patchewollock
Hopetoun
Speed
Tempy
Turriff
Lascelles
SUNSET COUNTRY
MURRAY–SUNSET NATIONAL PARK
HATTAH–KULKYNE NATIONAL PARK
WYPERFELD NATIONAL PARK
BIG DESERT
BIG DESERT WILDERNESS PARK
SCORPION SPRINGS CONSERVATION PARK
NGARKAT CONSERVATION PARK
CHOWILLA REGIONAL RESERVE
MALLEE
Murray River
Lake Victoria
Wonga Campground and Information Centre
Lindemans Karadoc Winery

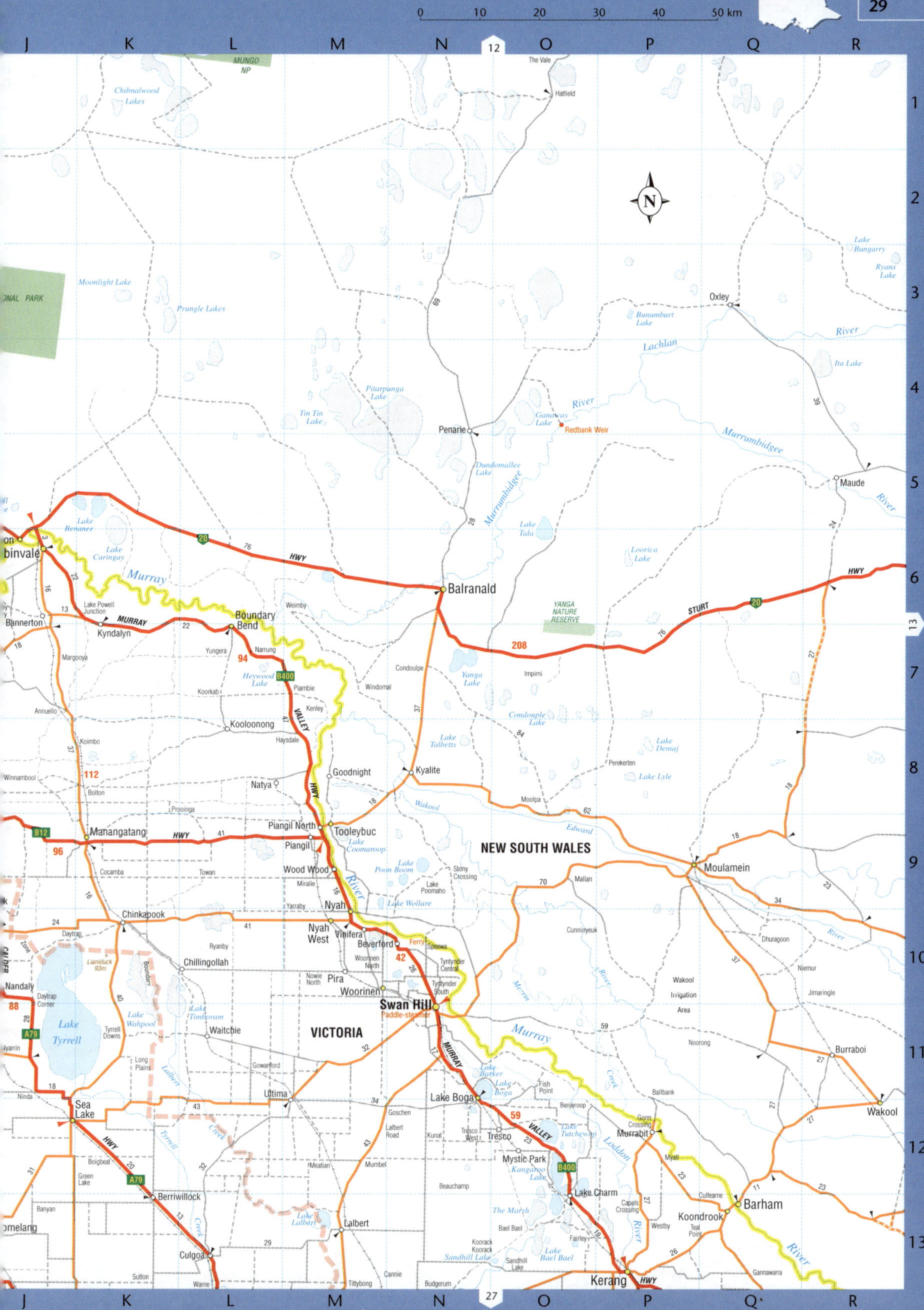

0 10 20 30 40 50 km
J K L M N O P Q R
12
MUNGO NP
The Vale
Hatfield
Chibnalwood Lakes
NAL PARK
Moonlight Lake
Prungle Lakes
Lake Bungarry
Ryans Lake
Oxley
Bunumburt Lake
Lachlan
River
Ita Lake
Pitarpunga Lake
Tin Tin Lake
Penarie
Ganaway Lake
River
Redbank Weir
Murrumbidgee
Dundomallee Lake
Maude
River
Murrumbidgee
Lake Benanee
Lake Caringay
Lake Tala
Loorica Lake
Robinvale
Murray
Balranald
HWY
STURT
HWY
YANGA NATURE RESERVE
208
Lake Powell Junction
MURRAY
Bannerton
Kyndalyn
Boundary Bend
Weimby
Margooya
Yungera
Narrung
94
B400
Heywood Lake
Piambie
Koorkab
Condoulpe
Impimi
Windomal
Yanga Lake
Kenley
Annuello
Kooloonong
VALLEY
Haysdale
Condouple Lake
Koimbo
Lake Talbetts
Lake Demaj
Perekerten
Goodnight
Kyalite
Winnamboo
112
Natya
Lake Lyle
Bolton
HWY
Wakool
Moolpa
Prooinga
Piangil North
Tooleybuc
Edward
B12
Manangatang
HWY
Piangil
Lake Coomaroop
NEW SOUTH WALES
96
Moulamein
Cocamba
Towan
Wood Wood
Lake Poon Boon
Stony Crossing
Mallan
Miralie
River
Lake Poomaho
Yarraby
Nyah
Lake Wollare
Chinkapook
Nyah West
Vinifera
Beverford
Ferry
Speewa
Dhuragoon
Daytrap
Ryanby
Cunninyeuk
River
Zone
CALDER
Lianiduck 93m
Chillingollah
42
Tyntynder Central
Woorinen North
Niemur
Nandaly
Nowie North
Pira
Woorinen
Tyntynder South
Wakool
Irrigation
Area
Jimaringle
Daytrap Corner
Swan Hill
Paddle-steamer
88
Lake Tyrrell
Lake Wahpool
Lake Timboram
Merran
Tyrrell Downs
Waitchie
VICTORIA
Murray
A79
Noorong
Burraboi
Long Plains
Gowanford
MURRAY
Lake Barker
Fish Point
Lake Boga
Ballbank
Ninda
Ultima
Lake Boga
Sea Lake
Benjeroop
Wakool
Goschen
Lalbert Road
Kunat
Tresco West
Tresco
59
VALLEY
Lake Tutchewop
Gonn Crossing
Murrabit
Loddon
Creek
Boigbeat
Tyrrell
Creek
Meatian
Mumbel
Mystic Park
Kangaroo Lake
B400
Myall
Green Lake
A79
Beauchamp
Lake Charm
Cullearne
Barham
Banyan
Berriwillock
Capels Crossing
Koondrook
Teal Point
Westby
The Marsh
Lake Lalbert
Lalbert
Bael Bael
River
Fairley
Koorack Koorack
Lake Bael Bael
Sandhill Lake
Culgoa
River
Sandhill Lake
Sutton
Warne
Tittybong
Cannie
Budgerum
Kerang
HWY
Gannawarra
27

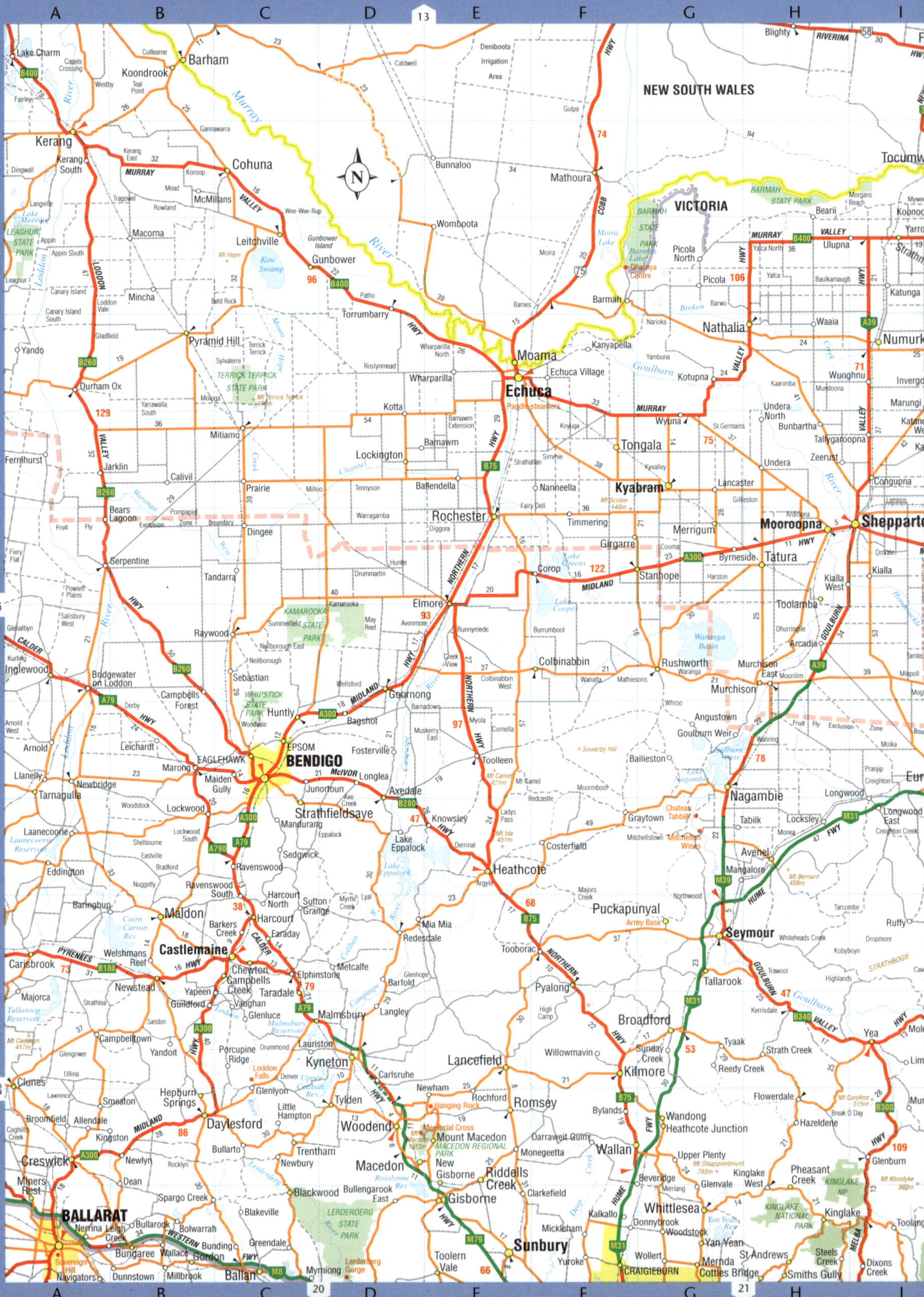
NEW SOUTH WALES
VICTORIA
Lake Charm
Barham
Koondrook
Kerang
Kerang South
Cohuna
McMillans
Leitchville
Gunbower
Torrumbarry
Macorna
Mincha
Pyramid Hill
Yando
Durham Ox
Mitiamo
Jarklin
Calivil
Prairie
Bears Lagoon
Dingee
Serpentine
Tandarra
Raywood
Sebastian
Inglewood
Bridgewater on Loddon
Campbells Forest
Huntly
EAGLEHAWK
EPSOM
BENDIGO
Marong
Maiden Gully
Arnold
Llanelly
Tarnagulla
Newbridge
Lockwood
Leichardt
Laanecoorie
Eddington
Ravenswood
Ravenswood South
Strathfieldsaye
Junortoun
Mandurang
Sedgwick
Harcourt
Harcourt North
Maldon
Castlemaine
Chewton
Campbells Creek
Newstead
Yapeen
Guildford
Vaughan
Glenluce
Taradale
Elphinstone
Metcalfe
Malmsbury
Carisbrook
Majorca
Campbelltown
Clunes
Smeaton
Hepburn Springs
Daylesford
Kyneton
Carlsruhe
Tylden
Woodend
Little Hampton
Trentham
Macedon
Mount Macedon
New Gisborne
Gisborne
Riddells Creek
Romsey
Lancefield
Sunbury
Creswick
Kingston
Allendale
Newlyn
Dean
Spargo Creek
Blackwood
Bullengarook
Greendale
Ballan
Myrniong
BALLARAT
Bungaree
Wallace
Gordon
Navigators
Dunnstown
Millbrook
Moama
Echuca
Echuca Village
Mathoura
Bunnaloo
Wombouta
Wharparilla
Kotta
Lockington
Bamawm
Ballendella
Rochester
Elmore
Goornong
Bagshot
Fosterville
Longlea
Axedale
Knowsley
Lake Eppalock
Heathcote
Toolleen
Colbinabbin
Corop
Nanneella
Timmering
Tongala
Kyabram
Girgarre
Stanhope
Rushworth
Murchison
Murchison East
Nagambie
Graytown
Costerfield
Puckapunyal
Seymour
Tooborac
Pyalong
Broadford
Kilmore
Wallan
Wandong
Heathcote Junction
Whittlesea
Donnybrook
Mernda
Craigieburn
Yan Yean
St Andrews
Kinglake
Kinglake West
Pheasant Creek
Glenburn
Flowerdale
Strath Creek
Yea
Tallarook
Avenel
Mangalore
Longwood
Locksley
Angustown
Goulburn Weir
Bailieston
Tatura
Mooroopna
Shepparton
Merrigum
Lancaster
Kotupna
Nathalia
Picola
Barmah
Kanyapella
Congupna
Toolamba
Arcadia
Undera
Katunga
Numurkah
Wunghnu
Blighty
Tocumwal
Murray River
Goulburn River
Loddon River
Campaspe River
BARMAH STATE PARK
KAMAROOKA STATE PARK
WHIPSTICK STATE PARK
TERRICK TERRICK STATE PARK
LERDERDERG STATE PARK
MACEDON REGIONAL PARK
KINGLAKE NATIONAL PARK
Lake Eppalock
Waranga Basin
Hanging Rock
Dharnya Centre
A B C D E F G H I
1 2 3 4 5 6 7 8 9 10 11 12 13

0 10 20 30 40 50 km
NEW SOUTH WALES
VICTORIA
Berrigan
Savenake
Rennie
Daysdale
Coreen
Lowesdale
Buraja
Balldale
Brocklesby
Walbundrie
Culcairn
Morven
Holbrook
Walla Walla
Burrumbuttock
Gerogery
Gerogery West
Woomargama
Mullengandra Village
Jindera
Barooga
Mulwala
Yarrawonga
Corowa
Wahgunyah
Howlong
Albury
Wodonga
Bundalong
Rutherglen
Barnawartha
Chiltern
Bandiana
Bellbridge
Bethanga
Granya
Talgarno
Katamatite
Tungamah
Wilby
Peechelba
Springhurst
Boorhaman
Baranduda
Staghorn Flat
Kiewa
Tangambalanga
Tallangatta
Old Tallangatta
Bonegilla
Ebden
St James
Lake Rowan
Dookie
Devenish
Thoona
Wangaratta
Eldorado
Beechworth
Wooragee
Yackandandah
Allans Flat
Osbornes Flat
Kergunyah
Silver Creek
Stanley
Tarrawingee
Goorambat
Glenrowan
Milawa
Oxley
Everton
Markwood
Murmungee
Dederang
Tallandoon
Eskdale
Mitta Mitta
Benalla
Winton
Greta West
Greta
Moyhu
Meadow Creek
Whorouly
Whorouly South
Gapsted
Myrtleford
Merriang
Mudgegonga
Carboor
Ovens
Baddaginnie
Molyullah
Eurobin
Havilah
Porepunkah
Bright
Freeburgh
Wandiligong
Mount Beauty
Tawonga
Tawonga South
Tawonga Gap
Mullindolingong
Warrenbayne
Swanpool
Tatong
King Valley
Myrrhee
Whitfield
Cheshunt
Edi
Buckland
Smoko
Harrietville
Bogong
Falls Creek Alpine Village
Hotham Heights Alpine Village
Dinner Plain Alpine Village
Strathbogie
Tolmie
Barjarg
Merton
Bonnie Doon
Maindample
Mansfield
Merrijig
Mirimbah
Mt Buller Alpine Village
Kanumbra
Alexandra
Eildon
Goughs Bay
Macs Cove
Howqua
Piries
Acheron
Thornton
Snobs Creek
Rubicon
Jamieson
Taggerty
Buxton
Kevington
Marysville
Gaffneys Creek
A1 Mine Settlement
Narbethong
Dargo
Waterford
Cobungra
Murray River
Lake Mulwala
Lake Hume
Lake Mokoan
Lake Eildon
Lake Buffalo
Lake Nillahcootie
Lake William Hovell
ALPINE NATIONAL PARK
MOUNT BUFFALO NATIONAL PARK
BOGONG HIGH PLAINS
GREAT DIVIDING RANGE
LAKE EILDON NATIONAL PARK
CHILTERN BOX-IRONBARK NP
WARBY RANGE STATE PARK
MOUNT SAMARIA STATE PARK
REEF HILLS PARK
CATHEDRAL RANGE STATE PARK
YARRA RANGES NATIONAL PARK
DARGO HIGH PLAINS
HOWITT PLAINS
HUME FWY
MURRAY VALLEY HWY
RIVERINA HWY
GREAT ALPINE RD
MIDLAND HWY
KIEWA VALLEY HWY
OLYMPIC HWY
MAROONDAH HWY
GOULBURN VALLEY HWY

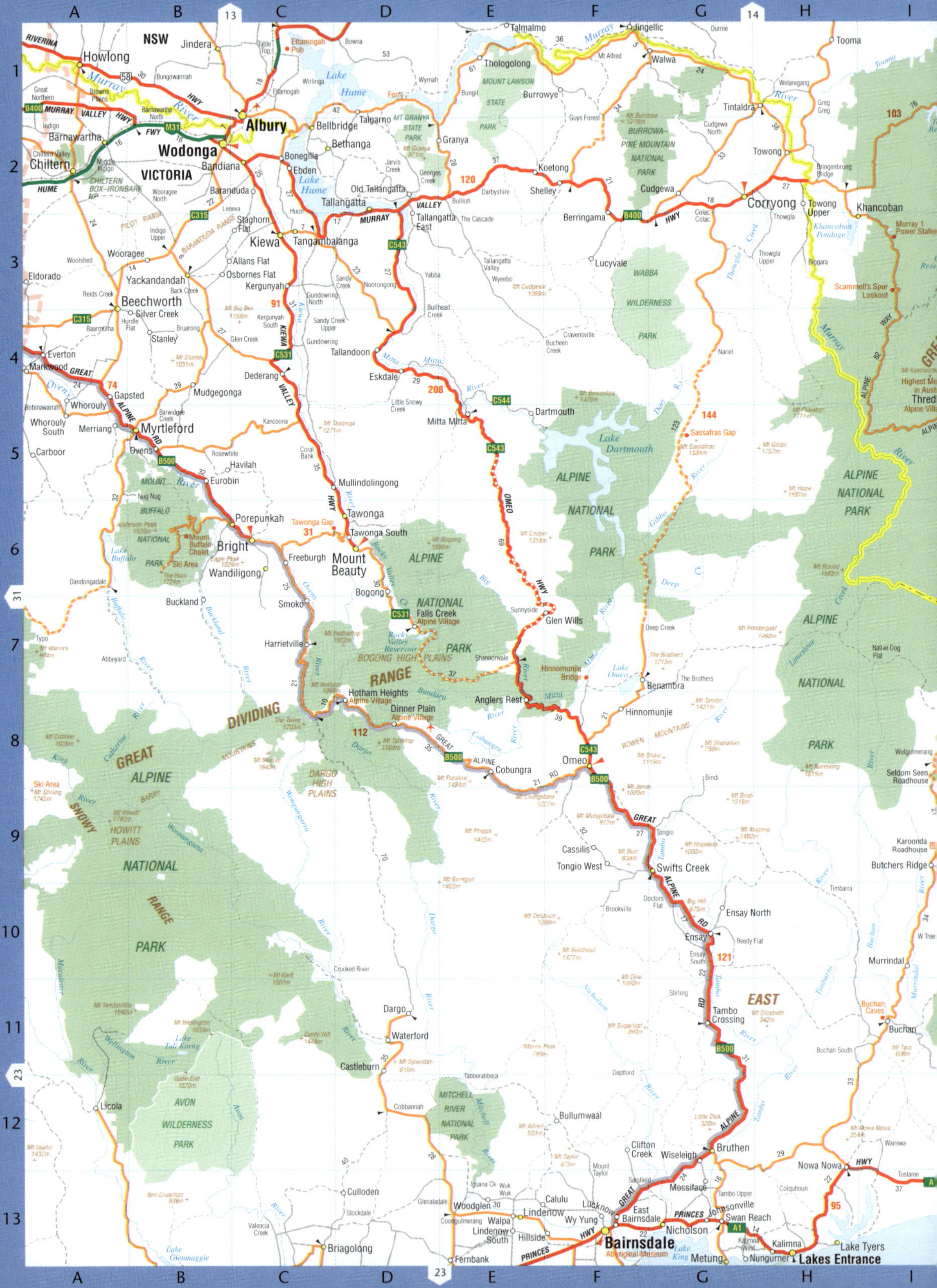

A B C D E F G H I
1 2 3 4 5 6 7 8 9 10 11 12 13
13
14
31
23
NSW
VICTORIA
RIVERINA
Howlong
Jindera
Albury
Wodonga
Chiltern
Barnawartha
Bandiana
Baranduda
Bellbridge
Bethanga
Talgarno
Bonegilla
Ebden
Lake Hume
Tallangatta
Old Tallangatta
Tallangatta East
Granya
Tholoegolong
Burrowye
Talmalmo
Jingellic
Walwa
Tintaldra
Towong
Tooma
Koetong
Shelley
Berringama
Cudgewa
Corryong
Towong Upper
Khancoban
Murray 1 Power Station
Scammell's Spur Lookout
Lucyvale
WABBA WILDERNESS PARK
BURROWA-PINE MOUNTAIN NATIONAL PARK
MOUNT LAWSON STATE PARK
MT GRANYA STATE PARK
Kiewa
Tangambalanga
Staghorn Flat
Allans Flat
Osbornes Flat
Kergunyah
Yackandandah
Wooragee
Eldorado
Beechworth
Silver Creek
Stanley
Everton
Markwood
Gapsted
Whorouly
Myrtleford
Merriang
Carboor
Ovens
Eurobin
Havilah
Mudgegonga
Dederang
Tallandoon
Eskdale
Mitta Mitta
Dartmouth
Lake Dartmouth
Mullindolingong
Tawonga
Tawonga South
Tawonga Gap
Mount Beauty
Bogong
Falls Creek Alpine Village
Porepunkah
Bright
Wandiligong
Freeburgh
Smoko
Buckland
Harrietville
Mount Buffalo Chalet
Ski Area
MOUNT BUFFALO NATIONAL PARK
ALPINE NATIONAL PARK
BOGONG HIGH PLAINS
Rocky Valley Reservoir
Glen Wills
Sunnyside
Shannonvale
Hinnomunjie Bridge
Anglers Rest
Benambra
Lake Omeo
The Brothers
Hinnomunjie
Sassafras Gap
Omeo
Hotham Heights Alpine Village
Dinner Plain Alpine Village
Cobungra
GREAT DIVIDING RANGE
DARGO HIGH PLAINS
GREAT ALPINE NATIONAL PARK
SNOWY RANGE
HOWITT PLAINS
GREAT ALPINE ROAD
Swifts Creek
Cassilis
Tongio West
Tongio
Doctors Flat
Ensay
Ensay North
Ensay South
Reedy Flat
Tambo Crossing
EAST
Buchan
Buchan Caves
Buchan South
Butchers Ridge
Murrindal
Seldom Seen Roadhouse
Karoonda Roadhouse
Dargo
Waterford
Castleburn
Crooked River
Lake Tali Karng
AVON WILDERNESS PARK
Licola
MITCHELL RIVER NATIONAL PARK
Cobbannah
Bullumwaal
Clifton Creek
Wiseleigh
Bruthen
Nowa Nowa
Mossiface
Sarsfield
Johnsonville
Swan Reach
Nicholson
East Bairnsdale
Bairnsdale
Aboriginal Museum
Lucknow
Wy Yung
Calulu
Lindenow
Lindenow South
Walpa
Hillside
Woodglen
Glenaladale
Culloden
Briagolong
Fernbank
Metung
Kalimna
Lakes Entrance
Lake Tyers
Nungurner
Lake King
PRINCES HWY
MURRAY VALLEY HWY
HUME FWY
KIEWA VALLEY HWY
OMEO HWY
ALPINE WAY
B400
B500
C531
C543
C544
C315
M31
A1

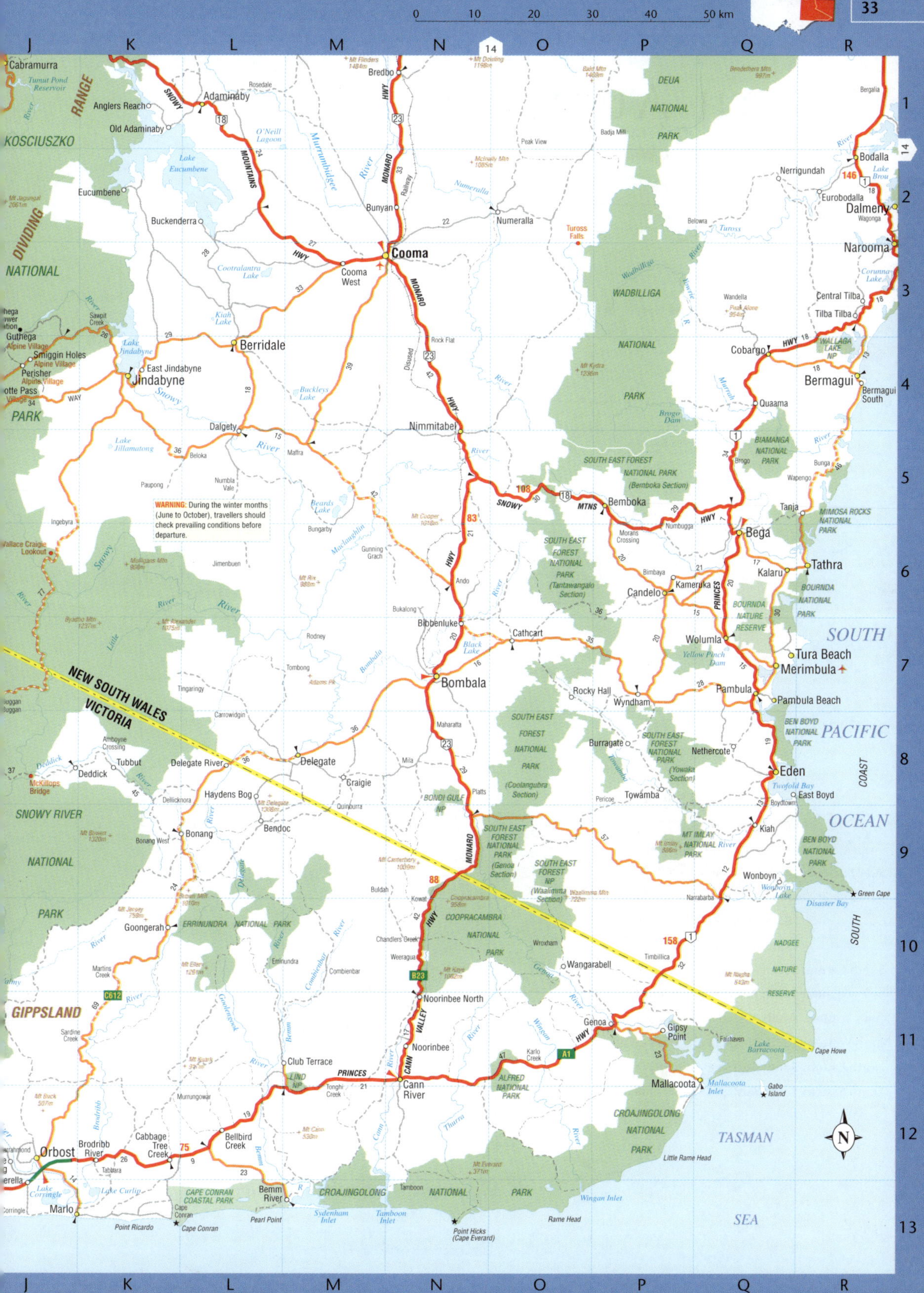

0 10 20 30 40 50 km
J K L M N O P Q R
1 2 3 4 5 6 7 8 9 10 11 12 13
14
Cabramurra
Tumut Pond Reservoir
RANGE
Adaminaby
Anglers Reach
Old Adaminaby
KOSCIUSZKO
Eucumbene
Lake Eucumbene
SNOWY MOUNTAINS
O'Neill Lagoon
Murrumbidgee
Bredbo
Mt Flinders 1484m
Mt Dowling 1198m
Baldi Mtn 1468m
Bendethera Mtn 987m
Bergalia
DEUA NATIONAL PARK
Rosedale
Peak View
Badja Mill
Mt McInally Mtn 1085m
Numeralla
Bunyan
Buckenderra
Cooma
Cooma West
Coolralantra Lake
DIVIDING
NATIONAL
Mt Jagungal 2061m
Tuross Falls
Belowra
Tuross
Bodalla
Lake Brou
Nerrigundah
Eurobodalla
Dalmeny
Wagonga
Narooma
Corunna Lake
Central Tilba
Tilba Tilba
Wandella
Peak Alone 954m
WADBILLIGA NATIONAL PARK
Kiah Lake
Sawpit Creek
Guthega
Smiggin Holes
Alpine Village
Perisher
Alpine Village
Berridale
East Jindabyne
Jindabyne
Lake Jindabyne
Buckleys Lake
Rock Flat
Disused
Cobargo
WALLAGA LAKE NP
Bermagui
Bermagui South
Quaama
Mt Kydra 1236m
PARK
Brogo Dam
Dalgety
Beloka
Lake Jillamatong
Maffra
Nimmitabel
BIAMANGA NATIONAL PARK
Brogo
Bunga
Wapengo
Paupong
Numbla Vale
SOUTH EAST FOREST NATIONAL PARK (Bemboka Section)
WARNING: During the winter months (June to October), travellers should check prevailing conditions before departure.
Beards Lake
Mt Cooper 1048m
SNOWY MTNS HWY
Bemboka
Tanja
MIMOSA ROCKS NATIONAL PARK
Ingebyra
Bungarby
Maclaughlin
Gunning Grach
Morans Crossing
Numbugga
Bega
Wallace Craigie Lookout
Jimenbuen
Ando
SOUTH EAST FOREST NATIONAL PARK (Tantawangalo Section)
Bimbaya
Candelo
Kameruka
PRINCES
Kalaru
Tathra
Mt Rix 988m
Mulligans Mtn 808m
Byadbo Mtn 1237m
Mt Alexander 1075m
Bukalong
Bibbenluke
Cathcart
BOURNDA NATURE RESERVE
BOURNDA NATIONAL PARK
Wolumla
SOUTH
Rodney
Black Lake
Yellow Pinch Dam
Tura Beach
Merimbula
Tombong
Adams Pk
Bombala
Rocky Hall
Wyndham
Pambula
Pambula Beach
NEW SOUTH WALES
VICTORIA
Tingaringy
Carrowidgin
SOUTH EAST FOREST NATIONAL PARK (Coolangubra Section)
Burragate
SOUTH EAST FOREST NATIONAL PARK (Yowaka Section)
Nethercote
BEN BOYD NATIONAL PARK
PACIFIC
Amboyne Crossing
Tubbut
Deddick
McKillops Bridge
Delegate River
Delegate
Maharatta
Mila
Craigie
Eden
Twofold Bay
East Boyd
Boydtown
COAST
Hayden's Bog
Dellicknora
Mt Delegate 1308m
Quidong
Bendoc
BONDI GULF NP
Platts
Pericoe
Towamba
SNOWY RIVER
Bonang
Bonang West
Mt Bowen 1320m
SOUTH EAST FOREST NATIONAL PARK (Genoa Section)
SOUTH EAST FOREST NP (Waalimma Section)
Waalimma Mtn 722m
MT IMLAY NATIONAL PARK
Mt Imlay 886m
Kiah
OCEAN
BEN BOYD NATIONAL PARK
NATIONAL
Mt Canterbury 1009m
Buldah
Kowat
Coopracambra 958m
COOPRACAMBRA NATIONAL PARK
Wonboyn
Wonboyn Lake
Narrabarba
Green Cape
Disaster Bay
Goongerah
Mt Jersey 759m
Brown Mtn 1016m
ERRINUNDRA NATIONAL PARK
PARK
Chandlers Creek
Weeragua
Wroxham
Timbillica
NADGEE NATURE RESERVE
SOUTH
Errinundra
Combienbar
Mt Ellery 1291m
Mt Kaye 1002m
Wangarabell
Mt Nadgee 543m
Martins Creek
GIPPSLAND
Noorinbee North
Noorinbee
CANN VALLEY HWY
Genoa
Gipsy Point
Fairhaven
Lake Barracoota
Cape Howe
Sardine Creek
Club Terrace
LIND NP
PRINCES
Tonghi Creek
Cann River
ALFRED NATIONAL PARK
Karlo Creek
Mallacoota
Mallacoota Inlet
Gabo Island
Mt Buck 587m
Murrungowar
Brodribb
Bellbird Creek
Mt Cann 530m
Thurra
CROAJINGOLONG NATIONAL PARK
TASMAN
Orbost
Brodribb River
Cabbage Tree Creek
Tablara
Mt Everard 371m
Little Rame Head
Lake Corringle
Lake Curlip
CAPE CONRAN COASTAL PARK
Bemm River
CROAJINGOLONG NATIONAL PARK
Tamboon
Wingan Inlet
Marlo
Corringle
Cape Conran
Point Ricardo
Pearl Point
Sydenham Inlet
Tamboon Inlet
Point Hicks (Cape Everard)
Rame Head
SEA
N

South Australia

Location Map

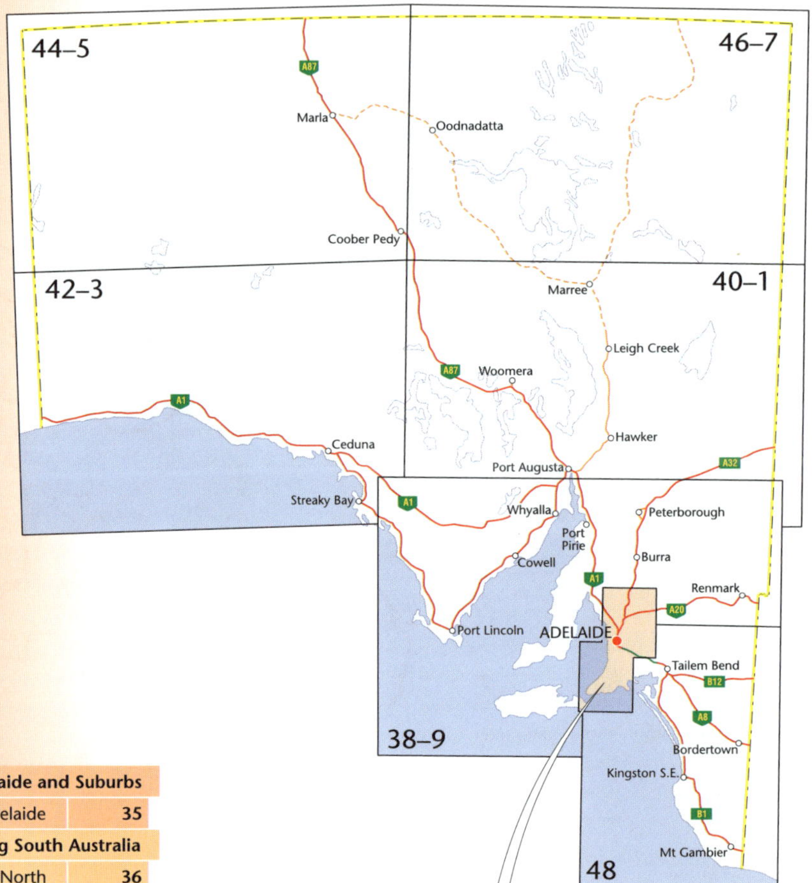

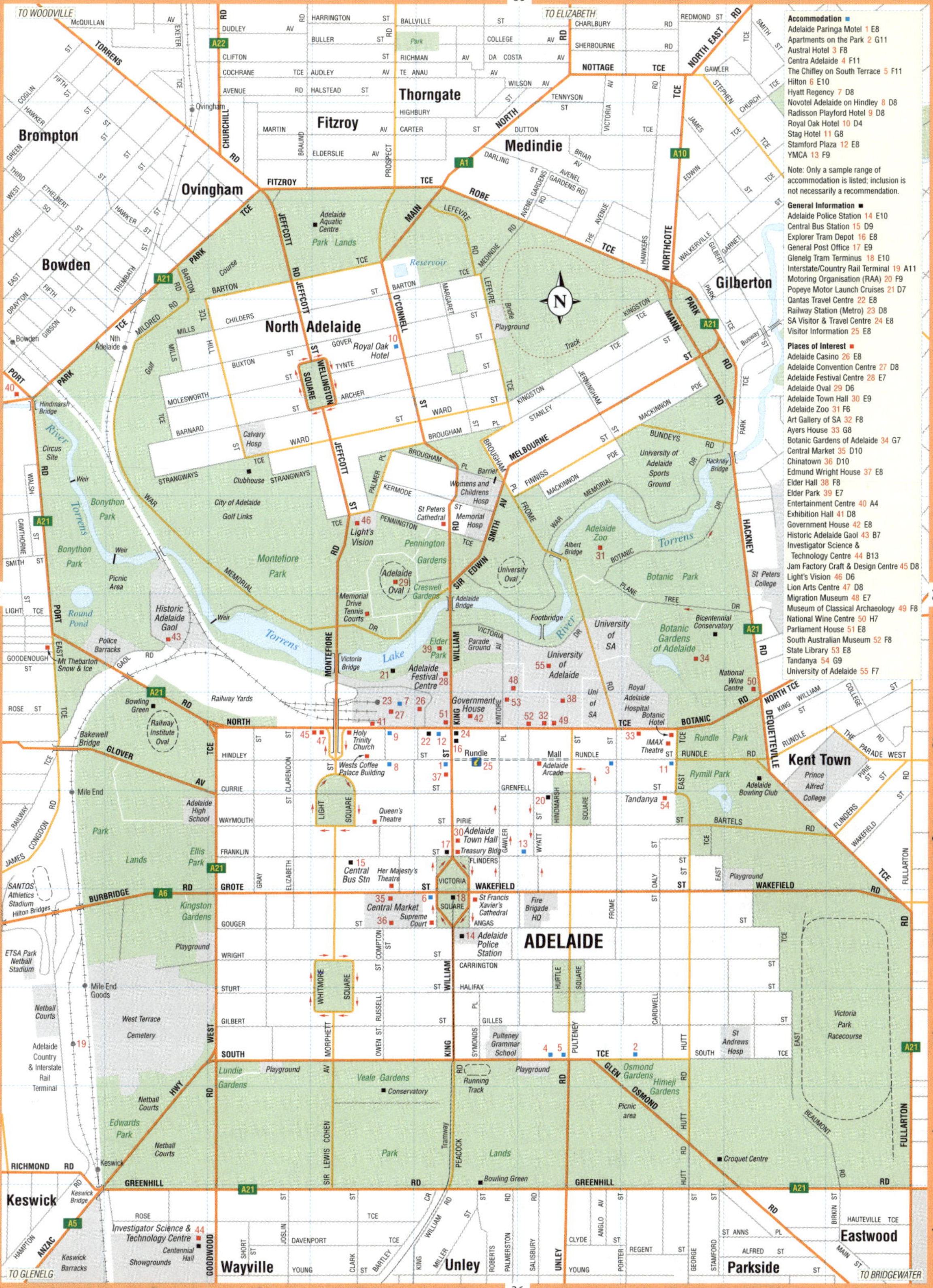
0 0.5 1 1.5 km
TO WOODVILLE
TO ELIZABETH
TO GLENELG
TO BRIDGEWATER
Brompton
Ovingham
Bowden
Fitzroy
Thorngate
Medindie
Gilberton
North Adelaide
ADELAIDE
Kent Town
Keswick
Wayville
Unley
Parkside
Eastwood
Accommodation
Adelaide Paringa Motel 1 E8
Apartments on the Park 2 G11
Austral Hotel 3 F8
Centra Adelaide 4 F11
The Chifley on South Terrace 5 F11
Hilton 6 E10
Hyatt Regency 7 D8
Novotel Adelaide on Hindley 8 D8
Radisson Playford Hotel 9 D8
Royal Oak Hotel 10 D4
Stag Hotel 11 G8
Stamford Plaza 12 E8
YMCA 13 F9
Note: Only a sample range of accommodation is listed; inclusion is not necessarily a recommendation.
General Information
Adelaide Police Station 14 E10
Central Bus Station 15 D9
Explorer Tram Depot 16 E8
General Post Office 17 E9
Glenelg Tram Terminus 18 E10
Interstate/Country Rail Terminal 19 A11
Motoring Organisation (RAA) 20 F9
Popeye Motor Launch Cruises 21 D7
Qantas Travel Centre 22 E8
Railway Station (Metro) 23 D8
SA Visitor & Travel Centre 24 E8
Visitor Information 25 E8
Places of Interest
Adelaide Casino 26 E8
Adelaide Convention Centre 27 D8
Adelaide Festival Centre 28 E7
Adelaide Oval 29 D6
Adelaide Town Hall 30 E9
Adelaide Zoo 31 F6
Art Gallery of SA 32 F8
Ayers House 33 G8
Botanic Gardens of Adelaide 34 G7
Central Market 35 D10
Chinatown 36 D10
Edmund Wright House 37 E8
Elder Hall 38 F8
Elder Park 39 E7
Entertainment Centre 40 A4
Exhibition Hall 41 D8
Government House 42 E8
Historic Adelaide Gaol 43 B7
Investigator Science & Technology Centre 44 B13
Jam Factory Craft & Design Centre 45 D8
Light's Vision 46 D6
Lion Arts Centre 47 D8
Migration Museum 48 E7
Museum of Classical Archaeology 49 F8
National Wine Centre 50 H7
Parliament House 51 E8
South Australian Museum 52 F8
State Library 53 E8
Tandanya 54 G9
University of Adelaide 55 F7

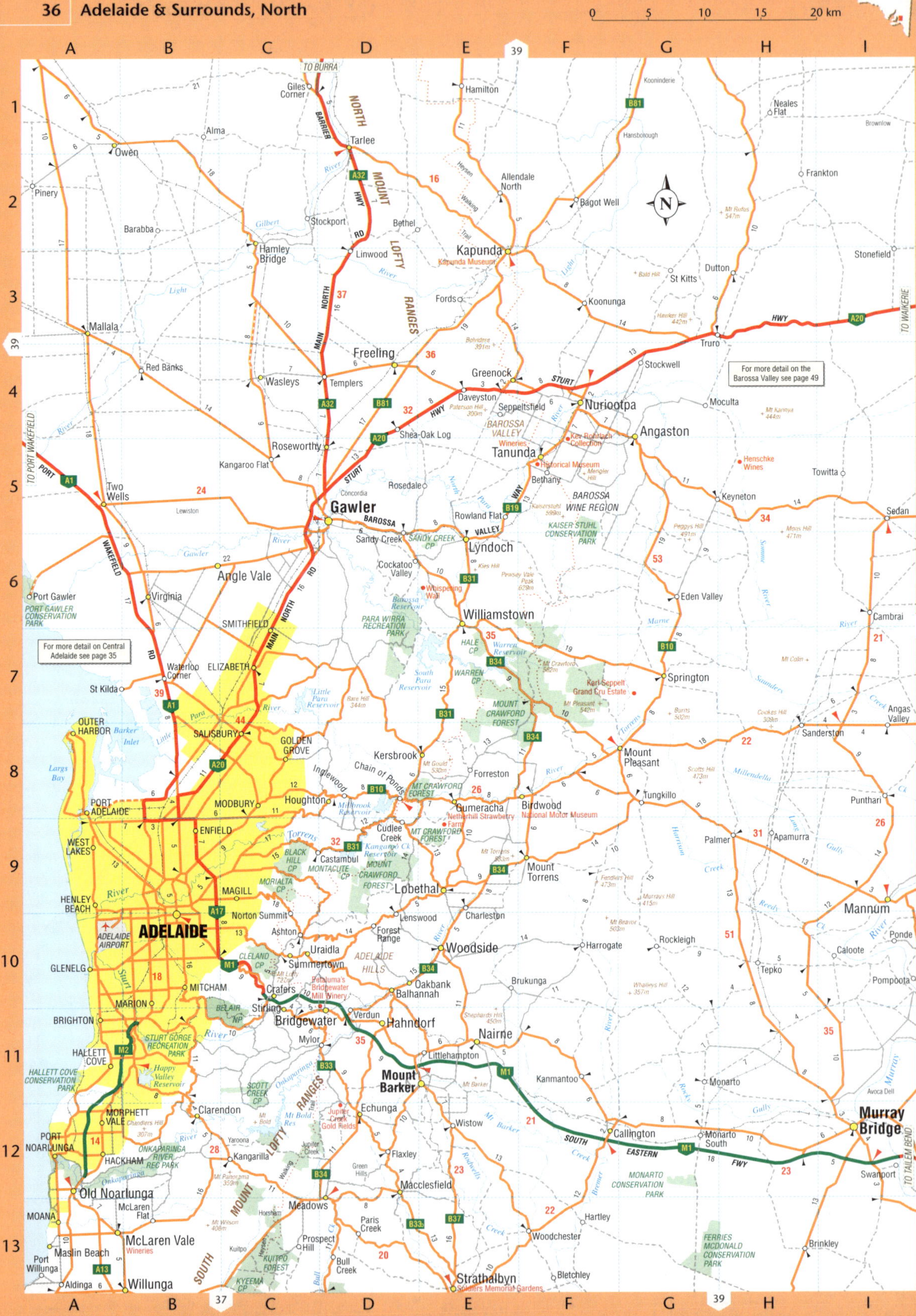
0 5 10 15 20 km
For more detail on the Barossa Valley see page 49
For more detail on Central Adelaide see page 35
TO BURRA
TO WAIKERIE
TO PORT WAKEFIELD
TO TAILEM BEND
Giles Corner
Hamilton
Koonindere
Neales Flat
Brownlow
Owen
Alma
Tarlee
Pinery
Allendale North
Bagot Well
Frankton
Barabba
Stockport
Bethel
Hamley Bridge
Linwood
Kapunda
Kapunda Museum
St Kitts
Dutton
Stonefield
Fords
Koonunga
Truro
Mallala
Freeling
Stockwell
Red Banks
Wasleys
Templers
Greenock
Daveyston
Seppeltsfield
Nuriootpa
Moculta
BAROSSA VALLEY
Angaston
Shea-Oak Log
Roseworthy
Kangaroo Flat
Tanunda
Historical Museum
Bethany
Henschke Wines
Towitta
Two Wells
Rosedale
Concordia
BAROSSA WINE REGION
Keyneton
Gawler
Rowland Flat
Lewiston
KAISER STUHL CONSERVATION PARK
Sedan
Sandy Creek
SANDY CREEK CP
Lyndoch
Angle Vale
Cockatoo Valley
Port Gawler
Virginia
PORT GAWLER CONSERVATION PARK
Whispering Wall
Barossa Reservoir
Eden Valley
Cambrai
Williamstown
PARA WIRRA RECREATION PARK
SMITHFIELD
HALE CP
Warren Reservoir
Waterloo Corner
ELIZABETH
Springton
St Kilda
WARREN CP
South Para Reservoir
Karl Seppelt Grand Cru Estate
Little Para Reservoir
MOUNT CRAWFORD FOREST
Angas Valley
OUTER HARBOR
Barker Inlet
SALISBURY
GOLDEN GROVE
Sanderston
Largs Bay
Kersbrook
Mount Pleasant
Chain of Ponds
Forreston
PORT ADELAIDE
Inglewood
Houghton
MT CRAWFORD FOREST
Gumeracha
Birdwood
National Motor Museum
Netherhill Strawberry Farm
Tungkillo
Punthari
MODBURY
Millbrook Reservoir
WEST LAKES
ENFIELD
Cudlee Creek
Palmer
Apamurra
BLACK HILL CP
Castambul
Kangaroo Ck Reservoir
MONTACUTE CP
Mount Torrens
HENLEY BEACH
MAGILL
MORIALTA CP
Lobethal
Mannum
ADELAIDE AIRPORT
ADELAIDE
Norton Summit
Lenswood
Charleston
Ashton
Forest Range
Woodside
Harrogate
Rockleigh
Ponde
GLENELG
CLELAND CP
Uraidla
Summertown
ADELAIDE HILLS
Caloote
Tepko
Pompoota
MITCHAM
Crafers
Petaluma's Bridgewater Mill Winery
Oakbank
Balhannah
Brukunga
MARION
BELAIR NP
Stirling
Bridgewater
Verdun
Hahndorf
BRIGHTON
Mylor
Nairne
Littlehampton
HALLETT COVE
STURT GORGE RECREATION PARK
Happy Valley Reservoir
HALLETT COVE CONSERVATION PARK
SCOTT CREEK CP
Mount Barker
Kanmantoo
Monarto
Avoca Dell
MORPHETT VALE
Clarendon
Echunga
Jupiter Creek Gold Fields
Wistow
Murray Bridge
PORT NOARLUNGA
ONKAPARINGA RIVER REC PARK
Callington
Monarto South
HACKHAM
Kangarilla
Flaxley
SOUTH EASTERN FWY
Swanport
Old Noarlunga
MONARTO CONSERVATION PARK
Macclesfield
MOANA
McLaren Flat
Meadows
Hartley
McLaren Vale
Wineries
Paris Creek
Woodchester
Brinkley
Maslin Beach
Prospect Hill
FERRIES MCDONALD CONSERVATION PARK
Port Willunga
KUITPO FOREST
Bull Creek
Aldinga
Willunga
KYEEMA CP
Strathalbyn
Soldiers Memorial Gardens
Bletchley
NORTH MOUNT LOFTY RANGES
SOUTH MOUNT LOFTY RANGES
BARRIER HWY
MAIN NORTH RD
STURT HWY
BAROSSA VALLEY WAY
PORT WAKEFIELD RD

0 5 10 15 20 km
GULF
ST VINCENT
FLEURIEU
PENINSULA
SOUTHERN
OCEAN
BACKSTAIRS
PASSAGE
KANGAROO ISLAND
DUDLEY
PENINSULA
Encounter Bay
TO ENFIELD
ADELAIDE AIRPORT
GLENELG
MITCHAM
MARION
BRIGHTON
HALLETT COVE CP
HALLETT COVE
STURT GORGE RECREATION PARK
Happy Valley Reservoir
MORPHETT VALE
PORT NOARLUNGA
HACKHAM
ONKAPARINGA RIVER REC PARK
Old Noarlunga
MOANA
Maslin Beach
Port Willunga
Aldinga Beach
Aldinga
ALDINGA SCRUB CONSERVATION PARK
Aldinga Bay
Silver Sands
Sellicks Beach
Sellicks Hill
McLaren Flat
McLaren Vale
Wineries
Willunga
CLELAND CP
BELAIR NP
Ashton
Uraidla
Summertown
Crafers
Stirling
Bridgewater
Mylor
Forest Range
Woodside
Oakbank
Balhannah
ADELAIDE HILLS
Petaluma's Bridgewater Mill Winery
Verdun
Hahndorf
Littlehampton
Mount Barker
TO MURRAY BRIDGE
Echunga
Wistow
Jupiter Creek Gold Fields
Flaxley
Macclesfield
Clarendon
Kangarilla
SCOTT CREEK CP
Mt Bold Res
MOUNT LOFTY RANGES
SOUTH
Meadows
Paris Creek
Prospect Hill
Bull Creek
Strathalbyn
Soldiers Memorial Gardens
Lookout
KUITPO FOREST
KYEEMA CP
Hope Forest
Kuitpo Colony
McHarg Creek
Ashbourne
MT MAGNIFICENT CP
COX SCRUB CONSERVATION PARK
Pages Flat
Mount Compass
Nangkita
Sandergrove
Finniss
Begonia Farm (Open Oct.–Apr.)
Myponga Beach
Myponga Reservoir
Lookout
Myponga
NIXON-SKINNER CP
MYPONGA CONSERVATION PARK
Carrickalinga
Normanville
Yankalilla
Yankalilla Bay
Paradise Wirrina Cove Resort
Rapid Bay
Second Valley
Delamere
Cape Jervis Lighthouse
Cape Jervis
Lands End
Fishery Beach
TALISKER CONSERVATION PARK
DEEP CREEK CONSERVATION PARK
Porpoise Head
Tunkalilla Beach
Tunk Head
Parsons Beach
Waitpinga Beach
Newland Head
NEWLAND HEAD CONSERVATION PARK
Waitpinga
SPRING MOUNTAIN CONSERVATION PARK
Hindmarsh Falls
Glacier Rock
Inman Valley
SECOND VALLEY FOREST
Back Valley
Newland
Victor Harbor
Horse-drawn Tram
Granite Island
Fairy Penguins
SA Whale Centre
Rosetta Head (The Bluff)
King Beach
West Island
WEST ISLAND CONSERVATION PARK
Urimbirra Wildlife Park
Greenhills Adventure Park
Hindmarsh Valley
Middleton
Middleton Winery
Crows Nest Lookout
Port Elliot
Boomer Beach
Steam Ranger (train)
Malleebaa Woolshed
Goolwa
Goolwa River
Narnu Bay
Hindmarsh Island
Barrage
Murray Mouth
Currency Creek
Currency Creek Winery
Canoe Tree
SCOTT CONSERVATION PARK
Mosquito Flat
Tooperang
Gilberts
Snapper Point
Cape Coutts
LASHMAR CP
Antechamber Bay
Chapman River
Cape St Albans
Moncrieff Bay
Cape Willoughby
CAPE HART CONSERVATION PARK
Cape Hart
4WD only
Kangaroo Island Vehicular & Passenger Ferry

GREAT AUSTRALIAN BIGHT
SOUTHERN OCEAN
SPENCER GULF
INVESTIGATOR STRAIT
EYRE PENINSULA
YORKE PENINSULA
KANGAROO ISLAND
Cungena
Poochera
Minnipa
Yaninee
Wudinna
Pygery
Kyancutta
Koongawa
Kimba
Iron Knob
Iron Baron
Whyalla
Buckleboo
Port Kenny
Venus Bay
Talia
Elliston
Bramfield
Warramboo
Waddikee
Caralue
Darke Peak
Lock
Kielpa
Rudall
Cleve
Mangalo
Cowell
Lucky Bay
Carpa
Elbow Hill
Arno Bay
Sheringa
Murdinga
Tooligie
Wharminda
Karkoo
Mount Hope
Kapinnie
Yeelanna
Port Neill
Butler Tanks
Cockaleechie
Ungarra
Cummins
Lipson
Warrow
Coulta
Yallunda Flat
Tumby Bay
Edillilie
Koppio
White Flat
Wanilla
Wangary
Louth Bay
Poonindie
North Shields
Coffin Bay
Port Lincoln
GAWLER RANGES NP
PINKAWILLINIE CONSERVATION PARK
LAKE GILLES CONSERVATION PARK
LINCOLN NATIONAL PARK
COFFIN BAY NATIONAL PARK
Wallaroo
Kadina
Moonta
Maitland
Port Victoria
Minlaton
Warooka
Yorketown
Edithburgh
Marion Bay
Stenhouse Bay
Kingscote
American River
Parndana
Vivonne Bay
Karatta
Rocky River
FLINDERS CHASE NATIONAL PARK

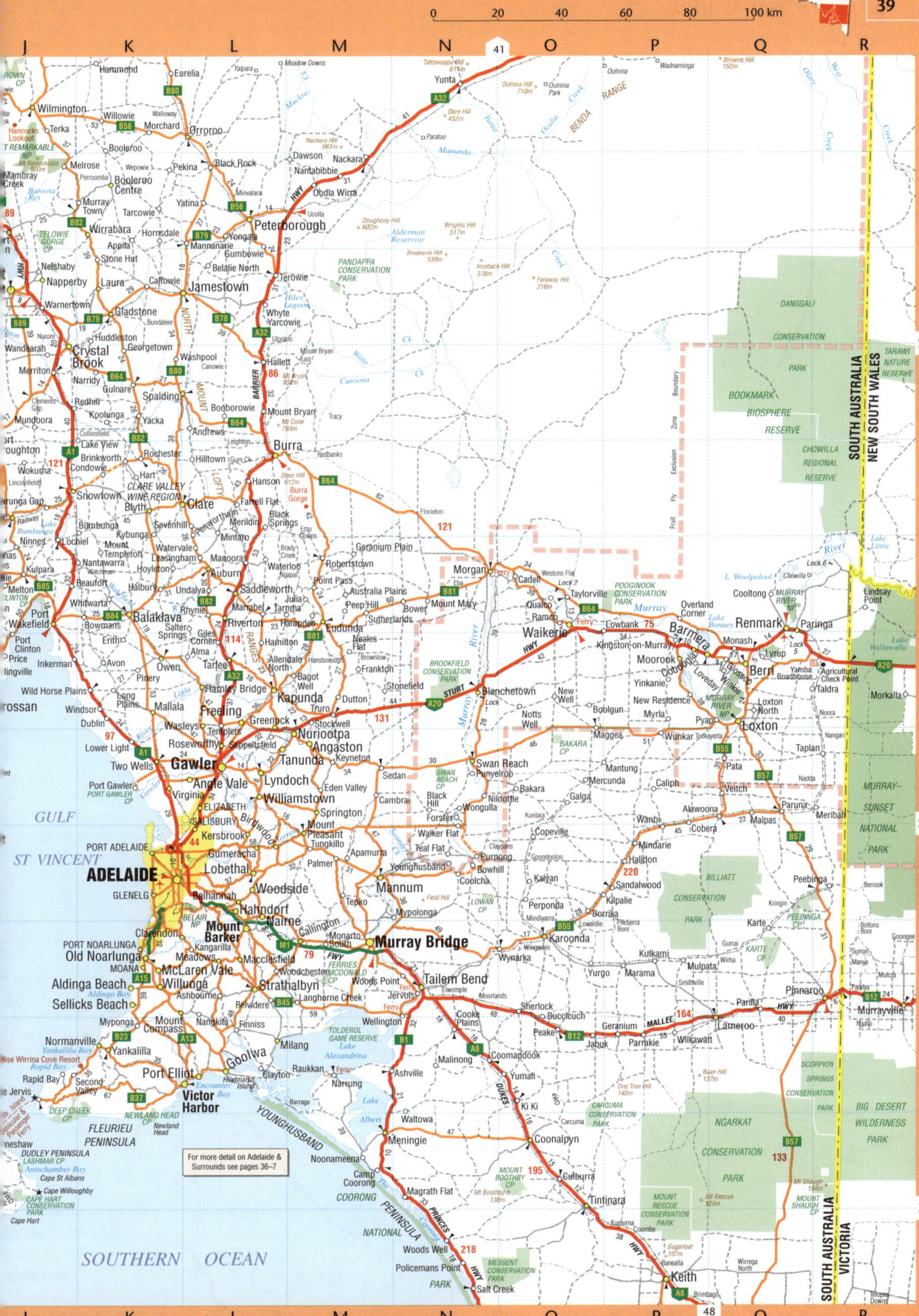
0 20 40 60 80 100 km
J K L M N O P Q R
1 2 3 4 5 6 7 8 9 10 11 12 13
41
12
28
26
48
Hammond
Eurelia
Yalpara
Meadow Downs
Tattawuppa Hill 611m
Yunta
Oulnina Hill 710m
Oulnina Park
Oulnina
Wadnaminga
Browns Hill 152m
Wilmington
Willowie
Walloway
Morchard
Orroroo
Terka
Hancocks Lookout
MT REMARKABLE NP
Booleroo
Nackara Hill 661m
Dawson
Nackara
Dare Hill 452m
Paratoo
Manunda
BENDA RANGE
Olary Creek
Melrose
Wepowie
Pekina
Black Rock
Nantabibbie
Oodla Wirra
Mambray Creek
Booleroo Centre
Murray Town
Tarcowie
Yatina
Minvalara
Peterborough
Ucolta
Doughboy Hill 602m
Alderman Reservoir
Wrights Hill 517m
Wirrabara
Hornsdale
Yongala
Appila
Mannanarie
Gumbowie
TELOWIE GORGE CP
Stone Hut
Belalie North
Boiekevie Hill 539m
Ironback Hill 378m
PANDAPPA CONSERVATION PARK
Nelshaby
Napperby
Laura
Caltowie
Jamestown
Jerowie
Faraway Hill 216m
Warnertown
Gladstone
Bundaleer
Whyte Yarcowie
Hiles Lagoon
DANGGALI CONSERVATION PARK
Huddleston
Georgetown
Ulooloo
Wandearah
Crystal Brook
Washpool
Canowie
Hallett
Mount Bryan East
Mt Bryan 932m
Curoona
TARAWI NATURE RESERVE
Merriton
Narridy
Gulnare
Spalding
BOOKMARK BIOSPHERE RESERVE
Redhill
Koolunga
Booborowie
Mount Bryan
Tracy
Mt Cone 793m
SOUTH AUSTRALIA
NEW SOUTH WALES
Mundoora
Yacka
Andrews
Leighton
Burra
Redbanks
Fruit Fly Exclusion Zone Boundary
Lake View
Brinkworth
Rochester
Hilltown
Gum Creek
CHOWILLA REGIONAL RESERVE
Wokurna
Condowie
Hart
Stein Hill 612m
Burra Gorge
Snowtown
CLARE VALLEY WINE REGION
Blyth
Clare
Hanson
Farrell Flat
Florieton
Bumbunga
Sevenhill
Penwortham
Merildin
Black Springs
Lake Bumbunga
Lochiel
Kybunga
Mintaro
Emu Downs
Ninnes
Mount Templeton
Watervale
Leasingham
Manoora
Geranium Plain
Brady Creek
Robertstown
Nantawarra
Hoyleton
Auburn
Waterloo
Ngapal
Kulpara
Beaufort
Halbury
Undalya
Saddleworth
Point Pass
Australia Plains
Morgan
Cadell
Westons Flat
Lock 2
Taylorville
POOGINOOK CONSERVATION PARK
L. Woolpolool
Chowilla
Lock 6
Melton
Whitwarta
Rhynie
Marrabel
Julia
Tarnma
Peep Hill
Bower
Mount Mary
Qualco
Ramco
Overland Corner
Cooltong
MURRAY RIVER NP
Lindsay Point
Port Wakefield
Bowmans
Balaklava
Salter Springs
Riverton
Hamley
Sutherlands
Waikerie
Cobdogla
Lowbank
Barmera
Lake Bonney
Renmark
Paringa
Port Clinton
Erith
Giles Corner
Hampden
Eudunda
Kingston-on-Murray
Monash
Lyrup
Lake Wallawalla
Price
Inkerman
Avon
Alma
Hamilton
Neales Flat
Brownlow
Moorook
Berri
Glossop
Winkie
Loveday
Yamba
Agricultural Check Point
Wild Horse Plains
Owen
Tarlee
Allendale North
Hansborough
Frankton
BROOKFIELD CONSERVATION PARK
Yinkanie
Boadhouse
Taldra
Morkalla
Pinery
Hamley Bridge
Kapunda
Bagot Well
Stonefield
Blanchetown
New Well
New Residence
Loxton North
Windsor
Long Plains
Mallala
Freeling
Truro
Dutton
Lock 1
Notts Well
Bookpurnong
Myrla
Pyap
Loxton
Noora
Dublin
Wasleys
Greenock
Stockwell
Nuriootpa
Maggea
Wunkar
Taplan
Nangari
Lower Light
Roseworthy
Templers
Seppeltsfield
Angaston
Tanunda
Keyneton
BAKARA CP
Two Wells
Gawler
Angle Vale
Lyndoch
Swan Reach
Punyelroo
Mantung
Pata
Nadda
Port Gawler
PORT GAWLER CP
Virginia
Sedan
Eden Valley
Williamstown
Black Hill
SWAN REACH CP
Nildottie
Mercunda
Bakara
Galga
Caliph
Veitch
MURRAY-SUNSET NATIONAL PARK
GULF
ST VINCENT
ELIZABETH
SALISBURY
Springton
Cambrai
Wongulla
Forster
Kunlara
Wanbi
Alawoona
Paruna
Meribah
Kersbrook
Mount Pleasant
Tungkillo
Walker Flat
Copeville
Cobera
Malpas
PORT ADELAIDE
Gumeracha
Teal Flat
Claypans
Mindarie
Halidon
ADELAIDE
Lobethal
Palmer
Apamurra
Purnong
Goondooloo
BILLIATT CONSERVATION PARK
GLENELG
Woodside
Younghusband
Bowhill
Coolcha
Kalyan
Sandalwood
Peebinga
Berrook
Balhannah
Hahndorf
Tepko
Mannum
Field Hill
Kilpalie
Kringin
BELAIR NP
Nairne
Mypolonga
LOWAN CP
Perponda
Mindiyarra
Borrika
Pinkerra Bore
Karte
PEEBINGA CP
Boltons Bore
Goongee
PORT NOARLUNGA
Old Noarlunga
Clarendon
Mount Barker
Kangarilla
Callington
Monarto South
Murray Bridge
Wynarka
Karoonda
Wingamin
Lowaldie
Gurrai
Wirha
KARTE CP
Sunset
Mamja
MOANA
Meadows
Macclesfield
Kulkami
Mulpata
Yurgo
Marama
Smithville
Mulcra
Aldinga Beach
McLaren Vale
Willunga
Woodchester
FERRIES McDONALD CP
Tailem Bend
Elwomple
Moorlands
Pinnaroo
Parilla
Panitya
Murrayville
Sellicks Beach
Ashbourne
Strathalbyn
Woods Point
Jervois
Langhorne Creek
Wellington
Cooke Plains
Sherlock
Bucclcuch
Peake
Geranium
MALLEE
Lameroo
Ngallo
Myponga
Nangkita
Mount Compass
Belvidere
Finniss
TOLDEROL GAME RESERVE
Lake Alexandrina
Jabuk
Parrakie
Wilkawatt
Normanville
Yankalilla
Yankalilla Bay
Milang
Coomandook
Malinong
Baan Hill 137m
SCORPION SPRINGS CONSERVATION PARK
Wirrina Cove Resort
Port Elliot
Goolwa
Clayton
Raukkan
Narrung
Ashville
Yumali
One Tree Hill 140m
Rapid Bay
Second Valley
Encounter Bay
Hindmarsh Island
Victor Harbor
Lake Albert
Ki Ki
CARCUMA CONSERVATION PARK
Carcuma
BIG DESERT WILDERNESS PARK
NGARKAT CONSERVATION PARK
Cape Jervis
DEEP CREEK CP
NEWLAND HEAD CP
Newland Head
Barrage
Waltowa
FLEURIEU PENINSULA
YOUNGHUSBAND
Meningie
Coonalpyn
DUDLEY PENINSULA
LASHMAR CP
Antechamber Bay
Cape St Albans
Cape Willoughby
CAPE HART CONSERVATION PARK
Cape Hart
For more detail on Adelaide & Surrounds see pages 36–7
Noonameena
Camp Coorong
COORONG
MOUNT BOOTHBY CP
Mt Boothby 130m
Culburra
Magrath Flat
Tintinara
Mt Shaugh 184m
MOUNT SHAUGH CP
NATIONAL PARK
THE COORONG
PENINSULA
Kunjora
Coombe
MOUNT RESCUE CONSERVATION PARK
Mt Rescue 129m
SOUTHERN OCEAN
Woods Well
Policemans Point
Salt Creek
MESSENT CONSERVATION PARK
Sugarloaf 107m
Beneilla
Wirrega North
Keith
Brimbago
Tellopea Downs
VICTORIA
PRINCES HWY
DUKES HWY
MALLEE HWY
STURT HWY
BARRIER HWY
MOUNT LOFTY RANGES
NORTH

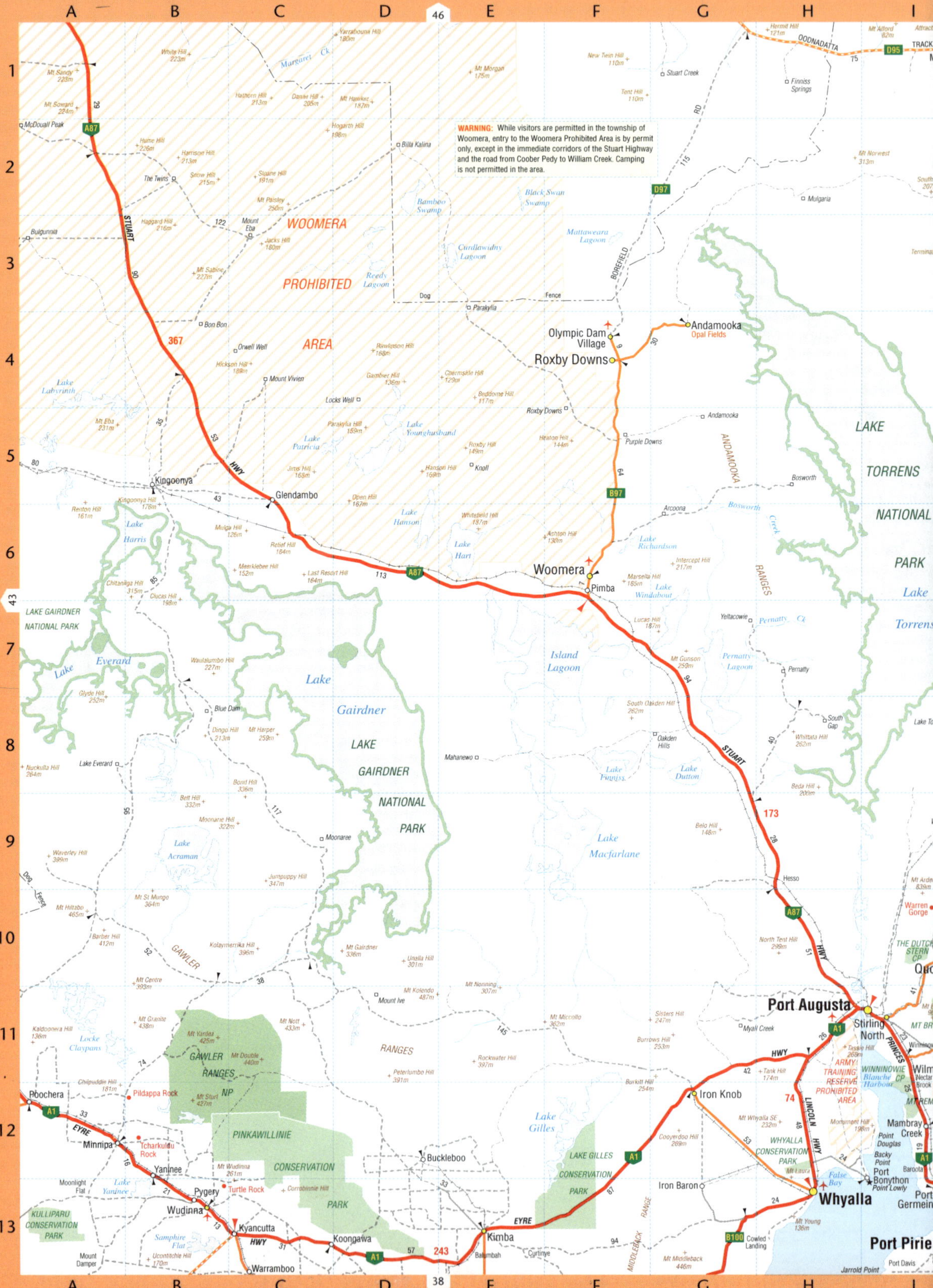
WARNING: While visitors are permitted in the township of Woomera, entry to the Woomera Prohibited Area is by permit only, except in the immediate corridors of the Stuart Highway and the road from Coober Pedy to William Creek. Camping is not permitted in the area.
WOOMERA PROHIBITED AREA
STUART HWY
LAKE GAIRDNER NATIONAL PARK
Lake Gairdner
LAKE TORRENS NATIONAL PARK
Lake Torrens
GAWLER RANGES NP
PINKAWILLINIE CONSERVATION PARK
LAKE GILLES CONSERVATION PARK
WHYALLA CONSERVATION PARK
KULLIPARU CONSERVATION PARK
LAKE GAIRDNER NATIONAL PARK
ARMY TRAINING RESERVE PROHIBITED AREA
ANDAMOOKA RANGES
GAWLER RANGES
EYRE HWY
LINCOLN HWY
PRINCES HWY
OODNADATTA TRACK
BOREFIELD RD
Dog Fence
Olympic Dam Village
Roxby Downs
Andamooka
Opal Fields
Woomera
Pimba
Glendambo
Kingoonya
Port Augusta
Stirling North
Iron Knob
Iron Baron
Whyalla
Port Pirie
Port Germein
Kimba
Buckleboo
Kyancutta
Koongawa
Warramboo
Wudinna
Pygery
Yaninee
Minnipa
Poochera
Lake Everard
Lake Harris
Lake Hart
Lake Hanson
Island Lagoon
Lake Macfarlane
Lake Gilles
Lake Acraman
Lake Labyrinth
Lake Younghusband
Lake Richardson
Lake Windabout
Lake Finniss
Lake Dutton
Pernatty Lagoon
Mattaweara Lagoon
Black Swan Swamp
Bamboo Swamp
Curdlawidny Lagoon
Reedy Lagoon
Lake Patricia
Locke Claypans
Pildappa Rock
Tcharkulda Rock
Turtle Rock
Hesso
Mount Ive
Moonaree
Mahanewo
Bon Bon
Mount Eba
Billa Kalina
Stuart Creek
Finniss Springs
Mulgaria
Purple Downs
Bosworth
Arcoona
Yeltacowie
Pernatty
Oakden Hills
Myall Creek
A87
A1
B97
D97
D95
B100
367
173
243
74
43
46
38
A
B
C
D
E
F
G
H
I
1
2
3
4
5
6
7
8
9
10
11
12
13

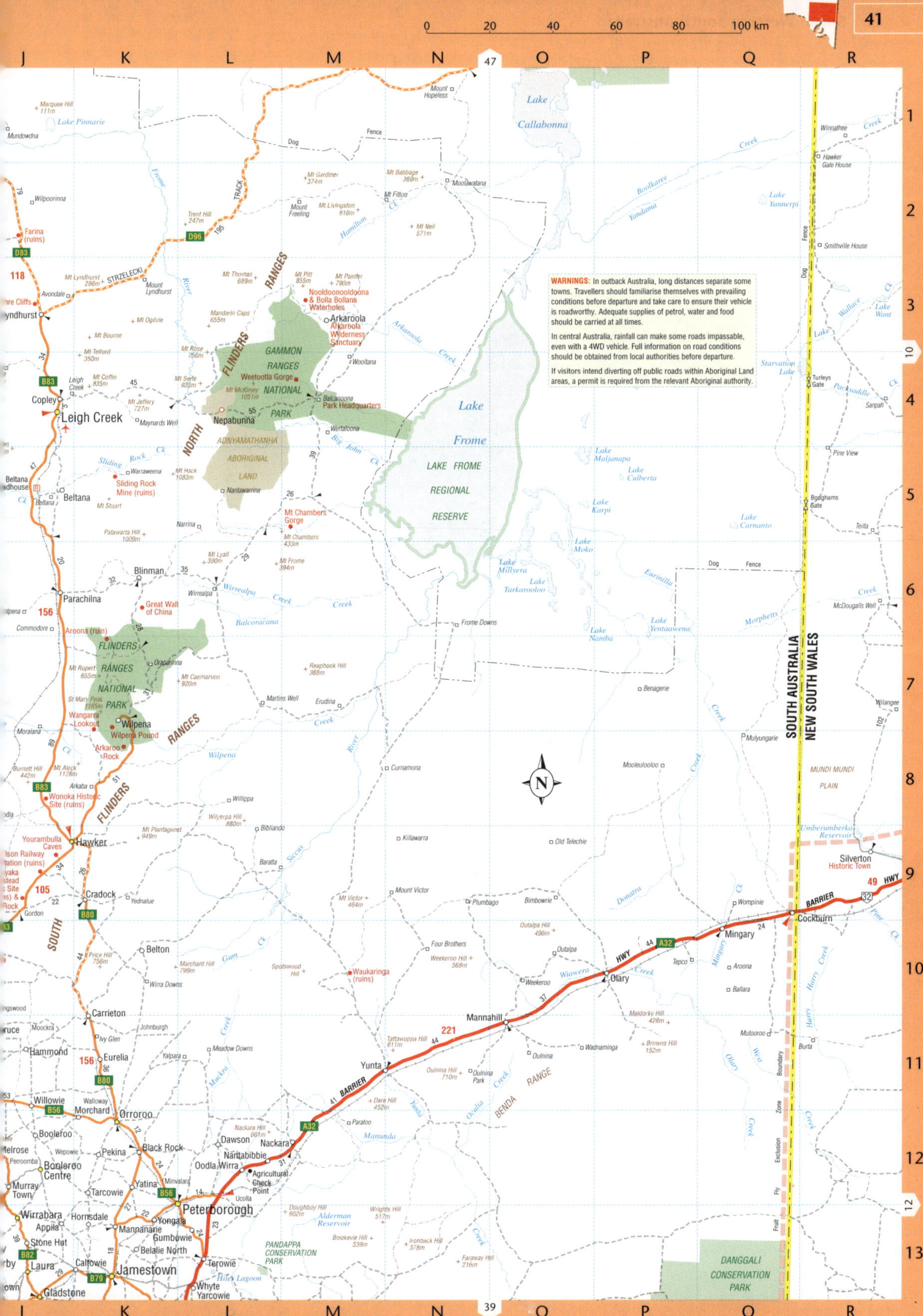
0 20 40 60 80 100 km
J K L M N O P Q R
1 2 3 4 5 6 7 8 9 10 11 12 13
47
39
WARNINGS: In outback Australia, long distances separate some towns. Travellers should familiarise themselves with prevailing conditions before departure and take care to ensure their vehicle is roadworthy. Adequate supplies of petrol, water and food should be carried at all times.
In central Australia, rainfall can make some roads impassable, even with a 4WD vehicle. Full information on road conditions should be obtained from local authorities before departure.
If visitors intend diverting off public roads into Aboriginal Land areas, a permit is required from the relevant Aboriginal authority.
Lake Callabonna
Lake Frome
LAKE FROME REGIONAL RESERVE
GAMMON RANGES NATIONAL PARK
ADNYAMATHANHA ABORIGINAL LAND
FLINDERS RANGES NATIONAL PARK
NORTH FLINDERS RANGES
SOUTH FLINDERS RANGES
SOUTH AUSTRALIA
NEW SOUTH WALES
Mount Hopeless
Dog Fence
Lake Pinnarie
Marquee Hill 111m
Mundowdna
Wilpoorinna
Farina (ruins)
D83
118
Mt Lyndhurst 286m
STRZELECKI TRACK
D96
Trent Hill 247m
Mount Lyndhurst
Avondale
Lyndhurst
Mt Gardiner 374m
Mt Babbage 369m
Moolawatana
Mt Fitton
Mount Freeling
Mt Livingston 616m
Mt Neil 571m
Hamilton Ck
Frome
River
Mt Thomas 689m
Mt Pitt 855m
Mt Painter 790m
Nooldoonooldoona & Bolla Bollana Waterholes
Arkaroola
Arkaroola Wilderness Sanctuary
Mandarin Caps 655m
Mt Ogilvie
Mt Bourne
Mt Telford 350m
Mt Rose 756m
Wooltana
Mt Coffin 835m
Leigh Creek
Mt Serle 938m
Weetootla Gorge
Mt McKinlay 1051m
Balcanoona Park Headquarters
Mt Jeffery 727m
Nepabunna
Maynards Well
Copley
Leigh Creek
B83
Wertaloona
Big John Ck
Arkaroola Creek
Sliding Rock Ck
Warraweena
Mt Hack 1083m
Sliding Rock Mine (ruins)
Nantawarrina
Beltana
Beltana Roadhouse
Mt Stuart
Mt Chambers Gorge
Mt Chambers 433m
Patawarta Hill 1009m
Narrina
Mt Lyall 390m
Mt Frome 394m
Blinman
Parachilna
Great Wall of China
Wirrealpa
Wirrealpa Creek
Balcoracana Creek
156
Commodore
Aroona (ruin)
Oraparinna
Mt Rupert 655m
Mt Caernarvon 920m
St Mary Peak 1165m
Wangarra Lookout
Wilpena
Wilpena Pound
Arkaroo Rock
Moralana
Martins Well
Erudina Creek
Reaphook Hill 388m
Frome Downs
Burnett Hill 442m
Mt Aleck 1128m
Arkaba
Wilpena River
Wonoka Historic Site (ruins)
Willippa
Wilyerpa Hill 880m
Bibliando
Mt Plantagenet 949m
Curnamona
Killawarra
Old Telechie
Yourambulla Caves
Hawker
Kanyaka Homestead
Wilson Railway Station (ruins)
105
Cradock
Yednalue
Gordon
Baratta
Siccus
Mount Victor
Mt Victor 464m
Plumbago
Bimbowrie
B80
Price Hill 756m
Belton
Marchant Hill 799m
Gum Ck
Spotswood Hill
Waukaringa (ruins)
Four Brothers
Weekeroo Hill 568m
Outalpa Hill 496m
Outalpa
Weekeroo
Wirra Downs
Carrieton
Moockra
Johnburgh
Hammond
Ivy Glen
Eurelia
Yalpara
Meadow Downs
Tattawuppa Hill 611m
221
Mannahill
Oulnina Hill 710m
Oulnina Park
Oulnina
BENDA RANGE
Yunta
BARRIER HWY
A32
Willowie
Walloway
Morchard
Orroroo
B56
Booleroo
Melrose
Wepowie
Pekina
Black Rock
Booleroo Centre
Murray Town
Tarcowie
Yatina
Minvalara
Peterborough
Ucolta
Wirrabara
Hornsdale
Appila
Mannanarie
Yongala
Stone Hut
Gumbowie
Belalie North
Laura
Caltowie
Jamestown
Terowie
Whyte Yarcowie
Gladstone
B82
B79
Hiles Lagoon
Dawson
Nackara
Nackara Hill 661m
Paratoo
Manunda
Nantabibbie
Oodla Wirra
Agricultural Check Point
Doughboy Hill 602m
Alderman Reservoir
Wrights Hill 517m
Boiokevie Hill 539m
Ironback Hill 378m
Faraway Hill 216m
PANDAPPA CONSERVATION PARK
DANGGALI CONSERVATION PARK
Olary
Wiawera Creek
Mingary
Tepco
Aroona
Ballara
Maldorky Hill 428m
Wadnaminga
Browns Hill 152m
Mutooroo
Burta
Wompinie
Cockburn
Silverton Historic Town
49 HWY
32
Umberumberka Reservoir
MUNDI MUNDI PLAIN
Mulyungarie
Mooleulooloo
Benagerie
Lake Maljanapa
Lake Culberta
Lake Karpi
Lake Moko
Lake Millyera
Lake Tarkarooloo
Lake Namba
Lake Yentaawena
Lake Carnanto
Eurinilla
Morphetts Creek
Lake Yannerpi
Bookaree
Yandama Creek
Winnathee
Hawker Gate House
Smithville House
Lake Want
Wallace Ck
Starvation Lake
Turleys Gate
Packsaddle Ck
Sanpah
Pine View
Boolghams Gate
Teilta
McDougalls Well
Wilangee
Fence
Dog Fence
Fruit Fly Exclusion Zone Boundary
Olary Creek
Harry Creek
Donatra
Pine Ck

A B C D E F G H I
1 2 3 4 5 6 7 8 9 10 11 12 13
44
57
GREAT VICTORIA DESERT NATURE RESERVE
UNNAMED CONSERVATION PARK
MARALINGA TJARUTJA ABORIGINAL LAND
OOLDEA RANGE
Maralinga
SOUTH AUSTRALIA
WESTERN AUSTRALIA
NULLARBOR PLAIN
Watson
31
O'Malley
Fisher
RAILWAY
Cook
AUSTRALIA
TRANS
Denman
Hughes
Deakin
125
NULLARBOR REGIONAL RESERVE
105
NULLARBOR NATIONAL PARK
Nullarbor Roadhouse
94
YALATA ABORIGINAL LAND
Whale-watching
Yalata Roadhouse
Head of Bight
GREAT AUSTRALIAN BIGHT MARINE PARK
HWY
42
A1
55
Lookout
293
Lookouts
89
EYRE
Border Village
Agricultural Check Point
13
Eucla
1
EUCLA NP
THE GREAT AUSTRALIAN BIGHT MARINE PARK: Extends almost 6 km off the coastline around Head of Bight. Between June and Oct., this area is transformed into a maritime nursery for visiting southern right whales and their calves. Permits for whale-watching can be purchased from the White Well Ranger Station near the viewing platform.
GREAT AUSTRALIAN BIGHT
N

0 20 40 60 80 100 km
WARNING: While visitors are permitted in the township of Woomera, entry to the Woomera Prohibited Area is by permit only, except in the immediate corridors of the Stuart Highway and the road from Coober Pedy to William Creek. Camping is not permitted in the area. Note the overlap with Aboriginal Lands where you need additional separate permits.
MARALINGA TJARUTJA ABORIGINAL LAND
WOOMERA PROHIBITED AREA
YELLABINNA REGIONAL RESERVE
YUMBARRA CONSERVATION PARK
PUREBA CONSERVATION PARK
LAKE GAIRDNER NATIONAL PARK
NUYTS ARCHIPELAGO CONSERVATION PARK
ISLES OF ST FRANCIS CONSERVATION PARK
ACRAMAN CREEK CONSERVATION PARK
CALPATANNA WATERHOLE CP
KULLIPARU CONSERVATION PARK
POINT LABATT CP
VENUS BAY CP
Wilkinson Lakes
Lake Anthony
Half Moon Lake
Ifould Lake
Lake Everard
Lake Labyrinth
Lake Moolkra
Locke Claypans
Lake Yaninee
West Point Hill 230m
Mt Christie 233m
Mt Finke 361m
Mt Soward 224m
Wilgena Hill 253m
Bulpara Hill 237m
Renton Hill 161m
Glyde Hill 252m
Nuckulla Hill 264m
Yaribrinda Hill 348m
Waverley Hill 399m
Mt Hiltaba 465m
Barber Hill 412m
Wallala Hill 166m
Pimbaacla Hill 121m
Kaldoonera Hill 136m
Chilpuddie Hill 181m
Oak Hill 111m
Nurka Hill 130m
Coppuduba Hill 147m
Koonibba Hill 169m
Woolshed Hill 134m
Cooper Hill 126m
Bookabie Hill 149m
Yalata Hill 84m
Mt Cooper 205m
Mt Hall 208m
Ingomar
McDouall Peak
Bulgunnia
Muckanippie
Mulgathing
Carnes
Gibraltar Rocks
Warrior
Malbooma
Tarcoola
PARTRIDGE RANGE
AUSTRALIAN CENTRAL RAILWAY
TRANS AUSTRALIA RAILWAY
Bates
Barton
Mungala
Mount Christie
Wynbring
Dog Fence
Fence
Colona
Nundroo Roadhouse
EYRE HWY
Bookabie
Gundillippy
Coorabie
Fowlers Bay
Point Fowler
Penong
Koonibba
Telstra Earth Station
Cactus Beach
Point Sinclair
Lake MacDonnell
McKenzie (ruins)
Ceduna
Agricultural Check Point
Thevenard
Denial Bay
Point Bell
St Peter Island
Smoky Bay
Eyre Island
Mudamuckla
Chinbingina
Nunjikompita
Wirrulla
Yantanabie
Carawa
Haslam
Pelina
Point de Mole
Point Brown
Streaky Bay
Chilpanunda
Cungena
Capietha
Poochera
Pildappa Rock
Minnipa
Eba Island
Cape Bauer
Olive Islands
Piednippie
Chandada
Corvisart Bay
Isles of St Francis
FLINDERS HWY
Point Westall
Yanerbie Beach
Sceale Bay
Murphy's Haystacks
Calca
Searcy Bay
Sea-lion Colony
Point Labatt
Cape Radstock
Baird Bay
Mount Cooper
Colley
Port Kenny
Venus Bay
Moonlight Flat
Mount Damper
A1
B100
202
222
109
124
45
40
38

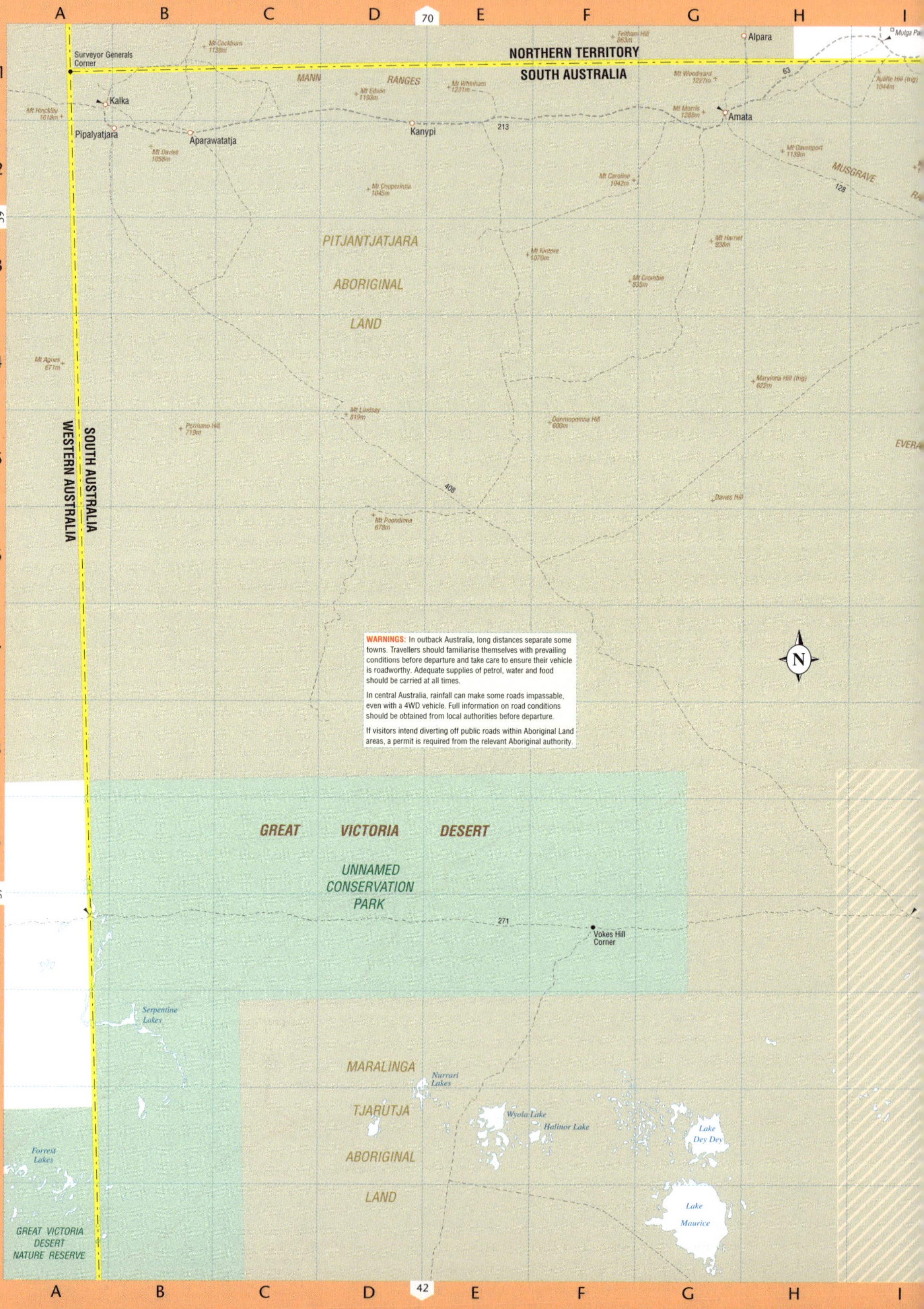

NORTHERN TERRITORY
SOUTH AUSTRALIA
WESTERN AUSTRALIA
Surveyor Generals Corner
Kalka
Pipalyatjara
Aparawatatja
Kanypi
Amata
Alpara
Mulga Park
MANN RANGES
MUSGRAVE
EVERARD
PITJANTJATJARA ABORIGINAL LAND
Mt Cockburn 1138m
Mt Edwin 1193m
Mt Whinham 1231m
Mt Hinckley 1018m
Mt Davies 1058m
Mt Woodward 1227m
Mt Morris 1288m
Mt Davenport 1139m
Mt Caroline 1042m
Mt Cooperinna 1045m
Mt Kintore 1070m
Mt Harriet 938m
Mt Crombie 835m
Mt Agnes 671m
Maryinna Hill (trig) 622m
Mt Lindsay 819m
Permano Hill 719m
Gonmooinna Hill 600m
Davies Hill
Mt Poondinna 678m
Feltham Hill 863m
Ayliffe Hill (trig) 1044m
213
63
128
408
271
WARNINGS: In outback Australia, long distances separate some towns. Travellers should familiarise themselves with prevailing conditions before departure and take care to ensure their vehicle is roadworthy. Adequate supplies of petrol, water and food should be carried at all times.
In central Australia, rainfall can make some roads impassable, even with a 4WD vehicle. Full information on road conditions should be obtained from local authorities before departure.
If visitors intend diverting off public roads within Aboriginal Land areas, a permit is required from the relevant Aboriginal authority.
N
GREAT VICTORIA DESERT
UNNAMED CONSERVATION PARK
Vokes Hill Corner
Serpentine Lakes
MARALINGA TJARUTJA ABORIGINAL LAND
Nurrari Lakes
Wyola Lake
Halinor Lake
Lake Dey Dey
Lake Maurice
Forrest Lakes
GREAT VICTORIA DESERT NATURE RESERVE
70
59
57
42

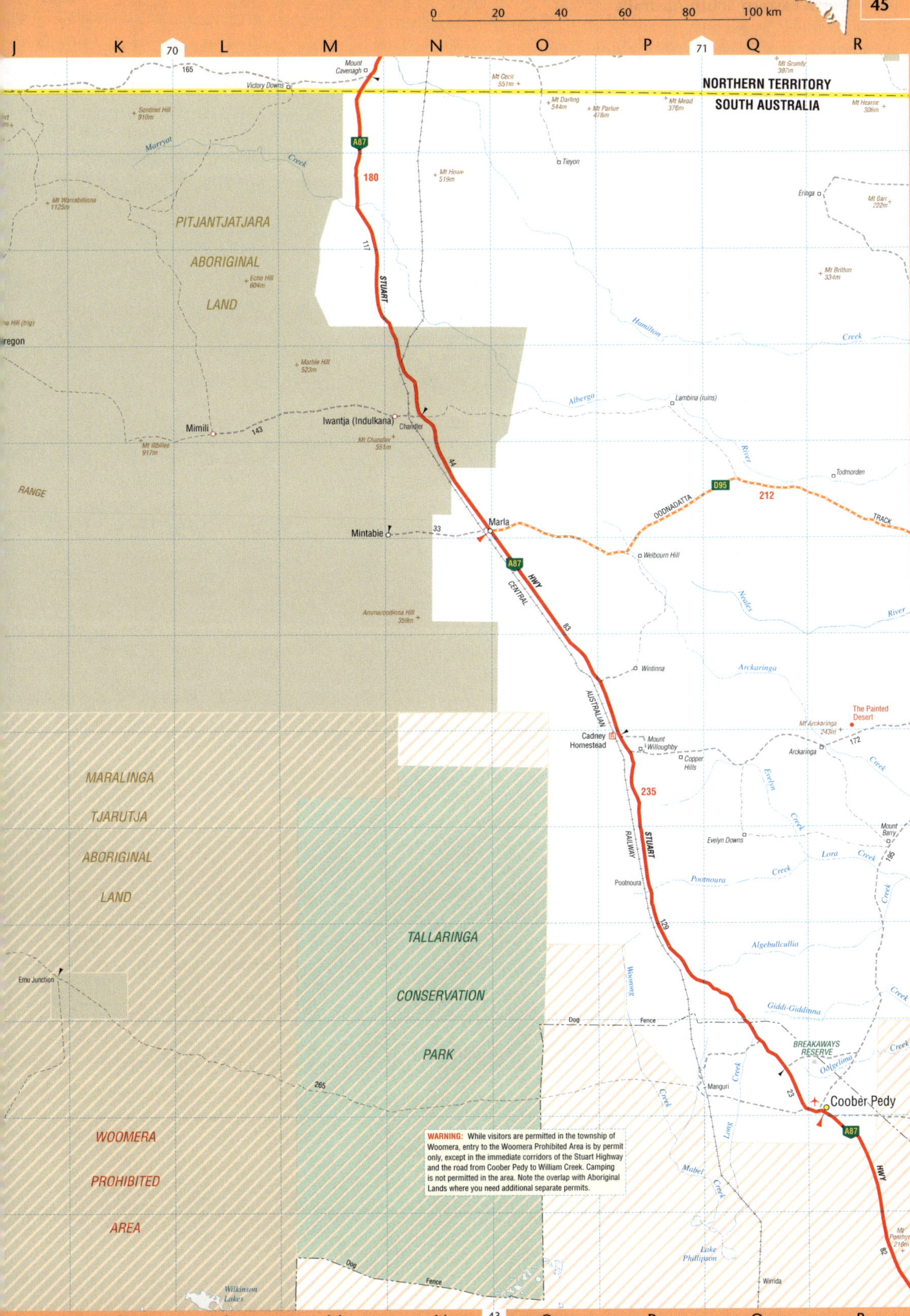
0 20 40 60 80 100 km
J K L M N O P Q R
70
71
NORTHERN TERRITORY
SOUTH AUSTRALIA
Mount Cavenagh
Victory Downs
165
Mt Cecil 551m
Mt Grundy 397m
Sentinel Hill 910m
Mt Darling 544m
Mt Parlue 478m
Mt Mead 376m
Mt Hearne 306m
Marryat
Creek
A87
180
Tieyon
Mt Howe 519m
Eringa
Mt Barr 222m
Mt Warrabillinna 1125m
PITJANTJATJARA
ABORIGINAL
LAND
Echo Hill 604m
117
STUART
Mt Britton 334m
Hamilton
Creek
regon
Marble Hill 523m
Alberga
Lambina (ruins)
Mimili
143
Iwantja (Indulkana)
Chandler
Mt Chandler 551m
Mt Illbillee 917m
River
44
Todmorden
RANGE
D95
212
OODNADATTA
TRACK
Marla
Mintabie
33
Welbourn Hill
A87
HWY
CENTRAL
Neales
River
Ammaroodinna Hill 359m
83
46
Wintinna
Arckaringa
AUSTRALIAN
The Painted Desert
Mt Arckaringa 243m
172
Cadney Homestead
Mount Willoughby
Copper Hills
Arckaringa
Creek
Evelyn
235
MARALINGA
TJARUTJA
ABORIGINAL
LAND
Creek
Mount Barry
RAILWAY
STUART
Evelyn Downs
Lora
Creek
195
Pootnoura
Pootnoura
Creek
Creek
129
TALLARINGA
CONSERVATION
PARK
Algebullcullia
Emu Junction
Woorong
Giddi-Giddinna
Creek
Dog
Fence
BREAKAWAYS RESERVE
Creek
Odlgelima
Creek
Manguri
265
Creek
23
Coober Pedy
WOOMERA
PROHIBITED
AREA
Long
A87
WARNING: While visitors are permitted in the township of Woomera, entry to the Woomera Prohibited Area is by permit only, except in the immediate corridors of the Stuart Highway and the road from Coober Pedy to William Creek. Camping is not permitted in the area. Note the overlap with Aboriginal Lands where you need additional separate permits.
Mabel
Creek
HWY
Mt Penrhyn 216m
Lake Phillipson
82
Dog
Fence
Wilkinson Lakes
Wirrida
43
1 2 3 4 5 6 7 8 9 10 11 12 13

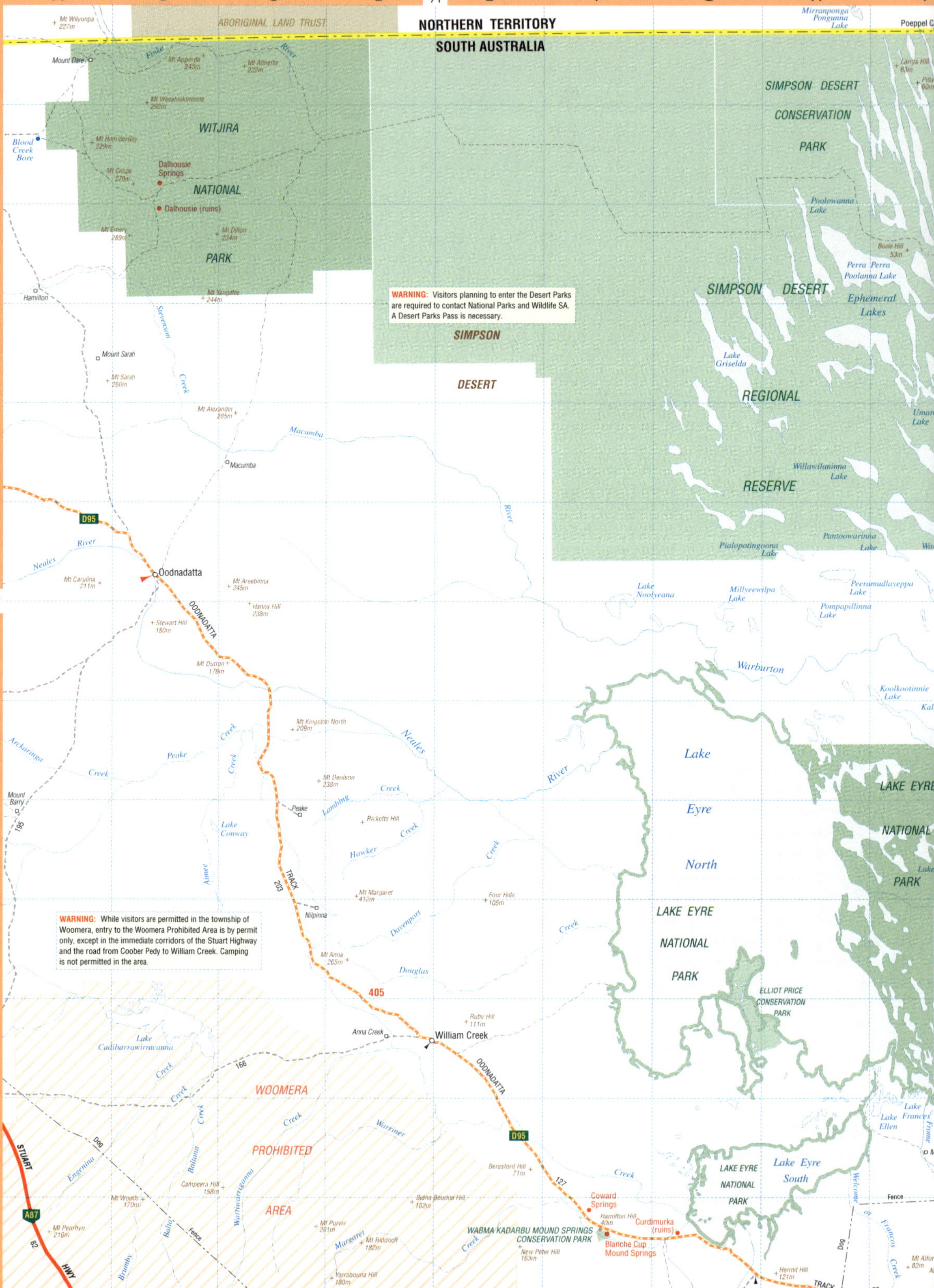

NORTHERN TERRITORY
SOUTH AUSTRALIA
ABORIGINAL LAND TRUST
Mt Wilyunpa 227m
Mount Dare
Finke River
Mt Apperda 245m
Mt Allnerta 222m
Mt Weeshilkiminne 292m
Blood Creek Bore
Mt Hammersley 229m
WITJIRA NATIONAL PARK
Dalhousie Springs
Dalhousie (ruins)
Mt Crispe 279m
Mt Emery 289m
Mt Dillon 234m
Hamilton
Mt Yangatee 244m
Stevenson Creek
Mount Sarah
Mt Sarah 260m
Mt Alexander 285m
Macumba River
Macumba
D95
Neales River
Oodnadatta
Mt Carulina 211m
Mt Areebinna 245m
Hanns Hill 238m
Stewart Hill 180m
OODNADATTA TRACK
Mt Dutton 176m
Mt Kingston North 209m
Arckaringa Creek
Peake Creek
Mount Barry
195
Mt Denison 238m
Peake
Lambing Creek
Ricketts Hill
Lake Conway
Hawker Creek
Aimee
203
Mt Margaret 412m
Four Hills 105m
Nilpinna
Davenport Creek
Mt Anna 265m
Douglas
405
Ruby Hill 111m
Anna Creek
William Creek
Lake Cadibarrawirracanna
166
WOOMERA PROHIBITED AREA
Warriner Creek
Dog Fence
STUART HWY
A87
82
Engenina
Bulluna Creek
Campeera Hill 158m
Mt Woods 170m
Wattiwarriganna
Budna Boouna Hill 182m
Beresford Hill 71m
127
Coward Springs
Hamilton Hill 40m
Curdimurka (ruins)
WABMA KADARBU MOUND SPRINGS CONSERVATION PARK
Blanche Cup Mound Springs
New Peter Hill 163m
Mt Penrhyn 216m
Mt Purvis 201m
Mt Riddoch 182m
Margaret Creek
Yarrabouna Hill 180m
Brumby
SIMPSON DESERT
WARNING: Visitors planning to enter the Desert Parks are required to contact National Parks and Wildlife SA. A Desert Parks Pass is necessary.
SIMPSON DESERT CONSERVATION PARK
Mirranponga Pongunna Lake
Poeppel Co
Larrys Hill 63m
Pillan 60m
Poolowanna Lake
Beale Hill 53m
Perra Perra Poolanna Lake
SIMPSON DESERT REGIONAL RESERVE
Ephemeral Lakes
Lake Griselda
Umaroo Lake
Willawilaninna Lake
Pialpotingoona Lake
Pantoowarinna Lake
Lake Noolyeana
Millyeewilpa Lake
Peeramudlayeppa Lake
Pompapillinna Lake
Warburton
Koolkootinnie Lake
Lake Eyre North
LAKE EYRE NATIONAL PARK
ELLIOT PRICE CONSERVATION PARK
Lake Eyre South
Lake Ellen
Lake Frances
Fence
Welcome
Hermit Hill 121m
Mt Alford 82m
TRACK
75
WARNING: While visitors are permitted in the township of Woomera, entry to the Woomera Prohibited Area is by permit only, except in the immediate corridors of the Stuart Highway and the road from Coober Pedy to William Creek. Camping is not permitted in the area.

71
45
40

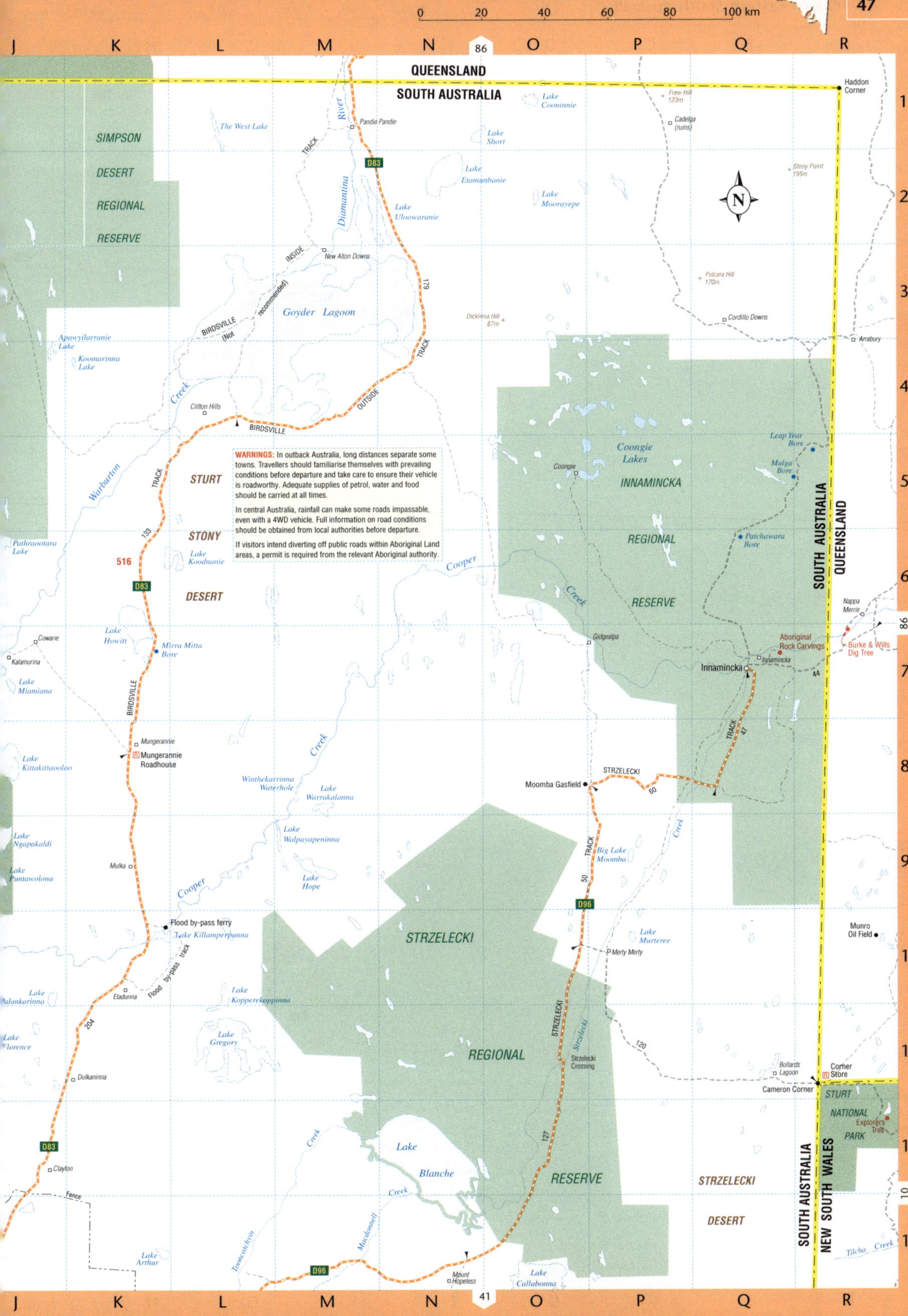
0 20 40 60 80 100 km
J K L M N O P Q R
86
QUEENSLAND
SOUTH AUSTRALIA
Haddon Corner
SIMPSON
DESERT
REGIONAL
RESERVE
The West Lake
River
Pandie Pandie
TRACK
D83
Diamantina
Lake Cooninnie
Frew Hill 123m
Cadelga (ruins)
Lake Short
Lake Etamunbanie
Stony Point 195m
Lake Uloowaranie
Lake Moorayepe
INSIDE
New Alton Downs
179
Pulcara Hill 170m
BIRDSVILLE (Not recommended)
Goyder Lagoon
Dickinna Hill 87m
Cordillo Downs
Arrabury
Apawyilarranie Lake
Koomarinna Lake
TRACK
Creek
Clifton Hills
OUTSIDE
BIRDSVILLE
Coongie Lakes
Coongie
Leap Year Bore
Mulga Bore
INNAMINCKA
REGIONAL
RESERVE
Patchawarra Bore
SOUTH AUSTRALIA
QUEENSLAND
Warburton
TRACK
STURT
STONY
DESERT
WARNINGS: In outback Australia, long distances separate some towns. Travellers should familiarise themselves with prevailing conditions before departure and ensure that their vehicle is roadworthy. Adequate supplies of petrol, water and food should be carried at all times.
In central Australia, rainfall can make some roads impassable, even with a 4WD vehicle. Full information on road conditions should be obtained from local authorities before departure.
If visitors intend diverting off public roads within Aboriginal Land areas, a permit is required from the relevant Aboriginal authority.
Pathraootara Lake
133
516
Lake Koodnanie
Cooper
Creek
Nappa Merrie
Cowarie
Kalamurina
Lake Howitt
Mirra Mitta Bore
Gidgealpa
Aboriginal Rock Carvings
Burke & Wills Dig Tree
Innamincka
44
Lake Miamiana
BIRDSVILLE
TRACK
47
Mungerannie
Mungerannie Roadhouse
Lake Kittakittaooloo
Creek
STRZELECKI
Moomba Gasfield
60
Winthekarrinna Waterhole
Lake Warrakalanna
Lake Ngapakaldi
Lake Walpayapeninna
TRACK
Big Lake Moomba
Creek
Lake Puntawolona
Mulka
Lake Hope
50
Cooper
D96
Flood by-pass ferry
Lake Killamperpunna
STRZELECKI
Lake Murteree
Munro Oil Field
Merty Merty
Flood by-pass track
Lake Palankarinna
Etadunna
Lake Kopperekoppinna
204
Lake Florence
Lake Gregory
REGIONAL
STRZELECKI
Strzelecki
120
Strzelecki Crossing
Bollards Lagoon
Corner Store
Cameron Corner
Dulkaninna
STURT
NATIONAL
PARK
Explorers Tree
Creek
Lake
Blanche
127
D83
Clayton
RESERVE
STRZELECKI
DESERT
SOUTH AUSTRALIA
NEW SOUTH WALES
Fence
Creek
Macdonnell
Toonculchyin
Lake Arthur
Tilcha Creek
D96
Mount Hopeless
Lake Callabonna
41
10
1 2 3 4 5 6 7 8 9 10 11 12 13

0 20 40 60 80 100 km

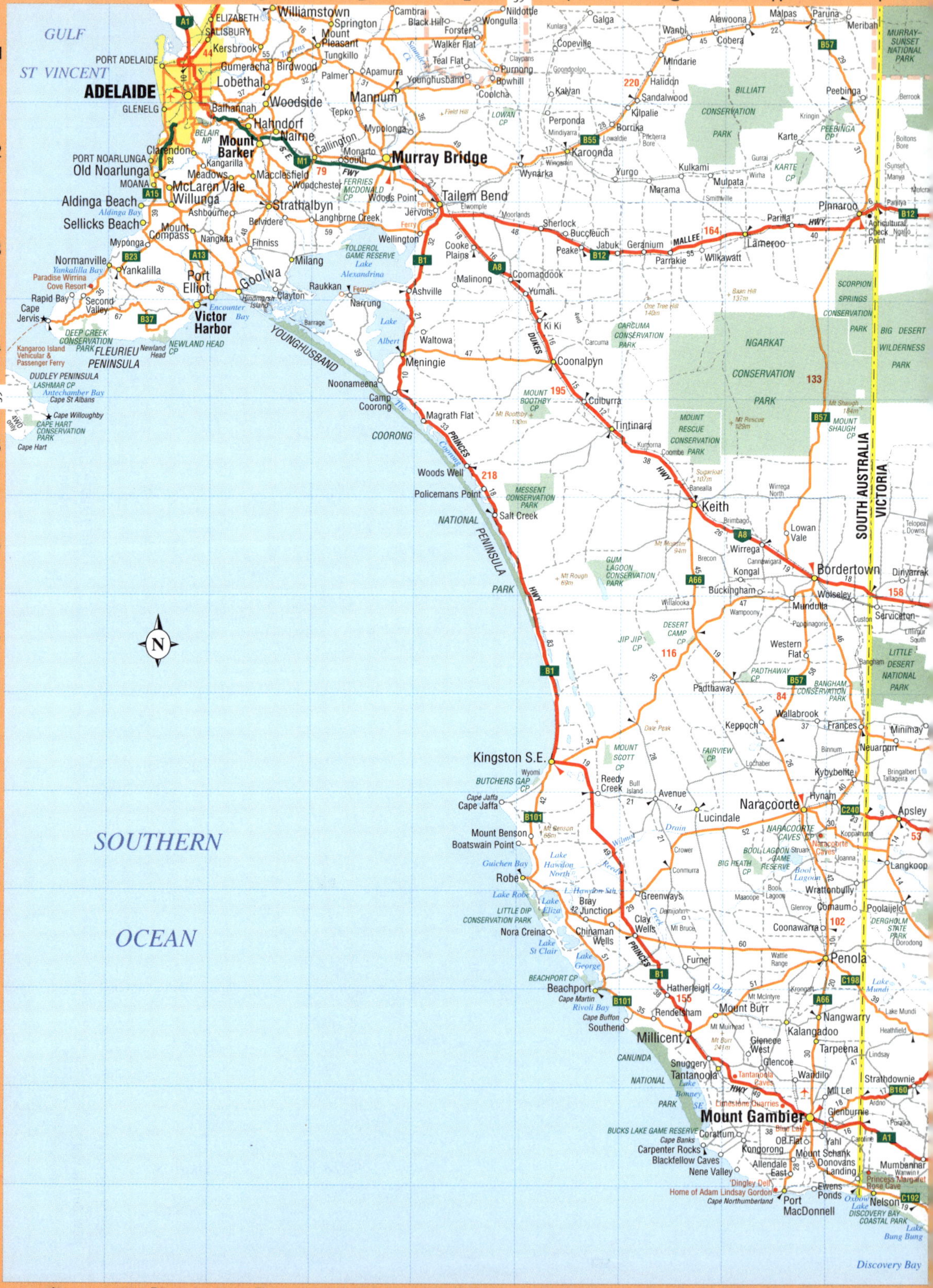

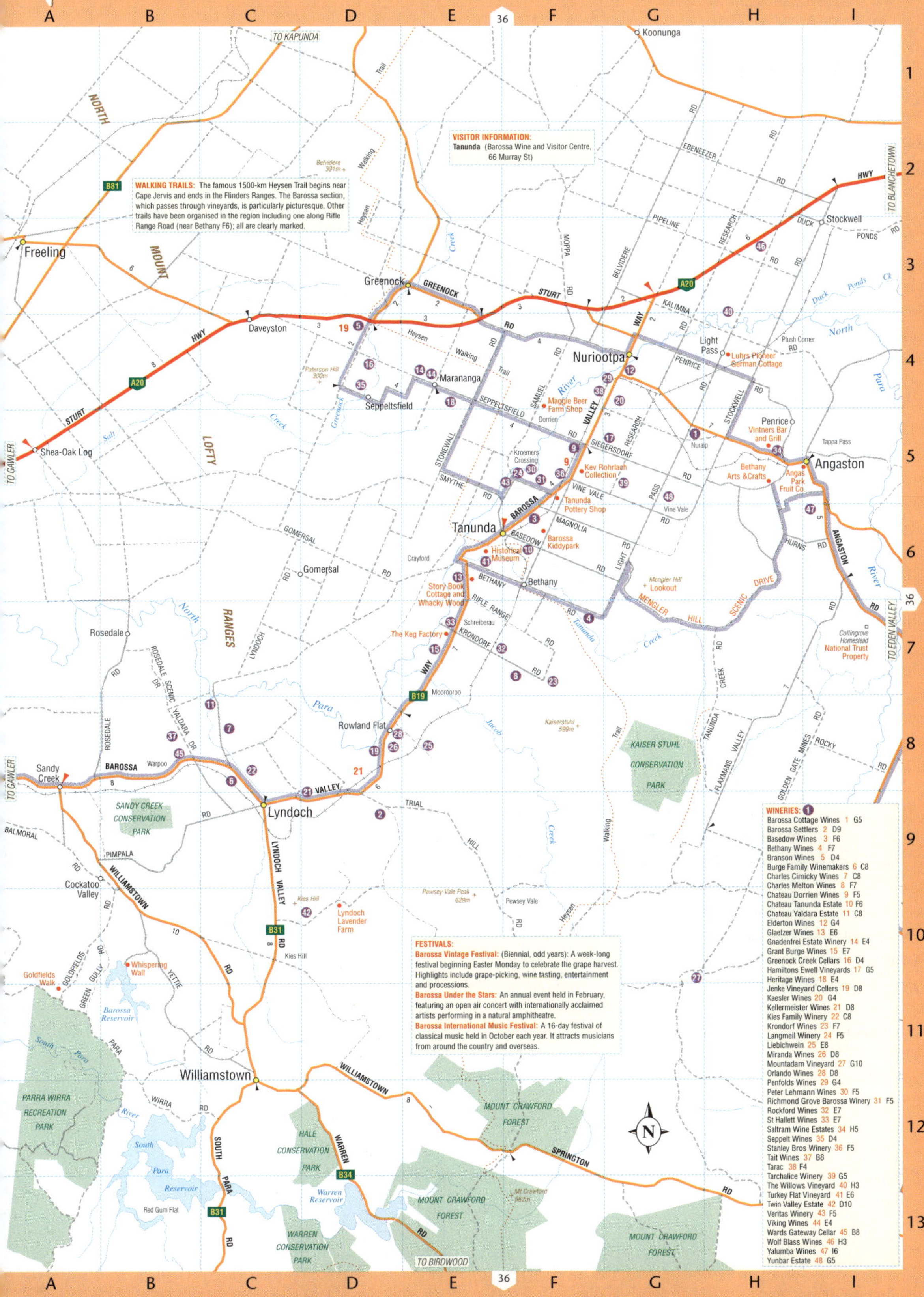

VISITOR INFORMATION: **Tanunda** (Barossa Wine and Visitor Centre, 66 Murray St)

WALKING TRAILS: The famous 1500-km Heysen Trail begins near Cape Jervis and ends in the Flinders Ranges. The Barossa section, which passes through vineyards, is particularly picturesque. Other trails have been organised in the region including one along Rifle Range Road (near Bethany F6); all are clearly marked.

FESTIVALS:
Barossa Vintage Festival: (Biennial, odd years): A week-long festival beginning Easter Monday to celebrate the grape harvest. Highlights include grape-picking, wine tasting, entertainment and processions.
Barossa Under the Stars: An annual event held in February, featuring an open air concert with internationally acclaimed artists performing in a natural amphitheatre.
Barossa International Music Festival: A 16-day festival of classical music held in October each year. It attracts musicians from around the country and overseas.

WINERIES: 1

- Barossa Cottage Wines 1 G5
- Barossa Settlers 2 D9
- Basedow Wines 3 F6
- Bethany Wines 4 F7
- Branson Wines 5 D4
- Burge Family Winemakers 6 C8
- Charles Cimicky Wines 7 C8
- Charles Melton Wines 8 F7
- Chateau Dorrien Wines 9 F5
- Chateau Tanunda Estate 10 F6
- Chateau Yaldara Estate 11 C8
- Elderton Wines 12 G4
- Glaetzer Wines 13 E6
- Gnadenfrei Estate Winery 14 E4
- Grant Burge Wines 15 E7
- Greenock Creek Cellars 16 D4
- Hamiltons Ewell Vineyards 17 G5
- Heritage Wines 18 E4
- Jenke Vineyard Cellars 19 D8
- Kaesler Wines 20 G4
- Kellermeister Wines 21 D8
- Kies Family Winery 22 C8
- Krondorf Wines 23 F7
- Langmeil Winery 24 F5
- Liebichwein 25 E8
- Miranda Wines 26 D8
- Mountadam Vineyard 27 G10
- Orlando Wines 28 D8
- Penfolds Wines 29 G4
- Peter Lehmann Wines 30 F5
- Richmond Grove Barossa Winery 31 F5
- Rockford Wines 32 E7
- St Hallett Wines 33 E7
- Saltram Wine Estates 34 H5
- Seppelt Wines 35 D4
- Stanley Bros Winery 36 F5
- Tait Wines 37 B8
- Tarac 38 F4
- Tarchalice Winery 39 G5
- The Willows Vineyard 40 H3
- Turkey Flat Vineyard 41 E6
- Twin Valley Estate 42 D10
- Veritas Winery 43 F5
- Viking Wines 44 E4
- Wards Gateway Cellar 45 B8
- Wolf Blass Wines 46 H3
- Yalumba Wines 47 I6
- Yunbar Estate 48 G5

Western Australia

Location Map

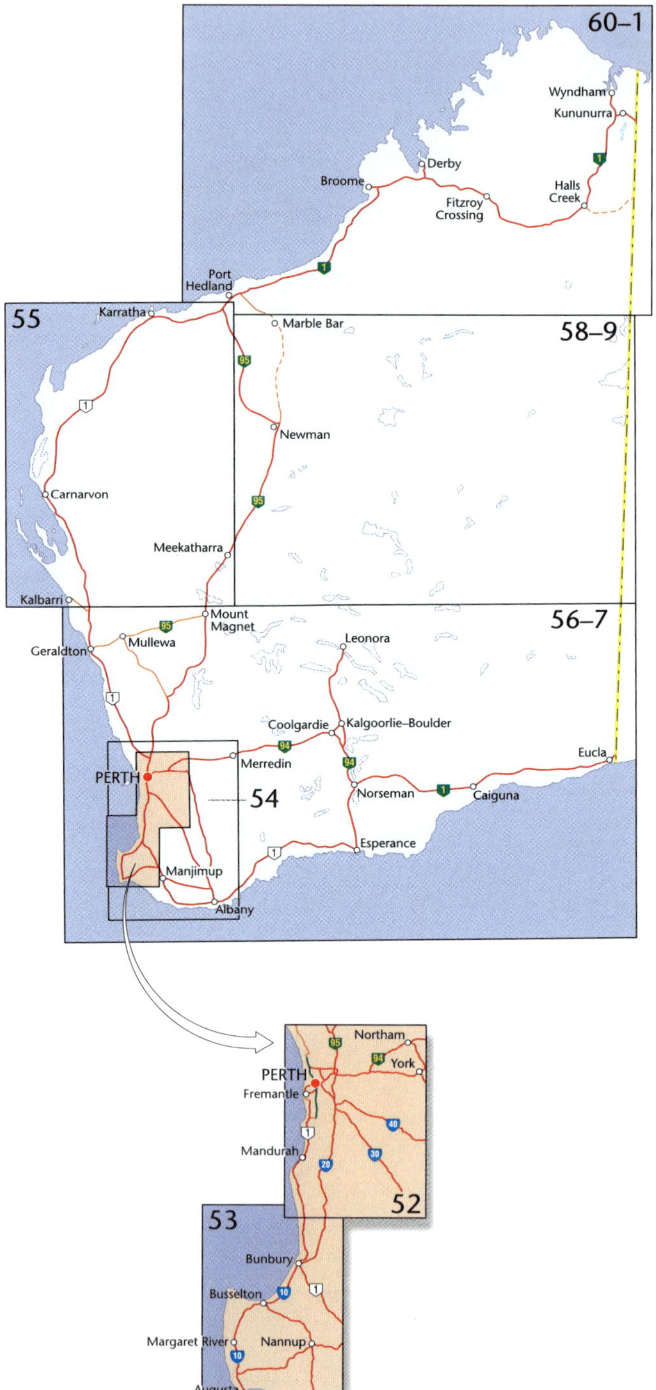

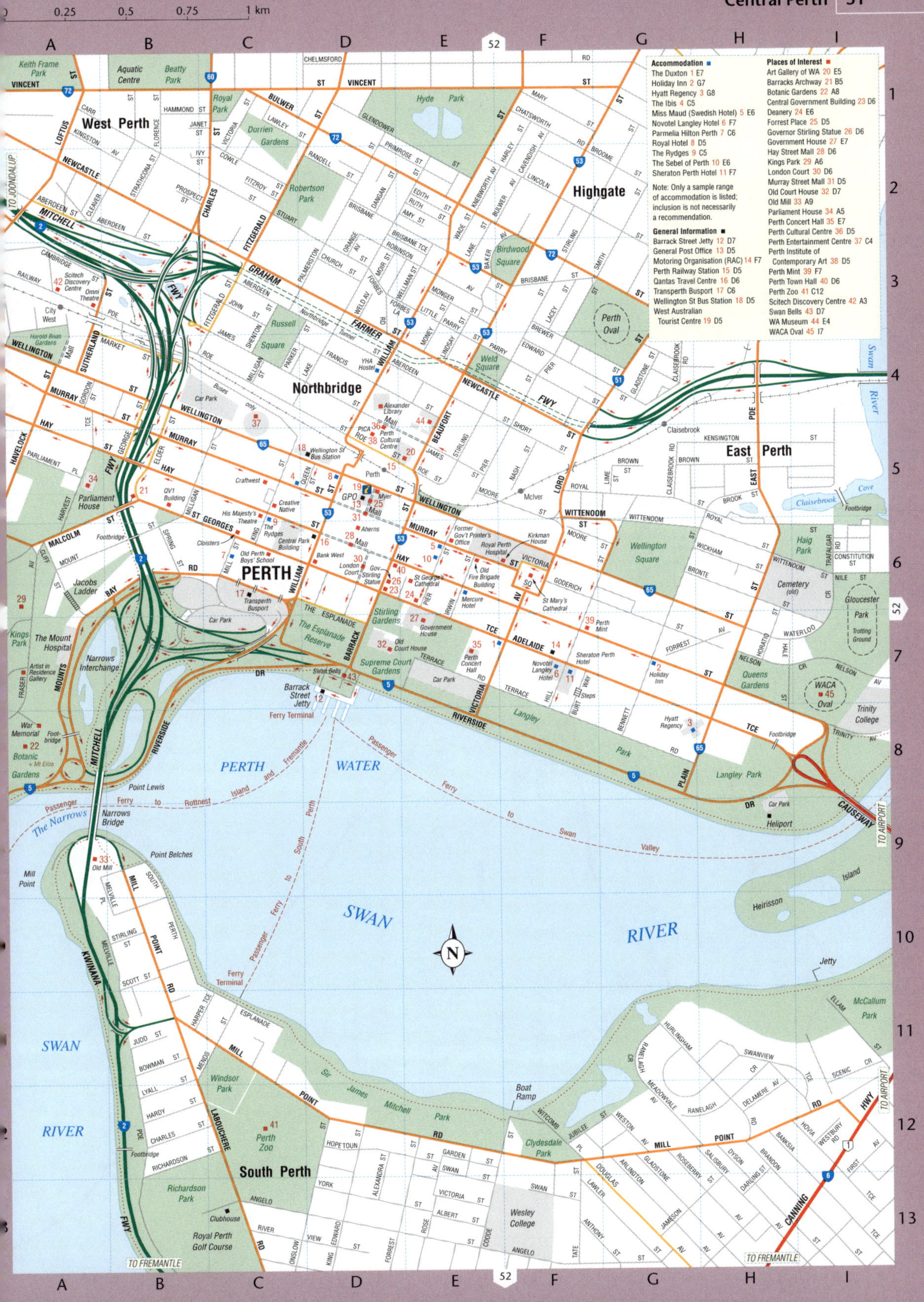
0 0.25 0.5 0.75 1 km
Accommodation
The Duxton 1 E7
Holiday Inn 2 G7
Hyatt Regency 3 G8
The Ibis 4 C5
Miss Maud (Swedish Hotel) 5 E6
Novotel Langley Hotel 6 F7
Parmelia Hilton Perth 7 C6
Royal Hotel 8 D5
The Rydges 9 C5
The Sebel of Perth 10 E6
Sheraton Perth Hotel 11 F7
Note: Only a sample range of accommodation is listed; inclusion is not necessarily a recommendation.
General Information
Barrack Street Jetty 12 D7
General Post Office 13 D5
Motoring Organisation (RAC) 14 F7
Perth Railway Station 15 D5
Qantas Travel Centre 16 D6
Transperth Busport 17 C6
Wellington St Bus Station 18 D5
West Australian Tourist Centre 19 D5
Places of Interest
Art Gallery of WA 20 E5
Barracks Archway 21 B5
Botanic Gardens 22 A8
Central Government Building 23 D6
Deanery 24 E6
Forrest Place 25 D5
Governor Stirling Statue 26 D6
Government House 27 E7
Hay Street Mall 28 D6
Kings Park 29 A6
London Court 30 D6
Murray Street Mall 31 D5
Old Court House 32 D7
Old Mill 33 A9
Parliament House 34 A5
Perth Concert Hall 35 E7
Perth Cultural Centre 36 D5
Perth Entertainment Centre 37 C4
Perth Institute of Contemporary Art 38 D5
Perth Mint 39 F7
Perth Town Hall 40 D6
Perth Zoo 41 C12
Scitech Discovery Centre 42 A3
Swan Bells 43 D7
WA Museum 44 E4
WACA Oval 45 I7
West Perth
Northbridge
Highgate
East Perth
PERTH
South Perth
PERTH WATER
SWAN RIVER
TO JOONDALUP
TO FREMANTLE
TO AIRPORT

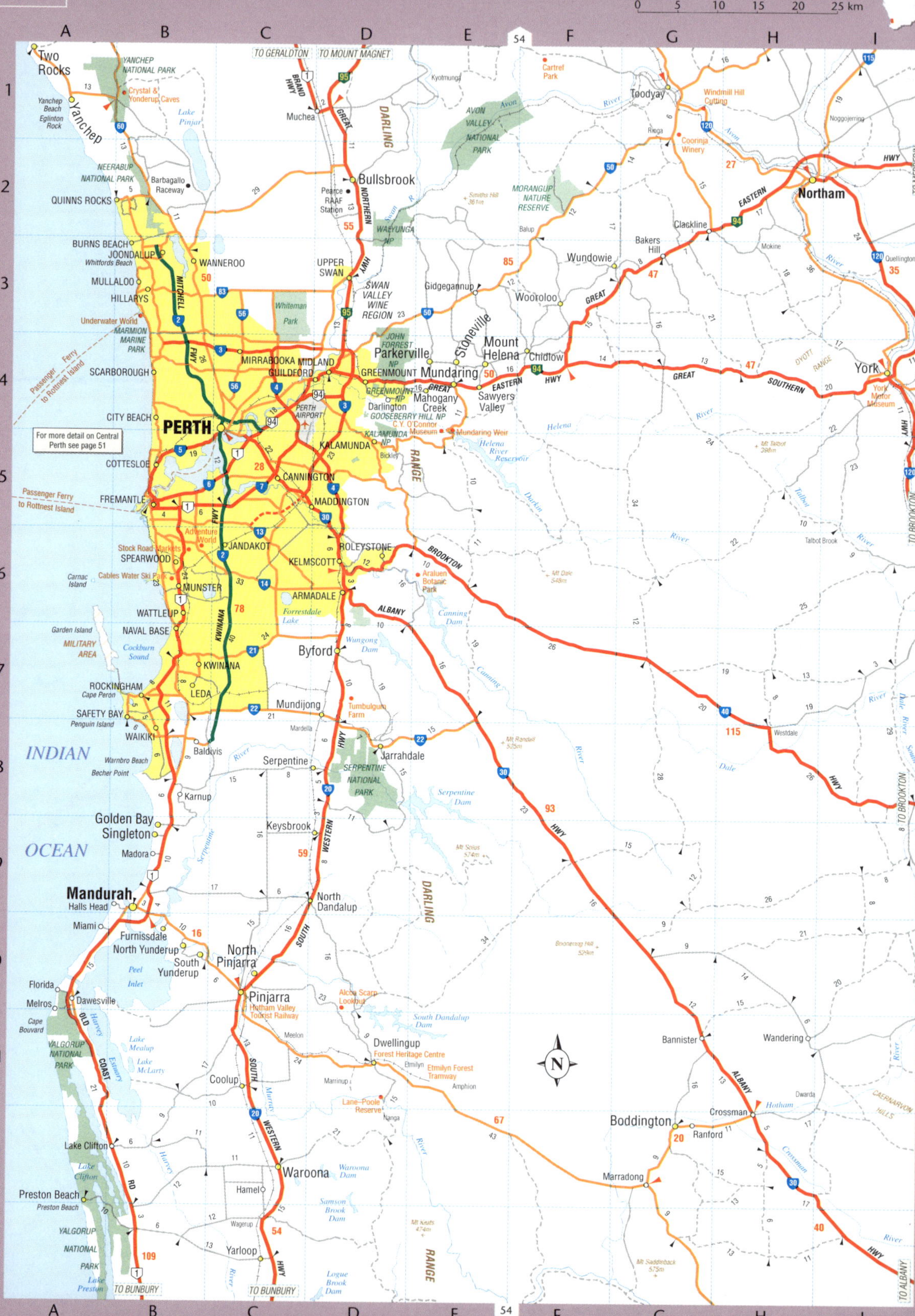
0 5 10 15 20 25 km
A B C D E F G H I
1 2 3 4 5 6 7 8 9 10 11 12 13
54
TO GERALDTON
TO MOUNT MAGNET
TO MERREDIN
TO BROOKTON
TO ALBANY
TO BUNBURY
Two Rocks
Yanchep
Yanchep Beach
Eglinton Rock
YANCHEP NATIONAL PARK
Crystal & Yonderup Caves
Lake Pinjar
NEERABUP NATIONAL PARK
Barbagallo Raceway
QUINNS ROCKS
BURNS BEACH
JOONDALUP
Whitfords Beach
WANNEROO
MULLALOO
HILLARYS
Underwater World
MARMION MARINE PARK
SCARBOROUGH
Passenger Ferry to Rottnest Island
CITY BEACH
PERTH
For more detail on Central Perth see page 51
COTTESLOE
FREMANTLE
Adventure World
Stock Road Markets
SPEARWOOD
Cables Water Ski Park
Carnac Island
MUNSTER
WATTLEUP
Garden Island
NAVAL BASE
MILITARY AREA
Cockburn Sound
KWINANA
LEDA
ROCKINGHAM
Cape Peron
SAFETY BAY
Penguin Island
WAIKIKI
Baldivis
Warnbro Beach
Becher Point
INDIAN OCEAN
Karnup
Golden Bay
Singleton
Madora
Mandurah
Halls Head
Miami
Furnissdale
North Yunderup
South Yunderup
Peel Inlet
Florida
Melros
Dawesville
Cape Bouvard
YALGORUP NATIONAL PARK
OLD COAST RD
Harvey Estuary
Lake Mealup
Lake McLarty
Lake Clifton
Preston Beach
Lake Preston
MITCHELL FWY
KWINANA FWY
MIRRABOOKA
MIDLAND
GUILDFORD
PERTH AIRPORT
CANNINGTON
MADDINGTON
KALAMUNDA
JANDAKOT
ROLEYSTONE
KELMSCOTT
ARMADALE
Forrestdale Lake
Byford
Mundijong
Mardella
Serpentine
Keysbrook
North Dandalup
North Pinjarra
Pinjarra
Hotham Valley Tourist Railway
Meelon
Coolup
Waroona
Hamel
Wagerup
Yarloop
Muchea
BRAND HWY
GREAT NORTHERN HWY
Bullsbrook
Pearce RAAF Station
UPPER SWAN
Swan River
WALYUNGA NP
SWAN VALLEY WINE REGION
Whiteman Park
JOHN FORREST NP
Parkerville
GREENMOUNT
GREENMOUNT NP
Darlington
GOOSEBERRY HILL NP
KALAMUNDA NP
Bickley
C.Y. O'Connor Museum
Mundaring Weir
Mundaring
Mahogany Creek
Stoneville
Mount Helena
Sawyers Valley
Chidlow
GREAT EASTERN HWY
Helena River Reservoir
DARLING RANGE
Kyotmunga
AVON VALLEY NATIONAL PARK
Avon River
MORANGUP NATURE RESERVE
Smiths Hill 361m
Balup
Gidgegannup
Wooroloo
Wundowie
Bakers Hill
Clackline
Toodyay
Cartref Park
Windmill Hill Cutting
Coorinja Winery
Noggojerring
Northam
Quellington
York
York Motor Museum
Mokine
GREAT SOUTHERN HWY
DYOTT RANGE
Mt Talbot 396m
Talbot Brook
Dale River
Mt Dale 546m
Araluen Botanic Park
BROOKTON HWY
ALBANY HWY
Canning Dam
Wungong Dam
Canning River
Tumbulgum Farm
Jarrahdale
SERPENTINE NATIONAL PARK
Serpentine Dam
Mt Randall 525m
Mt Solus 574m
Westdale
Dale River
Serpentine River
South Dandalup Dam
Alcoa Scarp Lookout
Dwellingup
Forest Heritage Centre
Etmilyn
Etmilyn Forest Tramway
Amphion
Marrinup
Lane-Poole Reserve
Nanga
Murray River
SOUTH WESTERN HWY
Waroona Dam
Samson Brook Dam
Logue Brook Dam
Mt Keats 474m
Mt Saddleback 575m
Boonering Hill 529m
Bannister
Wandering
Crossman
Dwarda
Hotham River
CAERNARVON HILLS
Boddington
Ranford
Marradong
Crossman River
N

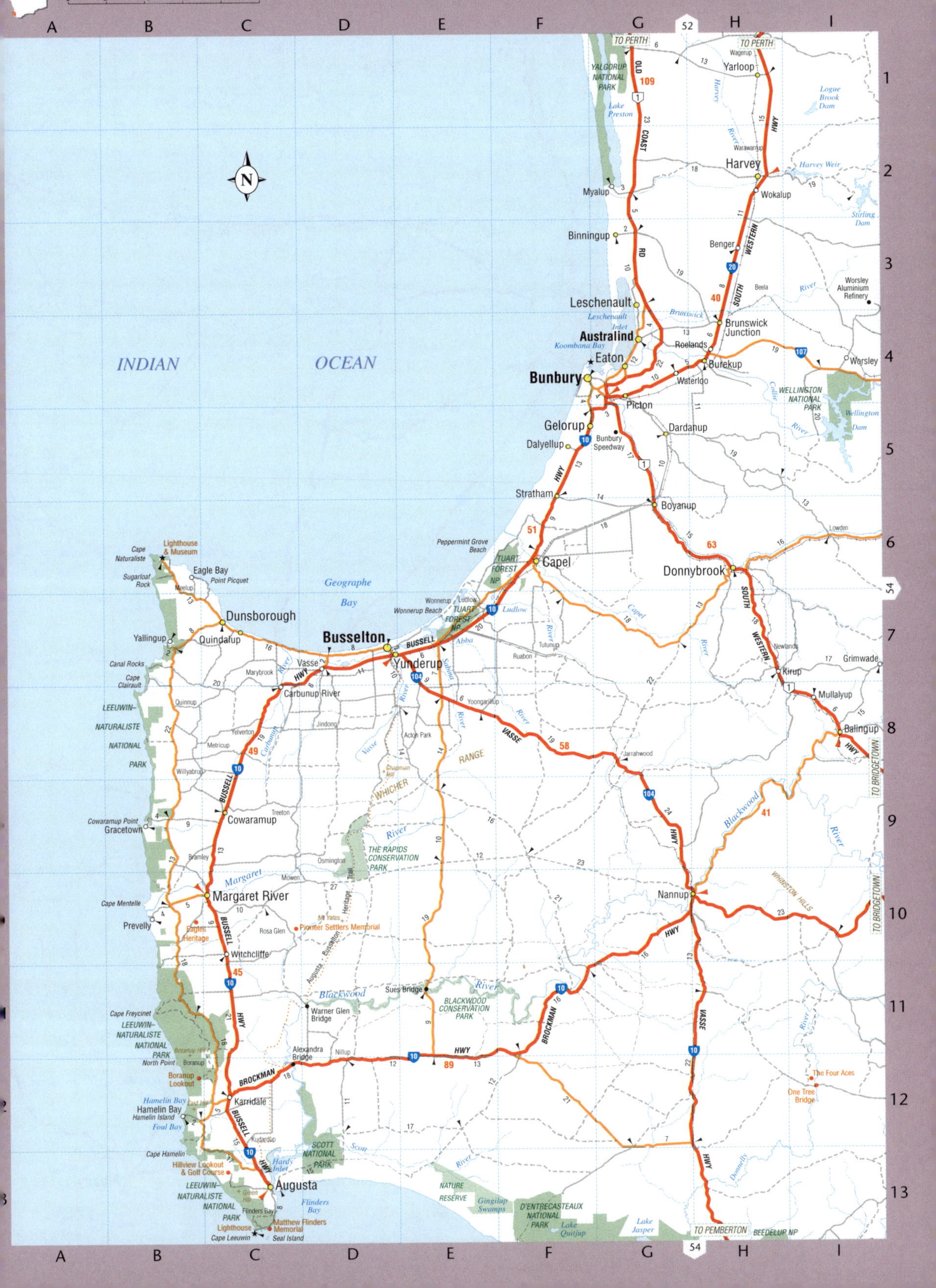
0 5 10 15 20 25 km
A B C D E F G H I
1 2 3 4 5 6 7 8 9 10 11 12 13
52
54
INDIAN
OCEAN
N
TO PERTH
TO PERTH
YALGORUP NATIONAL PARK
Lake Preston
OLD COAST RD
109
Wagerup
Yarloop
Harvey River
HWY
Logue Brook Dam
Warawarup
Harvey
Harvey Weir
Myalup
Wokalup
Stirling Dam
Binningup
Benger
SOUTH WESTERN
Worsley Aluminium Refinery
Beela
River
Leschenault
Leschenault Inlet
Brunswick
Brunswick Junction
40
Australind
Koombana Bay
Roelands
Eaton
Burekup
107
Worsley
Bunbury
Waterloo
WELLINGTON NATIONAL PARK
Collie
Wellington Dam
Picton
Gelorup
Dardanup
Bunbury Speedway
Dalyellup
Stratham
Boyanup
51
Capel
Peppermint Grove Beach
TUART FOREST NP
Donnybrook
63
Lowden
Cape Naturaliste
Lighthouse & Museum
Sugarloaf Rock
Eagle Bay
Point Picquet
Meelup
Geographe Bay
Wonnerup
Ludlow
Wonnerup Beach
Capel
SOUTH WESTERN
Dunsborough
Yallingup
Quindalup
Busselton
BUSSELL
Abba
Tutunup
Ruabon
Newlands
Grimwade
Vasse
Yunderup
Sabina
Kirup
Canal Rocks
Cape Clairault
Marybrook
Carbunup River
104
Yoongarillup
Mullalyup
LEEUWIN–NATURALISTE NATIONAL PARK
Quinnup
Jindong
Balingup
Yelverton
Carbunup
Acton Park
VASSE
58
Metricup
49
Chapman Hill
RANGE
Jarrahwood
TO BRIDGETOWN
Willyabrup
WHICHER
Blackwood
41
Cowaramup Point
Gracetown
Cowaramup
Treeton
THE RAPIDS CONSERVATION PARK
Bramley
Osmington
Margaret
Mowen
Heritage Trail
Nannup
WHINSTON HILLS
Cape Mentelle
Margaret River
Prevelly
Eagles Heritage
Rosa Glen
Mt Yates
Pioneer Settlers Memorial
TO BRIDGETOWN
Witchcliffe
45
Augusta – Busselton
Sues Bridge
BLACKWOOD CONSERVATION PARK
BROCKMAN
Cape Freycinet
LEEUWIN–NATURALISTE NATIONAL PARK
Warner Glen Bridge
Boranup Hill
North Point
Boranup
Alexandra Bridge
Nillup
HWY
89
The Four Aces
Boranup Lookout
BROCKMAN
Karridale
One Tree Bridge
Hamelin Bay
Hamelin Island
Foul Bay
Kudardup
Cape Hamelin
SCOTT NATIONAL PARK
Scott
Hillview Lookout & Golf Course
Hardy Inlet
River
Donnelly
LEEUWIN–NATURALISTE NATIONAL PARK
Augusta
Green Hill
NATURE RESERVE
Gingilup Swamps
D'ENTRECASTEAUX NATIONAL PARK
Flinders Bay
Flinders Bay
Matthew Flinders Memorial
Lighthouse
Cape Leeuwin
Seal Island
Lake Quitjup
Lake Jasper
TO PEMBERTON
BEEDELUP NP

0 20 40 60 80 km
INDIAN
OCEAN
SOUTHERN
OCEAN
PERTH
FREMANTLE
SCARBOROUGH
Rottnest Island
For more detail on Perth & Surrounds see page 52
For more detail on The South-West see page 53
Lancelin
Ledge Point
Seabird
Guilderton
Two Rocks
Yanchep
QUINNS ROCKS
WANNEROO
Regans Ford
Mogumber
New Norcia
Calingiri
Gingin
Bindoon
Muchea
Bullsbrook
Toodyay
Northam
Clackline
Wundowie
Bakers Hill
Gidgegannup
Mount Helena
Chidlow
Mundaring
Darlington
York
ARMADALE
KWINANA
ROCKINGHAM
Mundijong
Byford
Jarrahdale
Waikiki
Baldivis
Serpentine
Golden Bay
Singleton
Mandurah
North Yunderup
South Yunderup
Dawesville
Keysbrook
North Dandalup
North Pinjarra
Pinjarra
Dwellingup
Coolup
Lake Clifton
Waroona
Hamel
Preston Beach
Yarloop
Harvey
Myalup
Wokalup
Binningup
Benger
Australind
Eaton
Brunswick Junction
Roelands
Burekup
Bunbury
Gelorup
Dalyellup
Stratham
Waterloo
Allanson
Collie
Shotts
Collie Burn
Collie Cardiff
Dardanup
Boyanup
Capel
Donnybrook
Mumballup
Cape Naturaliste
Eagle Bay
Dunsborough
Yallingup
Vasse
Busselton
Kirup
Mullalyup
Balingup
Grimwade
Wilga
Boyup Brook
Greenbushes
Cowaramup
Gracetown
Margaret River
Nannup
Bridgetown
Karridale
Augusta
Cape Leeuwin
Manjimup
Deanmill
Jardee
Palgarup
Pemberton
Quinninup
Northcliffe
Windy Harbour
Point D'Entrecasteaux
Walpole
Nornalup
Peaceful Bay
Denmark
Albany
Little Grove
Mount Barker
Kendenup
Cranbrook
Tenterden
Frankland
Rocky Gully
Narrikup
Porongurup
Kalgan
Redmond
King River
Boddington
Bannister
Wandering
Crossman
Marradong
Quindanning
Williams
Darkan
Duranillin
Buckingham
Bowelling
Boscabel
Kojonup
Muradup
Kulikup
Dinninup
Mayanup
Jingalup
Katanning
Broomehill
Tambellup
Gnowangerup
Borden
Woodanilling
Wagin
Arthur River
Dumbleyung
Nyabing
Kukerin
Moulyinning
Narrogin
Cuballing
Highbury
Piesseville
Wickepin
Dudinin
Harrismith
Tincurrin
Toolibin
Jitarning
Kulin
Kondinin
Yealering
Pingelly
Popanyinning
Moorumbine
Brookton
Beverley
Beverley East
Corrigin
Bullaring
Babakin
South Kumminin
Quairading
Dangin
Caroling
Pantapin
Yoting
Kwolyin
Shackleton
Bruce Rock
Greenhills
Balkuling
Youndegin
Meckering
Cunderdin
Tammin
Kellerberrin
Doodlakine
Hines Hill
Merredin
Goomalling
Dowerin
Jennacubbine
Wyalkatchem
Minnivale
Ejanding
Konnongorring
Trayning
Kununoppin
Nungarin
Bolgart
Wyening
Dewars Pool
Great Eastern Hwy
Albany Hwy
Brookton Hwy
South Western Hwy
Brand Hwy
Great Northern Hwy
Bussell Hwy
Vasse Hwy
Brockman Hwy
Muirs Hwy
South Coast Hwy
Great Southern Hwy
Stirling Range National Park
Porongurup NP
Walpole-Nornalup National Park
Leeuwin-Naturaliste National Park
D'Entrecasteaux National Park
Shannon NP
Mount Frankland NP
Yalgorup National Park
Scott National Park
Torndirrup National Park
West Cape Howe National Park
William Bay NP
Two Peoples Bay Nature Reserve
Moore River NP
Yanchep NP
Avon Valley NP
Serpentine NP
Wellington NP
Beedelup NP
Warren NP
Brockman NP
Blackwood CP

0 50 100 150 200 km
A B C D E F G H I
1 2 3 4 5 6 7 8 9 10 11 12 13
INDIAN OCEAN
WITTENOOM: The blue asbestos dust present in and around Wittenoom may cause cancer if inhaled.
While the risk from such fibres to short term visitors is significantly less than to residents, the Ashbuton Shire Council advocates avoidance of the Wittenoom area.
BARROW ISLAND NATURE RESERVE
Barrow Island
Montebello Islands
MACKEREL ISLANDS
Karratha
Dampier
Wickham
Point Samson
Cossack
Roebourne
Cape Lambert
Enderby Island
Burrup Penin
Dolphin Island
Karratha Roadhouse
Cape Preston
Regnard Bay
Sholl Island
Cape Poivre
Whim Creek
Mallina
Depuch Is
Cape Cossigny
Mundabullangana
Yandeyarra
ABORIGINAL LAND
MUNGAROONA RANGE NATURE RESERVE
THE PILBARA
MILLSTREAM–CHICHESTER NATIONAL PARK
Python Pool
Pyramid
Sherlock
Mardie
Fortescue Roadhouse
Fortescue
Robe
Yarraloola
Pannawonica
Onslow
Beadon Point
North Murion Island
Wreck of SS Mildura
Point Murat
North West Cape
False Island Point
Low Point
Naval Communication Station -Restricted Area
CAPE RANGE
Shothole Canyon
Charles Knife Canyon
Exmouth
Exmouth Gulf
Learmonth
NINGALOO MARINE PARK
NINGALOO REEF
NP
Norwegian Bay
Ningaloo
Bullara
Giralia
GIRALIA RANGE
Coral Bay
Point Maud
Cardabia
Warroora
Bulbarli Point
Cape Farquhar
Gnarraloo Bay
Gnaraloo
Minilya
Minilya Roadhouse
Red Bluff
Lake MacLeod
Cape Cuvier
HMAS Sydney Memorial Cairn
Blowholes
Boolathana
Carnarvon
Bernier Island
BERNIER–DORRE ISLANDS NATURE RESERVE
Dorre Island
Geographe Channel
Shark Bay
Cape Peron North
FRANCOIS PERON NATIONAL PARK
Peron Homestead
Monkey Mia Dolphin-watching
Denham
Denham Sound
Dirk Hartog Island
Faure Island
Hamelin Pool
Useless Loop Mine
Steep Point
Eagle Bluff
110 km Shell Beach
Nanga Bay Resort
Henri Freycinet Harbour
Carrarang
Tamala
Zuytdorp Cliffs
ZUYTDORP NATURE RESERVE
Wooramel Roadhouse
Overlander Roadhouse
Billabong Roadhouse
TOOLONGA NATURE RESERVE
KALBARRI NATIONAL PARK
Kalbarri
NORTH WEST COASTAL HWY
Minderoo
Peedamulla
Cane River
Red Hill
Ashburton
Nanutarra Roadhouse
Mount Stuart
Duck Creek
Wyloo
Kooline
Glen Florrie
BARLEE RANGE NATURE RESERVE
Yanrey
Uaroo
Nyang
Towera
Winning
Mia Mia
Lyndon
Maroonah
Ullawarra
Ashburton Downs
TROPIC OF CAPRICORN
Edmund
Wandagee
Middalya
Williambury
Mangaroon
Gifford Creek
Wanna
Manberry
Moogooree
Minnie Creek
Cobra
Mt Augustus
MT AUGUSTUS NATIONAL PARK
Lyons River
Hill Springs
Mardathuna
Cooralya
KENNEDY RANGE NATIONAL PARK
Mt Sandiman
Eudamullah
Mount Phillips
Lyons River
Yinnetharra
Burringurrah
Doorawarrah
Meeragoolia
Mooka
Gascoyne Junction
Mooloo Downs
Gascoyne River
Landor
Mt Clere
Milgun
Woodlands
Mulgul
Waldburg
Dooley Downs
Pingandy
Mount Vernon
Galligiddy
Ella Valla
Yalbalgo
Edaggee
Marron
Wahroonga
Pimbee
Carey Downs
Glenburgh
Yalbra
Erong Springs
Errabiddy
Innouendy
Meedo
Callytharra Springs
Gilroyd
Wooramel River
Nth Branch
Moorarie
Yarlarweelor
Mount Padbury
Murchison River
Byro
Milly Milly
Beringarra
Woodleigh
Yalardy
Gladstone
Yaringa
Carbla
Nookawarra
Manfred
Mileura
Koonmarra
Belele
Peace Gorge (The Granites)
Meekatharra
Lake Annean
Wilgie Mia Red Ochre Mine
Annean
Beebyn
Kalli
Glen
Karbar
Tuckanarra
Coodardy
Taincrow
Cue
Lake Austin
Walga Rock
Lakeside
Mount Farmer
Woodthong
Mount Narryer
Muggon
Coburn
Murchison
Wooleen Homestead
Boolardy
NICHOLSON RANGE
Sanford River
Twin Peaks
Murgoo
Nerren Nerren
New Forest
Yallalong
Coolcalalya
Lake Nerramyne
Pinegrove
Bullardoo
Narloo
Yandi
Eurardy
Illingemarra
HAMERSLEY RANGE
Coolawanyah
Mount Florance
Hooley
Mulga Downs
Wittenoom
Hamersley Gorge
Hamersley
Mount Brockman
Dales Gorge
Tom Price
Marandoo
KARIJINI NATIONAL PARK
Juna Downs
Rocklea
Paraburdoo
Seven Mile Creek
Turee
Mininer
Hardey River
Irregully Creek
Boolgeeda
Bresnahan
NORTHERN HWY
GREAT NORTHERN HWY
58
56

55
58
INDIAN
OCEAN
SOUTHERN
For more detail on Perth & Surrounds see page 52
For more detail on South Western Western Australia see page 54
Murchison
Billabong Roadhouse
Kalbarri
Binnu
Northampton
Geraldton
Walkaway
Dongara
Port Denison
Mingenew
Mullewa
Pindar
Yalgoo
Cue
Tuckanarra
Mount Magnet
Sandstone
Leinster
Mount Keith
Leonora
Menzies
Paynes Find
Morawa
Perenjori
Three Springs
Carnamah
Coorow
Eneabba
Leeman
Green Head
Jurien Bay
Cervantes
Moora
Dalwallinu
Wubin
Kalannie
Wialki
Bonnie Rock
Beacon
Bencubbin
Mukinbudin
Koorda
Wongan Hills
Calingiri
Goomalling
Wyalkatchem
Nungarin
Merredin
Southern Cross
Kalgoorlie-Boulder
Coolgardie
Lancelin
Gingin
Bindoon
Toodyay
Northam
York
Two Rocks
Yanchep
WANNEROO
SCARBOROUGH
PERTH
FREMANTLE
KWINANA
ROCKINGHAM
ARMADALE
Mundaring
Beverley
Brookton
Quairading
Corrigin
Kondinin
Hyden
Narembeen
Bruce Rock
Kellerberrin
Cunderdin
Tammin
Singleton
Mandurah
Pinjarra
Dwellingup
Boddington
Waroona
Harvey
Australind
Bunbury
Collie
Williams
Narrogin
Wickepin
Pingelly
Wagin
Dumbleyung
Katanning
Kojonup
Lake Grace
Newdegate
Lake King
Ravensthorpe
Hopetoun
Jerramungup
Gnowangerup
Ongerup
Dunsborough
Busselton
Capel
Donnybrook
Balingup
Boyup Brook
Bridgetown
Margaret River
Nannup
Manjimup
Augusta
Pemberton
Northcliffe
Walpole
Denmark
Peaceful Bay
Mount Barker
Cranbrook
Frankland
Albany
Little Grove
Bremer Bay
Munglinup

0 50 100 150 200 km
J K L M N O P Q R
59
44
42
CENTRAL AUSTRALIA ABORIGINAL LAND TRUST
LENNIS HILLS
Tjukayirla Roadhouse
CENTRAL
RD
HWY)
Lake Throssel
Bandya
Cosmo Newbery
COSMO NEWBERY
ABORIGINAL LAND
GREAT (OUTBACK
YEO LAKE NATURE RESERVE
Yeo Lake
DUNGES TABLE
4WD only
CONNIE SUE 4WD
HWY only
Neale Junction
4WD
only
Laverton
Numerous Old Mine Workings
Windarra
Rason Lake
Wanna Lakes
Serpentine Lakes
GREAT VICTORIA DESERT
Lake Carey
Jubilee Lake
Shell Lakes
Lake Ilma
Carlisle Lakes
Forrest Lakes
GREAT VICTORIA DESERT NATURE RESERVE
CONSERVATION PARK
WARNINGS: In outback Australia, long distances separate some towns. Travellers should familiarise themselves with prevailing conditions before departure and take care to ensure their vehicle is roadworthy. Adequate supplies of petrol, water and food should be carried at all times.
In central Australia, rainfall can make some roads impassable. Full information on road conditions should be obtained from local authorities before departure.
If visitors intend diverting off public roads within Aboriginal Land areas, a permit is required from the relevant Aboriginal authority.
Plumridge Lakes
Lake Minigwai
Lake Raeside
Lake Rebecca
Lake Nyanga
WESTERN AUSTRALIA
SOUTH AUSTRALIA
QUEEN VICTORIA SPRING NATURE RESERVE
CUNDEELEE ABORIGINAL LAND
Cundeelee
Lake Roe
Lake Yindarlgooda
NULLARBOR PLAIN
Randell Karonie Chifley Zanthus Kitchener TRANS Naretha AUSTRALIA Haig Nurina RAILWAY Forrest Reid Deakin
Rawlinna
Loongana
NULLARBOR REGIONAL RESERVE
Lake Rivers
Harris Lake
Lake Lefroy
Lake Cowan
Agricultural Check Point
Eucla
Border Village
NULLARBOR NP
EUCLA NP
Lookouts
Mundrabilla Roadhouse
EYRE HWY
340
Madura Pass Oasis Motel & Roadhouse
Cocklebiddy Cave
Cocklebiddy
Eyre Bird Observatory
NUYTSLAND NATURE RESERVE
Red Rocks Point
Slessar Point
Norseman
373
Balladonia Roadhouse
Balladonia
Caiguna
Point Dover
Sheer Cliffs
NUYTSLAND NATURE RESERVE
Point Culver
Lake Dundas
Lake Halbert
CAPE ARID NATIONAL PARK
Israelite Bay
Point Dempster
Condingup
Esperance
Whistling Rock
CAPE LE GRAND NATIONAL PARK
Cape Arid
Cape Pasley
ARCHIPELAGO OF THE RECHERCHE
GREAT AUSTRALIAN BIGHT
OCEAN
N
1 2 3 4 5 6 7 8 9 10 11 12 13

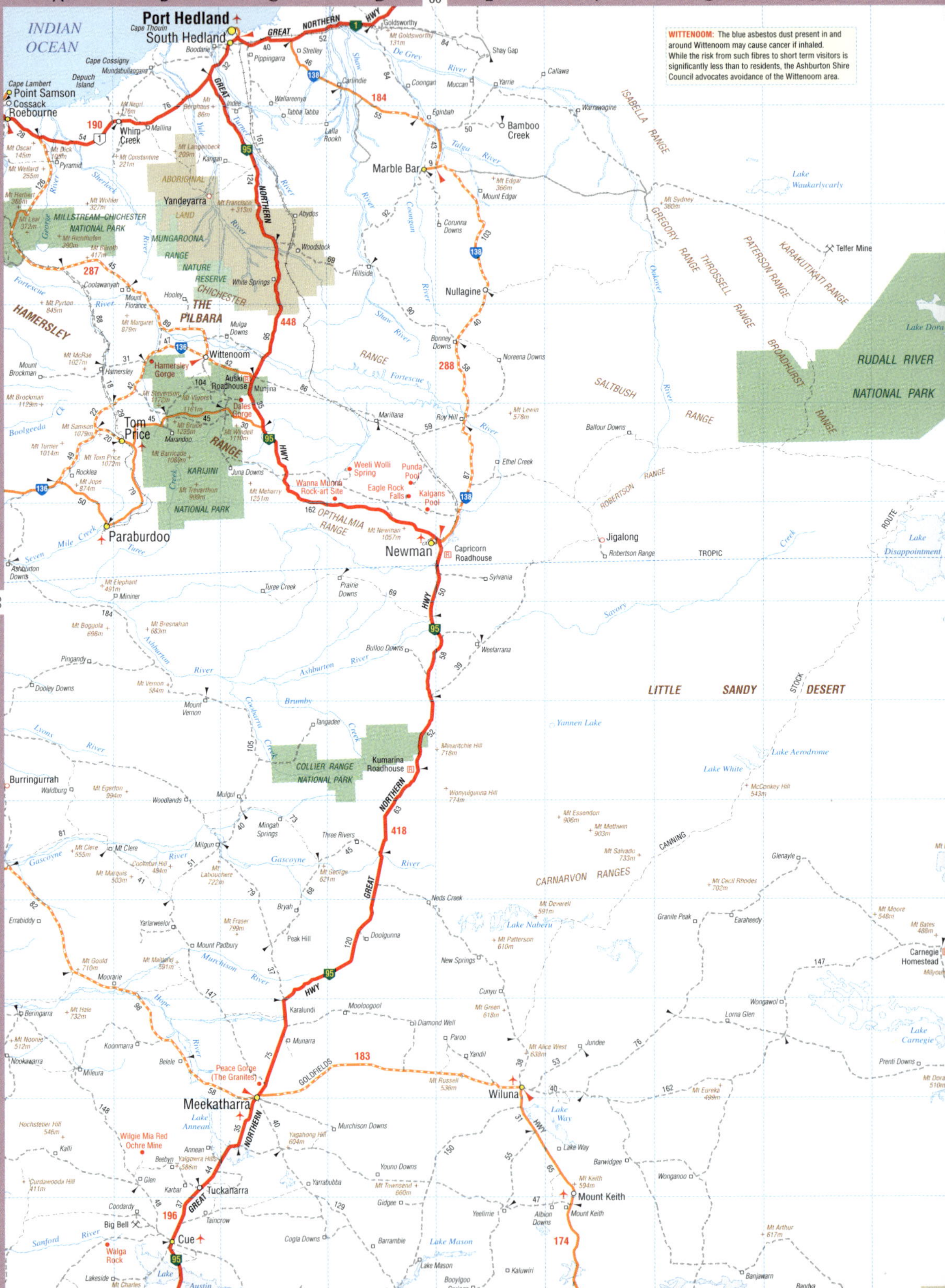
A B C D E F G H I
60
1 2 3 4 5 6 7 8 9 10 11 12 13
55
56
INDIAN OCEAN
Port Hedland
South Hedland
Cape Thouin
Boodarie
Cape Cossigny
Mundabullangana
Cape Lambert
Point Samson
Cossack
Roebourne
Depuch Island
Whim Creek
Mallina
Pippingarra
Strelley
Goldsworthy
Mt Goldsworthy 131m
De Grey River
Shay Gap
Callawa
Carlindie
Coongan
Muccan
Yarrie
Wallareenya
Tabba Tabba
Lalla Rookh
Egina
Bamboo Creek
Warrawagine
Marble Bar
Talga River
Mt Edgar 366m
Mount Edgar
Corunna Downs
Nullagine
Bonney Downs
Noreena Downs
WITTENOOM: The blue asbestos dust present in and around Wittenoom may cause cancer if inhaled.
While the risk from such fibres to short term visitors is significantly less than to residents, the Ashburton Shire Council advocates avoidance of the Wittenoom area.
ISABELLA RANGE
Lake Waukarlycarly
Mt Sydney 360m
GREGORY RANGE
THROSSELL RANGE
PATERSON RANGE
KARAKUTIKATI RANGE
Telfer Mine
BROADHURST RANGE
Lake Dora
RUDALL RIVER NATIONAL PARK
SALTBUSH RANGE
Oakover River
Balfour Downs
ROBERTSON RANGE
Jigalong
Robertson Range
TROPIC
Lake Disappointment
ROUTE
Mt Langenbeck 209m
Kangan
Yandeyarra
ABORIGINAL LAND
Abydos
Woodstock
Hillside
MILLSTREAM-CHICHESTER NATIONAL PARK
Mt Herbert 366m
Mt Wohler 327m
Mt Richthofen 390m
Mt Barloth 417m
MUNGAROONA RANGE NATURE RESERVE
CHICHESTER
White Springs
Coolawanyah
Mount Florance
Hooley
THE PILBARA
Mulga Downs
HAMERSLEY
Mt Pyrton 845m
Mt Margaret 879m
Mt McRae 1027m
Mount Brockman
Hamersley
Hamersley Gorge
Wittenoom
Auski Roadhouse
Munjina
Dales Gorge
Mt Brockman 1129m
Mt Stevenson 1172m
Mt Vigors 1161m
Mt Bruce 1235m
Marandoo
Mt Windell 1110m
Tom Price
Mt Samson 1079m
Mt Turner 1014m
Mt Tom Price 1072m
Rocklea
Mt Jope 874m
Mt Barricade 1069m
KARIJINI RANGE
Mt Trevarthon 909m
NATIONAL PARK
Juna Downs
Mt Meharry 1251m
Paraburdoo
Turee Creek
Seven Mile Creek
Ashburton Downs
Fortescue River
RANGE
Marillana
Roy Hill
Mt Lewin 578m
Ethel Creek
Weeli Wolli Spring
Punda Pool
Eagle Rock Falls
Kalgans Pool
Wanna Munna Rock-art Site
OPTHALMIA RANGE
Mt Newman 1057m
Newman
Capricorn Roadhouse
Sylvania
Prairie Downs
Mt Elephant 491m
Mininer
Mt Bresnahan 683m
Mt Boggola 898m
Pingandy
Ashburton River
Bulloo Downs
Weelarrana
Savory Creek
Dooley Downs
Mt Vernon 584m
Mount Vernon
Brumby Creek
LITTLE SANDY DESERT
STOCK
Yannen Lake
Lyons River
Tangadee
Minaritchie Hill 718m
Lake Aerodrome
Lake White
COLLIER RANGE NATIONAL PARK
Kumarina Roadhouse
Burringurrah
Waldburg
Mt Egerton 994m
Woodlands
Mulgul
Wonyulgunna Hill 774m
McConkey Hill 543m
Mingah Springs
Three Rivers
Mt Essendon 906m
Mt Methwin 903m
Mt Salvado 733m
CANNING
Mt Clere 555m
Mt Clere
Milgun
Gascoyne River
Glenayle
Mt Marquis 503m
Coolinbar Hill 484m
Mt Labouchere 722m
Mt George 621m
CARNARVON RANGES
Mt Cecil Rhodes 702m
Neds Creek
Errabiddy
Bryah
Mt Deverell 591m
Granite Peak
Earaheedy
Mt Moore 548m
Mt Bates 488m
Yarlarweelor
Mt Fraser 799m
Peak Hill
Doolgunna
Lake Nabberu
Mt Patterson 610m
Carnegie Homestead
Mount Padbury
New Springs
Mt Gould 710m
Mt Maitland 591m
Murchison River
Moorarie
Cunyu
Wongawol
Beringarra
Mt Hale 732m
Hope River
Karalundi
Mooloogool
Diamond Well
Mt Green 618m
Lorna Glen
Mt Noonie 512m
Nookawarra
Koonmarra
Munarra
Paroo
Yandil
Mt Alice West 638m
Jundee
Lake Carnegie
Mileura
Belele
Peace Gorge (The Granites)
GOLDFIELDS
Mt Russell 538m
Wiluna
Prenti Downs
Mt Eureka 498m
Mt Dora 510m
Meekatharra
Lake Annean
Lake Way
Murchison Downs
Hochstetter Hill 546m
Wilgie Mia Red Ochre Mine
Yagahong Hill 604m
Kalli
Annean
Beebyn
Yalgowra Hills 588m
Lake Way
Barwidgee
Youno Downs
Wonganoo
Curdawoodda Hill 411m
Glen
Yarrabubba
Karbar
Tuckanarra
Mt Townsend 660m
Mt Keith 594m
Mount Keith
Gidgee
Coodardy
Big Bell
Taincrow
Yeelirrie
Albion Downs
Mt Arthur 617m
Sanford River
Cue
Walga Rock
Cogla Downs
Barrambie
Lake Mason
Lake Mason
Kaluwiri
Lakeside
Mt Charles 646m
Lake Austin
Booylgoo Springs
Banjawarn
Bandya
GREAT NORTHERN HWY
1 95 136 138
190 184 287 288 448 418 183 196 174

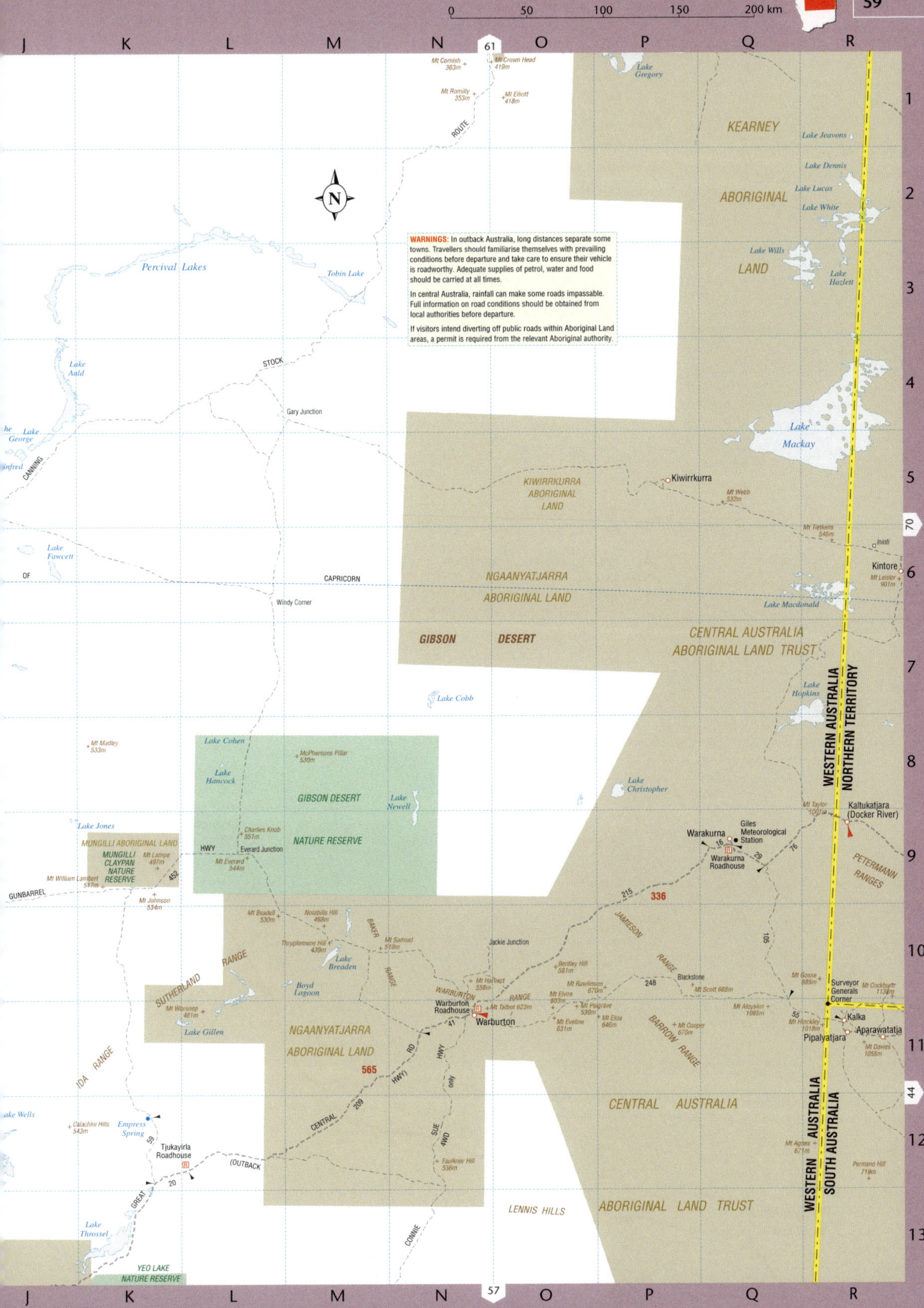
0 50 100 150 200 km
J K L M N O P Q R
1 2 3 4 5 6 7 8 9 10 11 12 13
61
70
44
57
WARNINGS: In outback Australia, long distances separate some towns. Travellers should familiarise themselves with prevailing conditions before departure and take care to ensure their vehicle is roadworthy. Adequate supplies of petrol, water and food should be carried at all times.
In central Australia, rainfall can make some roads impassable. Full information on road conditions should be obtained from local authorities before departure.
If visitors intend diverting off public roads within Aboriginal Land areas, a permit is required from the relevant Aboriginal authority.
Mt Cornish 363m
Mt Crown Head 419m
Mt Romilly 353m
Mt Elliott 418m
ROUTE
Lake Gregory
KEARNEY
ABORIGINAL
LAND
Lake Jeavons
Lake Dennis
Lake Lucas
Lake White
Lake Wills
Lake Hazlett
Percival Lakes
Tobin Lake
Lake Auld
STOCK
Gary Junction
Lake George
CANNING
Lake Mackay
Kiwirrkurra
KIWIRRKURRA ABORIGINAL LAND
Mt Webb 532m
Mt Tietkens 546m
Ininti
Kintore
Mt Leisler 901m
Lake Fawcett
OF
CAPRICORN
Windy Corner
NGAANYATJARRA ABORIGINAL LAND
Lake Macdonald
GIBSON DESERT
CENTRAL AUSTRALIA ABORIGINAL LAND TRUST
WESTERN AUSTRALIA
NORTHERN TERRITORY
Lake Cobb
Lake Hopkins
Mt Madley 533m
Lake Cohen
McPhersons Pillar 530m
Lake Hancock
GIBSON DESERT NATURE RESERVE
Lake Newell
Lake Christopher
Mt Taylor 1001m
Kaltukatjara (Docker River)
Lake Jones
MUNGILLI ABORIGINAL LAND
MUNGILLI CLAYPAN NATURE RESERVE
Mt Lampe 497m
Charles Knob 551m
HWY
Everard Junction
Mt Everard 544m
Mt William Lambert 517m
452
GUNBARREL
Mt Johnson 534m
Warakurna
Giles Meteorological Station
Warakurna Roadhouse
16
29
76
PETERMANN RANGES
215
336
Mt Beadell 530m
Notabilis Hill 468m
BAKER
Mt Samuel 519m
Thryptomene Hill 439m
JAMIESON
RANGE
Jackie Junction
105
Lake Breaden
RANGE
SUTHERLAND
Boyd Lagoon
Bentley Hill 581m
Mt Harvest 558m
WARBURTON
RANGE
Mt Rawlinson 670m
248
Blackstone
Mt Scott 668m
Mt Gosse 885m
Surveyor Generals Corner
Mt Cockburn 1138m
Mt Worsnop 461m
Lake Gillen
Warburton Roadhouse
Warburton
Mt Talbot 623m
Mt Elvire 603m
Mt Palgrave 539m
Mt Eveline 631m
Mt Eliza 646m
Mt Cooper 670m
BARROW RANGE
Mt Aloysius 1085m
55
Mt Hinckley 1018m
Kalka
Pipalyatjara
Aparawatatja
Mt Davies 1058m
41
NGAANYATJARRA ABORIGINAL LAND
RD
HWY
565
IDA RANGE
HWY)
only
CENTRAL
209
CENTRAL AUSTRALIA
ABORIGINAL LAND TRUST
WESTERN AUSTRALIA
SOUTH AUSTRALIA
Lake Wells
Calachini Hills 543m
Empress Spring
59
Tjukayirla Roadhouse
SUE
4WD
Faulkner Hill 536m
Mt Agnes 671m
Permano Hill 719m
(OUTBACK
20
GREAT
LENNIS HILLS
CONNIE
Lake Throssel
YEO LAKE NATURE RESERVE

INDIAN
OCEAN
N
Cape Leveque
One Arm Point
Thomas Bay
Cygnet Bay
Lombadina
LOMBADINA ABORIGINAL RESERVE
Pender Bay
Beagle Bay
Beagle Bay
BEAGLE BAY ABORIGINAL RESERVE
Lake Paterson
Cape Baskerville
Carnot Bay
DAMPIER PENINSULA
Cape Bertholet
POINT COULOMB NATURE RESERVE
Country Downs
Coulomb Point
Fraser
River
James Price Point
4WD only
Cape Boileau
Roebuck Roadhouse
Waterbank
BROOME HWY
NORTHERN
Taylors Lagoon
Lake Eda
Ungani Lakes
Yakka Munga
Cable Beach
Broome
Roebuck Plains
Gantheaume Point
Roebuck Bay
Thangoo
4WD only
Cape Villaret
Gourdon Bay
Cape Latouche Treville
GREAT
Port Smith
False Cape Bossut
La Grange Bay
Bidyadanga
Cape Bossut
Frazier Downs
Admiral Bay
Cape Frezier
Cape Jaubert
Desault Bay
Nita Downs
Cape Missiessy
286
Anna Plains
Mt Phire 90m
Beach
HWY
Mile
Mandora
Wallal Downs
Eighty
Sandfire Roadhouse
GREAT SANDY DESERT
NORTHERN
281
Pardoo Station
Pardoo Roadhouse
GREAT
De Grey
Port Hedland
Cape Thouin
South Hedland
Goldsworthy
Mt Goldsworthy 131m
De Grey River
Shay Gap
Cape Cossigny
Boodarie
Pippingarta
Strelley
Mundabullangana
Callawa
Depuch Island
Carlindie
Coongan
Muccan
Yarrie
Shaw R
145
115
34
30
80
73
103
45
94
50
40
52
46
84
32
75
122
138
1
55
58
A
B
C
D
E
F
G
H
I
1
2
3
4
5
6
7
8
9
10
11
12
13

WARNINGS: In outback Australia, long distances separate some towns. Travellers should familiarise themselves with prevailing conditions before departure and take care to ensure their vehicle is roadworthy. Adequate supplies of petrol, water and food should be carried at all times.

In northern Australia, rainfall during the wet season (October to March) can make some roads impassable. Full information on road conditions should be obtained from local authorities before departure.

If visitors intend diverting off public roads within Aboriginal Land areas, a permit is required from the relevant Aboriginal authority.

Beware of crocodiles in rivers, estuaries and coastal areas.

Northern Territory

Location Map

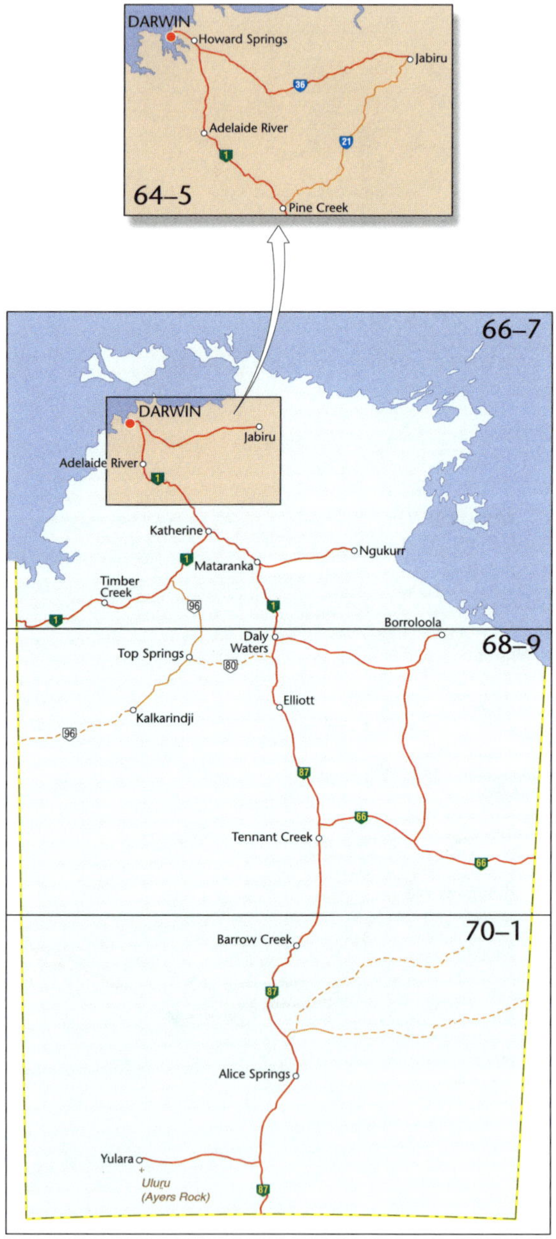

Accommodation

Banyan View Lodge 1 C7
Carlton Hotel Darwin 2 C8
MGM Grand Darwin Hotel 3 A3
Mirambeena Tourist Resort 4 E7
Novotel Atrium Darwin 5 D9
Poinciana Inn 6 D8
Rydges Plaza Hotel 7 F9
Top End Hotel 8 C7
YHA Backpackers International 9 E9
YMCA 10 B7

Note: Only a sample range of accommodation is listed; inclusion is not necessarily a recommendation.

General Information

Bus Terminal 11 G10
Darwin Civic Centre & Library 12 G9
Darwin Harbour seaplanes 13 H12
Darwin Tourist Precinct / Greyhound Pioneer Coaches 14 E9
Garuda Indonesia Airlines 15 F9
General Post Office 16 F8
McCafferty's Coaches 17 E8
Motoring Organisation (AANT) 18 D8
Police Station 19 F10
Qantas Travel Centre 20 G9
Visitor Information (Top End Tourism) 21 E9

Places of Interest

Aquascene 22 B7
Australian Pearling Exhibition 23 I11
Bicentennial Park 24 D9
Brown's Mart 25 G10
Burnett House 26 A4
Chinese Temple 27 G9
Christ Church Cathedral 28 G10
Darwin Botanic Gardens 29 D1
Darwin Entertainment Centre 30 D8
Deckchair Cinema 31 I9
Government House 32 F11
Indo Pacific Marine 33 I11
Lyons Cottage 34 E10
MGM Grand Casino 35 A3
Mindil Beach Sunset Market 36 B1
Old Admiralty House 37 E10
Old Police Station & Courthouse 38 G10
Overland Telegraph Memorial 39 G11
Palmerston (Darwin) Town Hall ruins 40 G10
Parliament House & NT Library 41 F10
Smith Street Mall 42 F9
Stokes Hill Wharf 43 H12
Supreme Court 44 F10
Survivors Lookout 45 G11
Tour Tub 46 F9
Tree of Knowledge 47 G10
Victoria Hotel 48 F9
WW II Oil Storage Tunnels 49 G11

A
B
C
D
E
F
G
H
I
66
BEAGLE GULF
Shoal Bay
Chambers Bay
For more detail on Central Darwin see page 63
DJUKBINJ NATIONAL PARK
MARY RIVER CONSERVATION RESERVE
Lee Point
Hope Inlet
CASUARINA
NIGHTCLIFF
KARAMA
Crocodylus Park
DARWIN AIRPORT
BERRIMAH
WINNELLIE
Charles Point
Mandorah
DARWIN
HOWARD SPRINGS NATURE PARK
Howard Springs
PALMERSTON
Night Markets (Fridays)
Howard Springs
Tapa Bay
Point Margaret
Port Darwin
East Arm
COX PENINSULA
Ida Bay
Mica Beach
Virginia
Coolalinga
McMinns Lagoon
Bees Creek
ARNHEM
Humpty Doo
DELISSAVILLE WAGAIT LARRAKIA ABORIGINAL LAND TRUST
Belyuen
Darwin Crocodile Farm
Haycock Reach
Noonamah
RAN Transmitting Station
Agricultural Check Point
Window on the Wetlands Visitor Centre
Adelaide River Cruises
FOGG DAM CONSERVATION RESERVE
Fogg Dam
Middle Point
Beatrice Hill
Humpty Doo (Wariuk)
Tommy Policeman Lagoon
Lake Finniss
Woolner
Koolpinyah
SHADY CAMP RESERVE
Point Stuart Wilderness Lodge
Wildman River Wilderness Lodge
North Rockhole
Corroboree Billabong
Couzens Lookout
MARY RIVER NATIONAL PARK (Delta Sector)
MARY RIVER NP (Bundey Sector)
Annaburroo
Mary River Crossing
Turnbull Bay
BERRY SPRINGS NATURE PARK
Territory Wildlife Park
Lakes Resort
Berry Springs
STUART
Bynoe Harbour
PENINSULA
RD
Observation Hill
LEANING TREE LAGOON NATURE PARK
Corroboree Park Tavern
Southport Siding Exotic Fruit Farm
Tumbling Waters Deer Park
Majestic Orchids
Acacia
Agricultural Check Point
DELISSAVILLE WAGAIT LARRAKIA ABORIGINAL LAND TRUST
Old Mount Bundy Outstation
HWY
Finniss River
MANTON DAM RECREATION AREA
Manton Dam
Darwin River Dam
Lake Bennett
Lake Bennett Wilderness Resort
Rum Jungle (Disused uranium mine)
FINNISS RIVER
Batchelor
DELISSAVILLE WAGAIT LARRAKIA ABORIGINAL LAND TRUST
Bamboo Creek Tin Mine (ruins)
Walker Creek
Florence Falls
Buley Rockhole
Magnetic Termite Mounds
Petherick's Rain Forest
Woolaning
Wangi Falls
Greenant Creek
Tolmer Falls
The Lost City
Tjaynera Falls
LITCHFIELD NATIONAL PARK
Mount Ringwood
Adelaide River
War Cemetery
Mount Bundy Station
Robin Falls
Goodilla
ALICE SPRINGS (under construction)
DARWIN RAILWAY
Labelle Downs Outstation
Wangi
Welltree
Blyth (ruins)
Keri
Litchfield
Litchfield Outstation
DORAT RD
Ban Ban Springs
Howley
Grove Hill
Brocks Creek
The Banyans
Hayes Creek Wayside Inn
Emerald Springs Wayside Inn
Douglas
Boomleera
MALAK MALAK ABORIGINAL LAND TRUST
Elizabeth Downs
Nauiyu
Daly River
Ceres Downs
Kumbyechants
Douglas Daly Park
Douglas Hot Springs
BUTTERFLY GORGE NATURE PARK
TJUWALIYN (DOUGLAS) HOT SPRINGS PARK
Douglas Daly Experimental Station
Pine Creek
Green Valley
Kybrook
Oolloo
WARNINGS: In northern Australia, long distances separate some towns. Travellers should familiarise themselves with prevailing conditions before departure and take care to ensure their vehicle is roadworthy. Adequate supplies of petrol, water and food should be carried at all times.
Rainfall during the wet season (November to April) can make some roads impassable, even with a 4WD vehicle. Full information on road conditions should be obtained from local authorities before departure.
If visitors intend diverting off public roads within Aboriginal Land areas, a permit is required from the relevant Aboriginal authority.
Beware of crocodiles in rivers, estuaries and coastal areas.

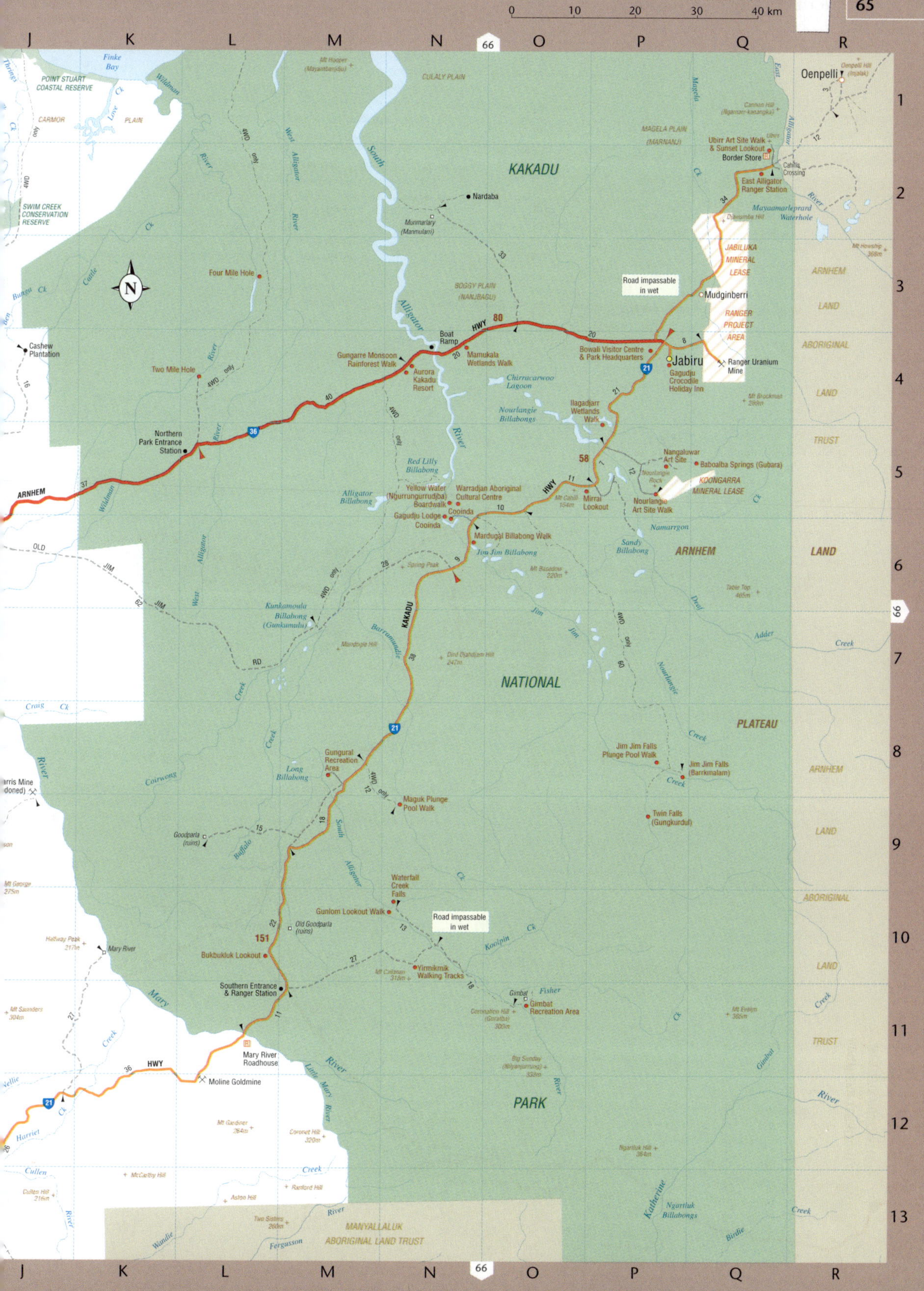
0 10 20 30 40 km
KAKADU
NATIONAL
PARK
ARNHEM LAND
ARNHEM PLATEAU
ARNHEM LAND ABORIGINAL LAND TRUST
MANYALLALUK ABORIGINAL LAND TRUST
POINT STUART COASTAL RESERVE
SWIM CREEK CONSERVATION RESERVE
JABILUKA MINERAL LEASE
RANGER PROJECT AREA
KOONGARRA MINERAL LEASE
Oenpelli
Ubirr Art Site Walk & Sunset Lookout
Border Store
Cahills Crossing
East Alligator Ranger Station
Mayaamarleprard Waterhole
Road impassable in wet
Mudginberri
Jabiru
Ranger Uranium Mine
Bowali Visitor Centre & Park Headquarters
Gagudju Crocodile Holiday Inn
Nardaba
Munmarlary (Manmulari)
Boat Ramp
Gungarre Monsoon Rainforest Walk
Aurora Kakadu Resort
Mamukala Wetlands Walk
Chirracarwoo Lagoon
Nourlangie Billabongs
Ilagadjarr Wetlands Walk
Four Mile Hole
Two Mile Hole
Cashew Plantation
Northern Park Entrance Station
Nangaluwar Art Site
Baboalba Springs (Gubara)
Nourlangie Art Site Walk
Mirrai Lookout
Red Lilly Billabong
Alligator Billabong
Yellow Water (Ngurrungurrudjba) Boardwalk
Warradjan Aboriginal Cultural Centre
Cooinda
Gagudju Lodge Cooinda
Mardugal Billabong Walk
Jim Jim Billabong
Sandy Billabong
Kunkamoula Billabong (Gunkumulu)
Gungural Recreation Area
Long Billabong
Maguk Plunge Pool Walk
Jim Jim Falls Plunge Pool Walk
Jim Jim Falls (Barrkmalam)
Twin Falls (Gungkurdul)
Goodparla (ruins)
Waterfall Creek Falls
Gunlom Lookout Walk
Old Goodparla (ruins)
Bukbukluk Lookout
Yirmikmik Walking Tracks
Gimbat Recreation Area
Southern Entrance & Ranger Station
Mary River Roadhouse
Moline Goldmine
Mary River
Ngarrluk Billabongs
ARNHEM HWY
KAKADU HWY
OLD JIM JIM RD
4WD only
Finke Bay
CARMOR PLAIN
MAGELA PLAIN (MARNANJ)
BOGGY PLAIN (NANJBAGU)
CULALY PLAIN
South Alligator River
West Alligator River
East Alligator River
Wildman River
Jim Jim Creek
Barramundie Creek
Koolpin Creek
Katherine River
Mary River

TIMOR
SEA
TIWI ISLANDS
Cape Van Diemen
Deception Point
Pirlangimpi
Milikapiti
TIWI ABORIGINAL LAND TRUST
Wurankuwu
BATHURST ISLAND
MELVILLE ISLAND
Nguiu
Paru
Pickertaramoor
Point Jahleel
Conder Point
Cape Gambier
Clarence Strait
Beagle Gulf
Gunn Point
Cape Hotham
DJUKBINJ NATIONAL PARK
Dundas Strait
Cape Don
Vashon Head
Smith Pt
Araru Pt
Lingi Pt
COBOURG PENINSULA
Port Essington
Gurig Store
Victoria Settlement
GURIG NATIONAL PARK
Danger Pt
Minjilang
Gul Gul
Cape Croker
CROKER ISLAND
McCluer Island
Grant Island
Cape Cockburn
COBOURG MARINE PARK
Greenhill Island
Morse Island
Endyalgout Island
Cape Keith
Murgenella
Warruwi
VAN DIEMEN GULF
Field Island
Point Stuart (Gurnaynjarr)
For more detail on Darwin & Surrounds see pages 64–5
DARWIN
Mandorah
PALMERSTON
Howard Springs
Belyuen
Noonamah
Humpty Doo
Dundee Beach
Fog Bay
Finniss River
Point Blaze
JOSEPH BONAPARTE GULF
DELISSAVILLE WAGAIT LARRAKIA ABORIGINAL LAND TRUST
Rum Jungle
Batchelor
Woolaning
Wangi Falls
North Peron Island
South Peron Island
Anson Bay
Cape Ford
Adelaide River
War Cemetery
LITCHFIELD NATIONAL PARK
Litchfield Outstation
MALAK MALAK ABORIGINAL LAND TRUST
Nauiyu
Daly River
Douglas Daly Park
Douglas Daly Experimental Station
Hayes Creek Wayside Inn
Emerald Springs Wayside Inn
TJUWALIYN (DOUGLAS) HOT SPRINGS PARK
Pine Creek
UMBRAWARRA GORGE NATURE PARK
Umbrawarra Gorge
MARY RIVER CONSERVATION RESERVE
MARY RIVER NP
MARY RIVER NATIONAL PARK
Annaburroo
Mount Ringwood
Two Mile Hole
KAKADU NATIONAL PARK
Aurora Kakadu Resort
Cooinda
Jabiru
Nourlangie Art Site Walk
Ubirr Art Site Walk & Sunset Lookout
Border Store
Oenpelli
Cahills Crossing
Jim Jim Falls (Barrkmalam)
Twin Falls (Gungkurdul)
Mary River Roadhouse
ARNHEM LAND
Gimbat
NITMILUK NATIONAL PARK
Edith Falls
Nitmiluk Gorge
George Camp
Katherine
Tindal RAAF Base
MANYALLALUK ABORIGINAL LAND TRUST
Manyallaluk
BESWICK ABORIGINAL LAND TRUST
Barunga
Beswick
Maranboy
CUTTA CUTTA CAVES NATURE PARK
Mataranka
Mataranka Thermal Pool
ELSEY NP
Elsey Cemetery
Jilkminggan
Larrimah
DALY RIVER PORT KEATS ABORIGINAL LAND TRUST
Cape Dombey
Wadeye
Pearce Point
Treachery Bay
Swamp Point
MACADAM RANGE
WINGATE MOUNTAINS
UPPER DALY ABORIGINAL LAND TRUST
FISH RIVER FORESTRY RESERVE
JAWOYN ABORIGINAL LAND TRUST
FLORA RIVER NATURE PARK
Turtle Point
Fitzmaurice River
YAMBARRAN RANGE
Victoria River
Marralum
Legune
Kneebone
Bullo River
KEEP RIVER NATIONAL PARK
NORTHERN TERRITORY
WESTERN AUSTRALIA
Agricultural Check Point
Bulla
Timber Creek
GREGORY NATIONAL PARK (Bullita Sector)
Limestone Gorge
NGALIWURRU / NUNGALI ABORIGINAL LAND TRUST
WANIMIYN ABORIGINAL LAND TRUST
Victoria River Roadhouse
GREGORY NATIONAL PARK (Victoria River Sector)
Jasper Gorge
Willeroo
Delamere
Old Delamere
Gilnockie
Sunday Creek
ALICE SPRINGS - DARWIN RAILWAY (under construction)
STUART HWY
ARNHEM HWY
KAKADU HWY
VICTORIA HWY
BUNTINE HWY
BUCHANAN HWY

0 50 100 150 km
J K L M N O P Q R
1 2 3 4 5 6 7 8 9 10 11 12 13
ARAFURA SEA
GULF OF CARPENTARIA
N
Cape Wessel
Marchinbar Island
WESSEL ISLANDS
Guluwuru Island
Drysdale Island
ELCHO ISLAND
Galiwinku
Point Napier
Point Wilberforce
Bremer Island
Nhulunbuy
Gunyangara
Yirrkala
Buku-Larrnggay Mulka (Aboriginal Art Museum)
Cape Arnhem
GOVE PENINSULA
Rorruwuy
Arnhem Bay
Gapuwiyak Landing Ground
Gapuwiyak
Gurrumuru
FREDERICK HILLS
Garrthalala
Birany Birany
Point Alexander
Cape Grey
Baniyala
Cape Shield
Isle Woodah
Cape Barrow
Milyakburra
Bickerton Island
Alyangula
Umbakumba
Angurugu
GROOTE EYLANDT
Tasman Point
Cape Beatrice
Numbulwar
JRN ISLANDS
Braithwaite Point
Cape Stewart
Mooroongga Is
HOWARD ISLAND
Maningrida
Ji-Marda
Milingimbi
Castlereagh Bay
Ngangalala
Ramingining
Old Arafura
Mirrngadja Village
Gulbuwangay River
Manmoyi
ARNHEM LAND ABORIGINAL LAND TRUST
ARNHEM 160 RD
CENTRAL
MITCHELL RANGE
BATH RANGE
PARSONS RANGE
Koolatong River
Walker River
Goyder
Maidjungu River
Liverpool
Mann
Wilton
Annie Creek
Bulman
Mt Marumba
776
Rose
Harris Creek
Phelp
Rose River
DOWNERS RANGE
COLLERA
MTNS
Mountain Valley
Mainoru
Mt Furner 188m
Lake Allen
Roper Bar
Roper Bar Store
HWY
Ngukurr
St Vidgeon (ruins)
Roper
198
20
Roper Valley
Mt Harris 167m
PORT ROPER RD
Port Roper
Limmen Bight
Maria Island
MARRA ABORIGINAL LAND TRUST
Towns River
NATHAN
Limmen Bight River Fishing Camp
Minyerri
HODGSON DOWNS LEASE
ALAWA ABORIGINAL LAND TRUST
Maryfield (ruins)
Hodgson River
Arnold River
Nathan River
Lorella Springs
Nutwood Downs
Minamia
Cox
Hodgson
Limmen Bight
RIVER RD
SIR EDWARD PELLEW GROUP
West Island
North Island
BARRANYI (NORTH ISLAND) NATIONAL PARK
Vanderlin Island
SW Is
Centre Island
Bing Bong
WADA WADALLA LEASE
King Ash Bay
Batten Creek
NARWINBI ABORIGINAL LAND
Manangoora
Mara
Wandangula
Borroloola
Garawa
69
WARNINGS: In northern Australia, long distances separate some towns. Travellers should familiarise themselves with prevailing conditions before departure and take care to ensure their vehicle is roadworthy. Adequate supplies of petrol, water and food should be carried at all times.
Rainfall during the wet season (November to April) can make some roads impassable, even with a 4WD vehicle. Full information on road conditions should be obtained from local authorities before departure.
If visitors intend diverting off public roads within Aboriginal Land areas, a permit is required from the relevant Aboriginal authority.
Beware of crocodiles in rivers, estuaries and coastal areas.

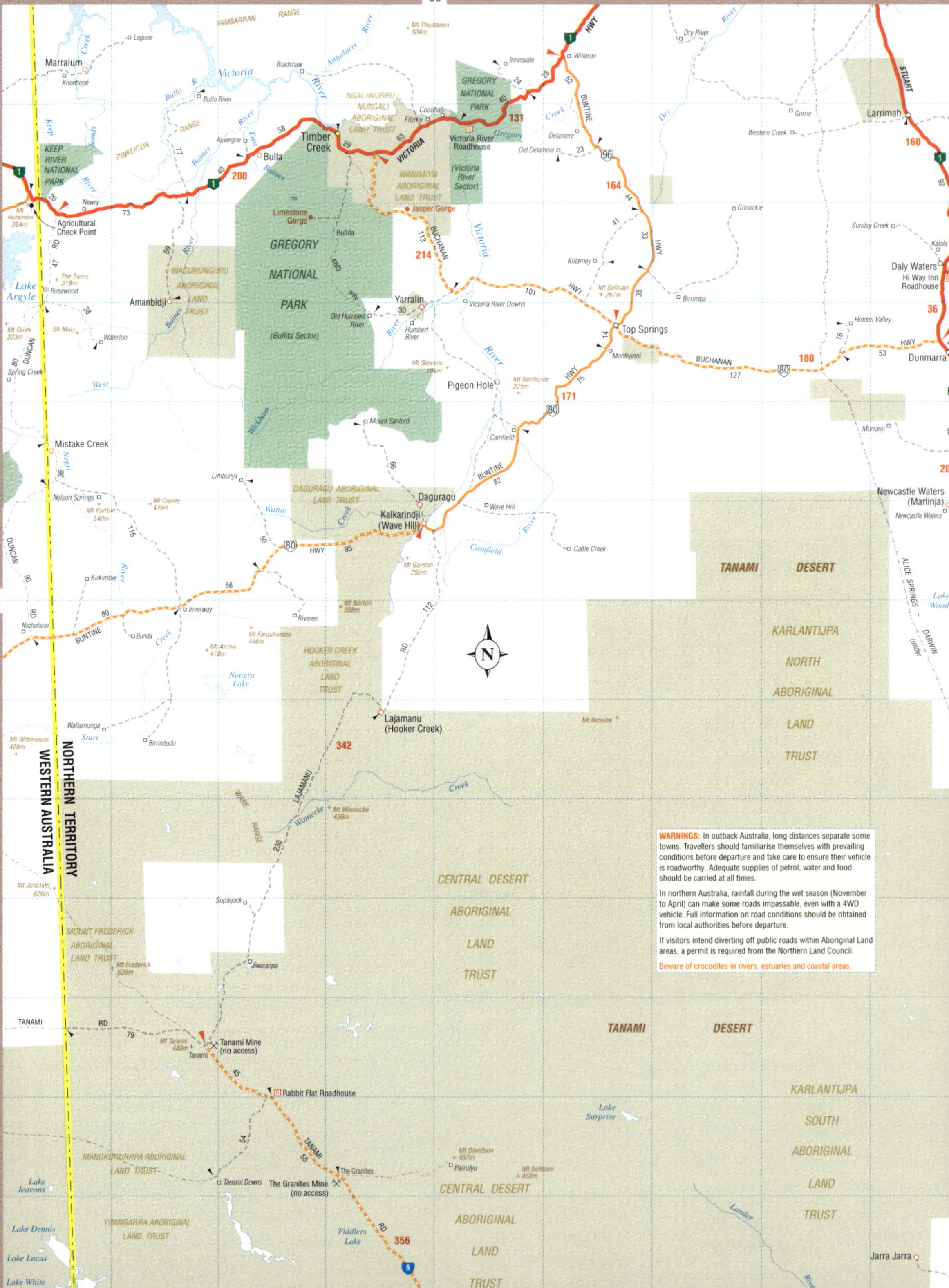

WARNINGS: In outback Australia, long distances separate some towns. Travellers should familiarise themselves with prevailing conditions before departure and take care to ensure their vehicle is roadworthy. Adequate supplies of petrol, water and food should be carried at all times.

In northern Australia, rainfall during the wet season (November to April) can make some roads impassable, even with a 4WD vehicle. Full information on road conditions should be obtained from local authorities before departure.

If visitors intend diverting off public roads within Aboriginal Land areas, a permit is required from the Northern Land Council.

Beware of crocodiles in rivers, estuaries and coastal areas.

0 50 100 150 km
GULF OF CARPENTARIA
SIR EDWARD PELLEW GROUP
BARRANYI (NORTH ISLAND) NATIONAL PARK
West Island
North Island
Vanderlin Island
Centre Island
SW Is
King Ash Bay
Bing Bong
WADA WADALLA LEASE
Limmen Bight River Fishing Camp
Minyerri
ALAWA ABORIGINAL LAND TRUST
Hodgson River
Maryfield (ruins)
Nutwood Downs
Minamia
Nathan River
Lorella Springs
Bauhinia Downs
Mara
Wandangula
Borroloola
Garawa
Manangoora
NARWINBI ABORIGINAL LAND TRUST
CARANBIRINI CON RES
McArthur River Mine
BUKALARA RANGE
Spring Creek
Doolgarina
Greenbank
Seven Emu
GARAWA ABORIGINAL LAND TRUST
Robinson River
Pungalina
Tawallah
Billengarrah (ruins)
Broadmere
Tanumbirini
Amungee Mungee
O T Downs
CARPENTARIA HWY
Cape Crawford
Lost City
Heartbreak Hotel
Balbirini
Mallapunyah
Kiana
Shenandoah
Beetaloo
Wollogorang Station & Roadhouse
Calvert Hills
Westmoreland
BARKLY
Ucharonidge
Mungabroom
Wallhallow
Cresswell Downs
CALVERT RD
BARKLY STOCK ROUTE
Eva Downs
Anthony Lagoon
Benmara
CHINA WALL
WAANYI/GARAWA ABORIGINAL LAND TRUST
Tarrabool Lake
Renner Springs
Helen Springs
Muckaty
Ngunarra
Corella Lake
Brunette Downs
Lake Sylvester
Springvale
Murun Murula
Musselbrook Mining Camp
LAWN HILL NATIONAL PARK
Mittiebah
CONNELLS LAGOON CONSERVATION RESERVE
TABLELAND
Banka Banka
Brunchilly
Rockhampton Downs
Wogyala
Alumpurlpa
Stuart Memorial
ATTACK CREEK HISTORICAL RESERVE
Alexandria
Gallipoli
Norfolk
WARUMUNGU ABORIGINAL LAND TRUST
Phillip Creek
John Flynn Memorial
Three Ways Roadhouse
Likkaparta
BARKLY
Alroy Downs
TABLELANDS
Warrego
The Pebbles
Tennant Creek
Historic Telegraph Station
Barkly Homestead
NORTHERN TERRITORY
QUEENSLAND
WAKAYA ABORIGINAL LAND TRUST
BARKLY HWY
Soudan
Avon Downs Police Station
Avon Downs
Camooweal
CAMOOWEAL CAVES NP
Six Mile Waterhole
Big Ranken Waterhole
22 Mile Waterhole
URANDANGI RD
Mungkarta
Kalinjarri
Wutunugurra
Epenarra
Austral Downs
Wooroona
DEVILS MARBLES CONSERVATION RESERVE
Devils Marbles
Wauchope
Canteen Creek
Singleton
Wycliffe Well Roadhouse
WARRABRI ABORIGINAL LAND TRUST
DAVENPORT RANGE NATIONAL PARK
ANURRETE ABORIGINAL LAND TRUST
Hatches Creek
Bullock Waterhole
Ali-Curung
Murray Downs
Imangara
SANDOVER HWY
Alpurrurulam
Lake Nash
Bullecourt

Rabbit Flat Roadhouse
MANGKURURRPA ABORIGINAL LAND TRUST
TANAMI
The Granites
Tanami Downs
The Granites Mine (no access)
Lake Jeavons
Lake Dennis
YININGARRA ABORIGINAL LAND TRUST
Lake Lucas
Lake White
Fiddlers Lake
Lake Surprise
TANAMI DESERT
KARLANTIJPA SOUTH ABORIGINAL LAND TRUST
CENTRAL DESERT ABORIGINAL LAND TRUST
Parrulyu
Lander River
Jarra Jarra
WIRIYAJARRAYI ABORIGINAL LAND TRUST
Willowra
Lake Hazlett
LAKE MACKAY ABORIGINAL LAND TRUST
Ranahan
MALA ABORIGINAL LAND TRUST
Mt Theo
Chilla Well
Mount Barkly
Old Mount Peake
Hanson
Anningie
Mount Esther
Mount Doreen
YUENDUMU ABORIGINAL LAND TRUST
MOUNT DENISON
Mount Denison
Coniston
Coniston (ruins)
Nturiya
Pmara Jutunta
Lake Mackay
Vaughan Springs
Yuendumu
Yuelamu
YALPIRAKINU ABORIGINAL LAND TRUST
STUART
Laramba
YUNKANJINI ABORIGINAL LAND TRUST
Nyirripi
Gurner
Newhaven
Aileron
RYANS WELL HISTORIC RESERVE
NATIVE GAP CONS RES
Lake Bennett
Central Mount Wedge
Tilmouth Well Roadhouse
Lake Lewis
Ininti
Pinpirnga
Kintore
Tinki
Derwent
Papunya
Narwietooma
Amburla
Warren Creek Bore
Mt Liebig
Ulambaura
Milton Park
Ilpilla
TROPIC OF CAPRICORN
HAASTS BLUFF ABORIGINAL LAND TRUST
Haasts Bluff
Hamilton Downs
Lake Macdonald
Ualki
Redbank Gorge
Ormiston Gorge
WEST MACDONNELL NATIONAL PARK
Standley Chasm
WARNING: Visitors planning to travel along Larapinta Drive through Aboriginal Land require a permit. Check road conditions before departing; 4WD vehicle may be required.
Glen Helen Resort
NAMATJIRA DR
Serpentine Gorge
TNORALA (GOSSE BLUFF) CON RES
Tnorala (Gosse Bluff)
ROULPMAULPMA ABORIGINAL LAND TRUST
Iwupataka
LARAPINTA (MEREENIE LOOP) RD
Ipolera
Hermannsburg
Lake Hopkins
NORTHERN TERRITORY
WESTERN AUSTRALIA
WATARRKA NATIONAL PARK
Kings Canyon
Kings Canyon Resort
Areyonga
Palm Valley
FINKE GORGE NATIONAL PARK
Wallace Rockhole
Lake Neale
ILLAMURTA SPRINGS CONSERVATION RES
Stuarts Well
Tempe Downs
Kings Creek Station (Camping ground)
LURITJA RD
Henbury Meteorite Craters
PETERMANN ABORIGINAL LAND TRUST
ERNEST GILES RD
Kaltukatjara (Docker River)
Lake Amadeus
Palmer Valley
LIDDLE HILLS
TJUKURURU (OUTBACK HWY) RD
PETERMANN RANGES
KATITI ABORIGINAL LAND TRUST
KERNOT RANGE
BASEDOW RANGE
Yulara
LASSETER (OUTBACK HWY)
Ayers Rock Resort
Kata Tjuta (The Olgas)
Uluru (Ayers Rock)
ULURU–KATA TJUTA NATIONAL PARK
Curtin Springs
Imanpa
Mt Ebenezer Roadhouse
Erldunda
Mygoora Lake
Mt Connor (ruins)
Lyndavale
Kulgera
Mulga Park
Alpara
Surveyor Generals Corner
NORTHERN TERRITORY
SOUTH AUSTRALIA
MANN RANGES
Victory Downs
Kalka
Pipalyatjara
Aparawatatja
Kanypi
Amata
Marryat Creek

0 50 100 150 km

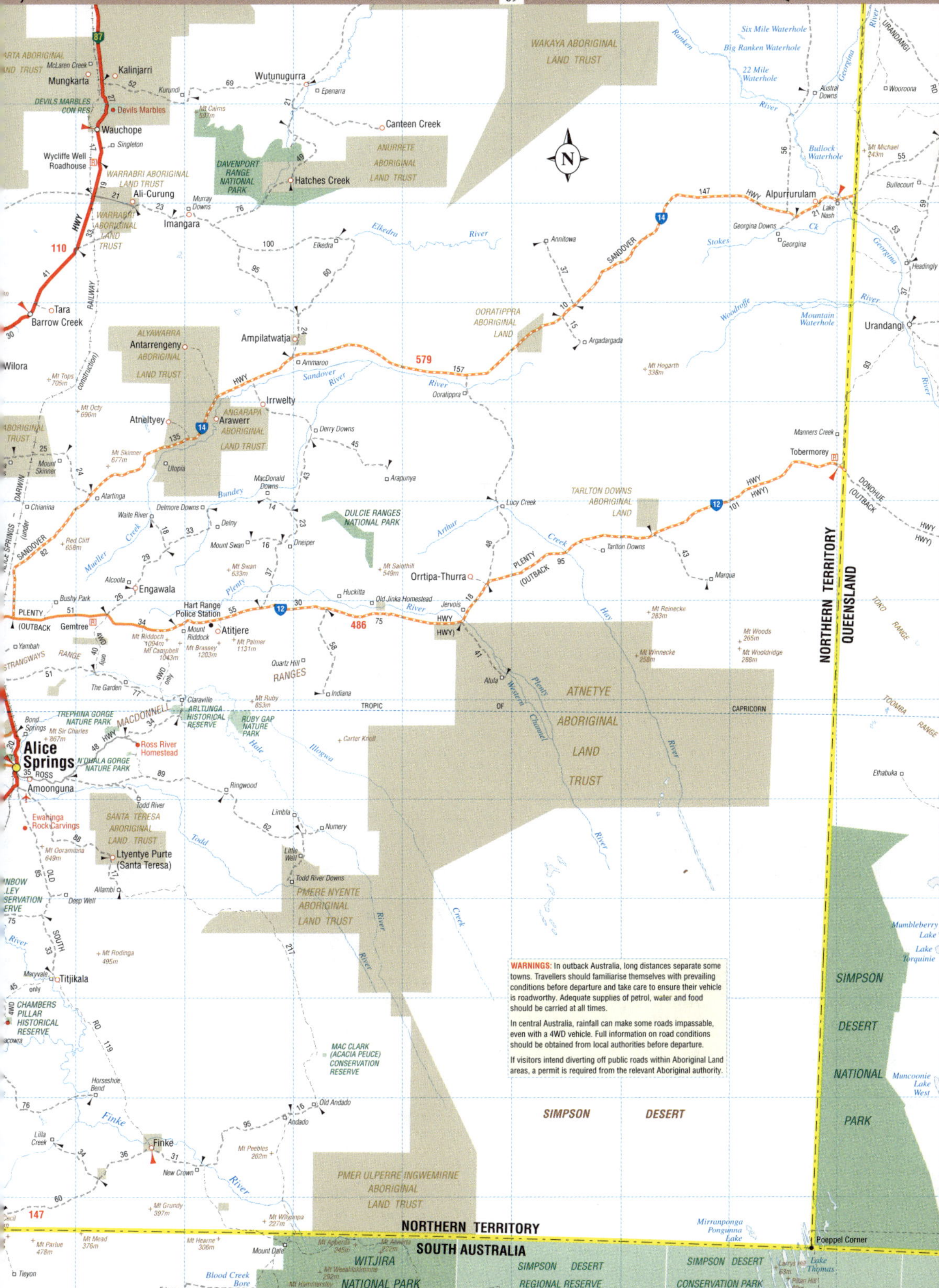

QUEENSLAND

LOCATION MAP

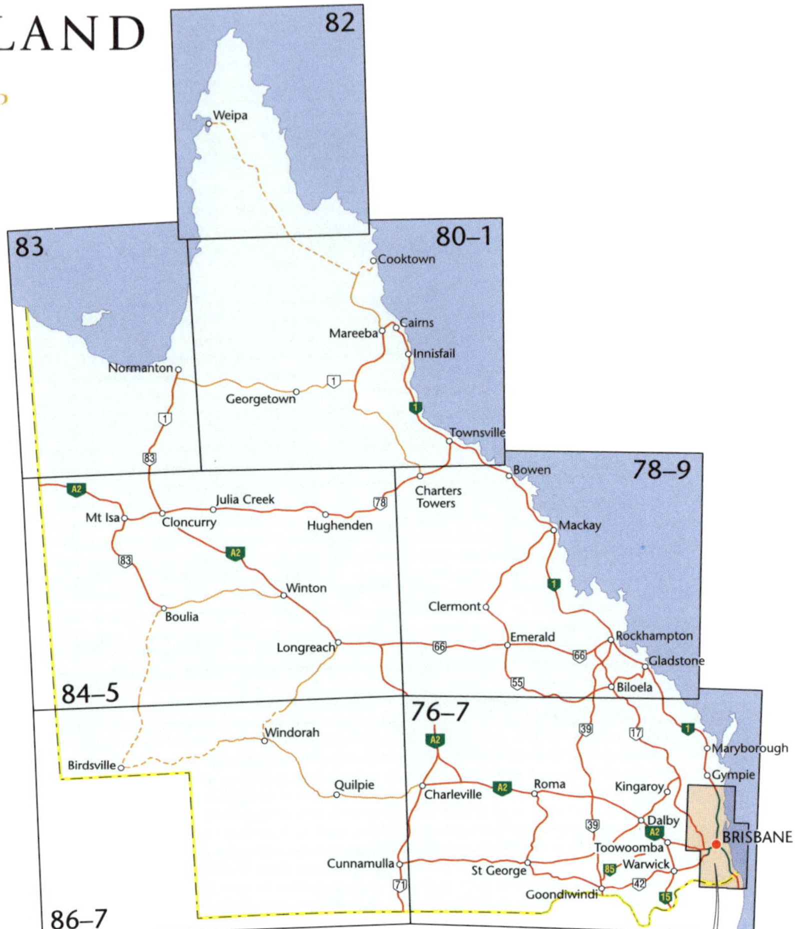

Accommodation
Brisbane City Travel Lodge 1 C5
Brisbane International Hilton 2 E6
Brisbane Marriott Hotel 3 G4
Conrad International Hotel 4 D8
Country Comfort Lennons Hotel 5 D7
Gazebo Hotel 6 C4
The Heritage Hotel 7 F7
Hotel Grand Chancellor 8 D4
Mercure Hotel Brisbane 9 C7
North Quay Hotel 10 B5
Novotel Brisbane 11 E4
Palace Backpackers 12 E5
Radisson Hotel and Suites Brisbane 13 G4
Ridge Hotel 14 E4
Rydges South Bank Hotel 15 C9
Sheraton Brisbane Hotel 16 E5
Story Bridge Motor Inn 17 H7

Note: Only a sample range of accommodation is listed; inclusion is not necessarily a recommendation.

General Information
Brisbane Transit Centre 18 C5
Central Railway Station 19 E5
City Police Station 20 F5
General Post Office 21 F6
Motoring Organisation (RACQ) 22 F6
Qantas Travel Centre 23 F5
Roma Street Station 24 C5
Visitor Information 25 D10, E7

Places of Interest
Brisbane City Hall 26 D6
Brisbane Cricket Ground (The Gabba) 27 I13
Brunswick Street Mall 28 H2
Chinatown 29 H2
City Botanic Gardens 30 F9
Commissariat Stores 31 E8
Conrad International Treasury Casino 32 D7
Customs House 33 G5
Eagle Street Pier 34 G6
IMAX Theatre 35 C10
Old Government House 36 F9
Old Windmill 37 D5
Parliament House 38 E9
Pauls Breaka Beach 39 D10
Queen Street Mall 40 E6
Queensland Art Gallery 41 C8
Queensland Maritime Museum 42 E11
Queensland Museum 43 B8
Queensland Performing Arts Complex 44 C8
St John's Cathedral 45 F4
St Stephen's Cathedral 46 F6
Sciencentre 47 E8
State Library of Queensland 48 B7

0 10 20 30 40 km
A B C D E F G H I
1 2 3 4 5 6 7 8 9 10 11 12 13
TO GYMPIE
Cooran
Pomona
Ringtail
GREAT SANDY NP
Amamoor
AMAMOOR STATE FOREST PARK
Toomcul
Kandanga
Manumbar Hill
Kandanga Creek
Kandanga Upper
Mt Kandanga
Gallangowan
Federal
BRUCE
Black Mountain
Black Mtn
YUROL STATE FOREST
Lake Cooroibah
Lake Macdonald
Tewantin
Tinbeerwah
Noosaville
Noosa Heads
NOOSA NP
Sunshine Beach
Laguna Bay
Cooroy
Mt Cooroy
Castaways Beach
Marcus Beach
Lake Weyba
NOOSA NATIONAL PARK
Peregian Beach
SUNSHINE
SOUTH
PACIFIC
OCEAN
Heritage Railway
Imbil
Derrier Flat
Brooloo
Carters Ridge
Ridgewood
BLACKALL RANGE
Mt Eerwah
Eumundi
Doonan
Thunder Egg Farm
Belli Park
North Arm
Coolum Beach
Yaroomba
MOUNT COOLUM NP
Marcoola
Mudjimba
Pacific Paradise
Bli Bli
Lake Borumba
Borumba Mtn
Yabba
JIMNA
RANGE
Moy Pocket
Cooloolabin Dam
Cooloolabin
The Ginger Factory
Mt Ninderry
Yandina
Kiamba
Maroochy River
Gheerulla
STATE FOREST
Kenilworth
Mapleton
Kureelpa
MAPLETON FALLS NP
Obi Obi
Dulong
Nambour
Woombye
Big Pineapple
Digilibah
Maroochydore
Alexandra Headland
Mooloolaba
Forest Glen
Buderim
Cambroon Bridge
Jimna
Fire Tower
Summer Mtn 789m
Mt Monsildale 726m
CONONDALE NATIONAL PARK
Mt Cabinet 732m
Mt Adelaide 754m
Mt Langley 868m
Mt Ramsden 792m
Donovans Knobs 662m
Flaxton
Hunchy
Palmwoods
KONDALILLA NP
Montville
Witta
Conondale
Chevallum
Eudlo
Warana
MOOLOOLAH RIVER NP
Bokarina
Wurtulla
CURRIMUNDI LAKE CONSERVATION PARK
Yednia
CONONDALE
Maleny
Reesville
Diamond Valley
Mooloolah
Bald Knob
DULARCHA NP
Wootha
Crohamhurst
Long Range Weather Forecasting Observatory
Currimundi
Caloundra
Golden Beach
Pelican Waters
Mt Spencer 445m
North West Mtn 599m
Bellthorpe
Mt Mellum 404m
Landsborough
Peachester
Beerwah
Campbellville
Mount Kilcoy
Mt Kilcoy 351m
Mt Marysmokes 657m
Commissioners Flat
Mt McLean 465m
Stanmore
Mt Pineview 432m
TO KINGAROY
Brisbane
Nurinda
Colinton
D'AGUILAR
HWY
Kilcoy
Winya
Kalangara
Mt Beerwah 556m
Mt Coonowrin 375m
GLASS HOUSE MOUNTAINS NP
Mt Ngungun 253m
Mt Tibrogargan 282m
Glass House Mountains
Coochin Creek
BRIBIE ISLAND
Pumicestone
Gregors Creek
Glenfern
Stanley
Neurum
Durundur
Villeneuve
Woodford
Mt Beerburrum 278m
Beerburrum
Harlin
Mt McConnel 489m
Mt Archer 460m
D'Aguilar
Mt Tunbubudla 294m
BRIBIE ISLAND NATIONAL PARK
Yimbun
CRESSBROOK NATURE RESERVE
Hazeldene
Cressbrook Lower
Mt Delaney 373m
Delaneys Creek
Bracalba
Elimbah
Six Mile
Donnybrook
Meldale
Ivory Creek
White Patch
BRIBIE ISLAND NATIONAL PARK
Banksia Beach
Wamuran
Caboolture Historical Village
Toorbul
Toogoolawah
Lake Somerset
Mt Brisbane 684m
Mt Mee 495m
Mount Mee
Wamuran Basin
Moodlu
Ningi
Bellara
Woorim
Skirmish Point
Bongaree
Campbells Pocket
Caboolture
Godwin Beach
Cooeeinbardi
Mount Beppo
Somerset Dam
Mt Byron 617m
Mt Pleasant 524m
Rocksberg
Morayfield
Caning
BUCKLEYS HOLE CONSERVATION PARK
Ottaba
Caboonbah
Beachmere
Deception Bay
Vehicle Ferry to Moreton Island
Biarra
BRISBANE
Coal Creek
Mount Pleasant
Crossdale
D'AGUILAR RANGE
BURPENGARY
DECEPTION BAY
Gallanani
Murrumba
Dayboro
Upper Laceys Creek
NARANGBA
SCARBOROUGH
Alma Park Zoo
DAKABIN
Esk
Glen Esk
VALLEY
Kobble
KALLANGUR
CLONTARF
REDCLIFFE
MARGATE
WOODY POINT
Mt Sim Jue 611m
Bryden
Lake Samsonvale
PETRIE
Main Channel
Bramble Bay
Moombra
Mount Hallen
Dundas
Lake Wivenhoe
Wivenhoe Lookout
Mt D'Aguilar 742m
Mt Samson 742m
D'AGUILAR NP
Mount Samson
STATE FOREST
STRATHPINE
SANDGATE
MORETON
BAY
Mt Hallen 388m
Buaraba
Hydro Power Station
Mt Glorious
Mount Glorious
Upper Cedar Creek
Yugar
Closeburn
River
Mud Island
Vehicle Ferry to Moreton Island
South Pine
Samford
BRISBANE FOREST PARK
BUNYAVILLE STATE FOREST PARK
BRISBANE AIRPORT
Fisherman Islands
St Helena Island
ST HELENA ISLAND NATIONAL PARK
CHERMSIDE
Coominya
Patrick Estate
Atkinson Dam
Clarendon
Ardmory
CABBAGE TREE RANGE
Mount Nebo
Highvale
Australian Woolshed
Buaraba Creek
Jollys Lookout
BRISBANE FOREST PARK
Lake Manchester
McAfees Lookout
NEWMARKET
Green Island
WYNNUM
MANLY
Waterloo Bay
Mount Tarampa
Wivenhoe Pocket
Fernvale
Lowood
BRISBANE
WOOLLOONGABBA
WELLINGTON POINT
Ormiston House
Lake Clarendon
Brightview
Tarampa
Fairneyview
INDOOROOPILLY
KENMORE
Glamorganvale
Wanora
Coolana
Old Court House
WARREGO
HWY
Glenore Grove
Minden
Marburg
Haigslea
Borallon
Mt Crosby
KARRANA DOWNS
CAPALABA
CLEVELAND
TO TOOWOOMBA
Agricultural College
Plainland
Hatton Vale
TO IPSWICH
MT OMMANEY
TO BEENLEIGH
77 75
N

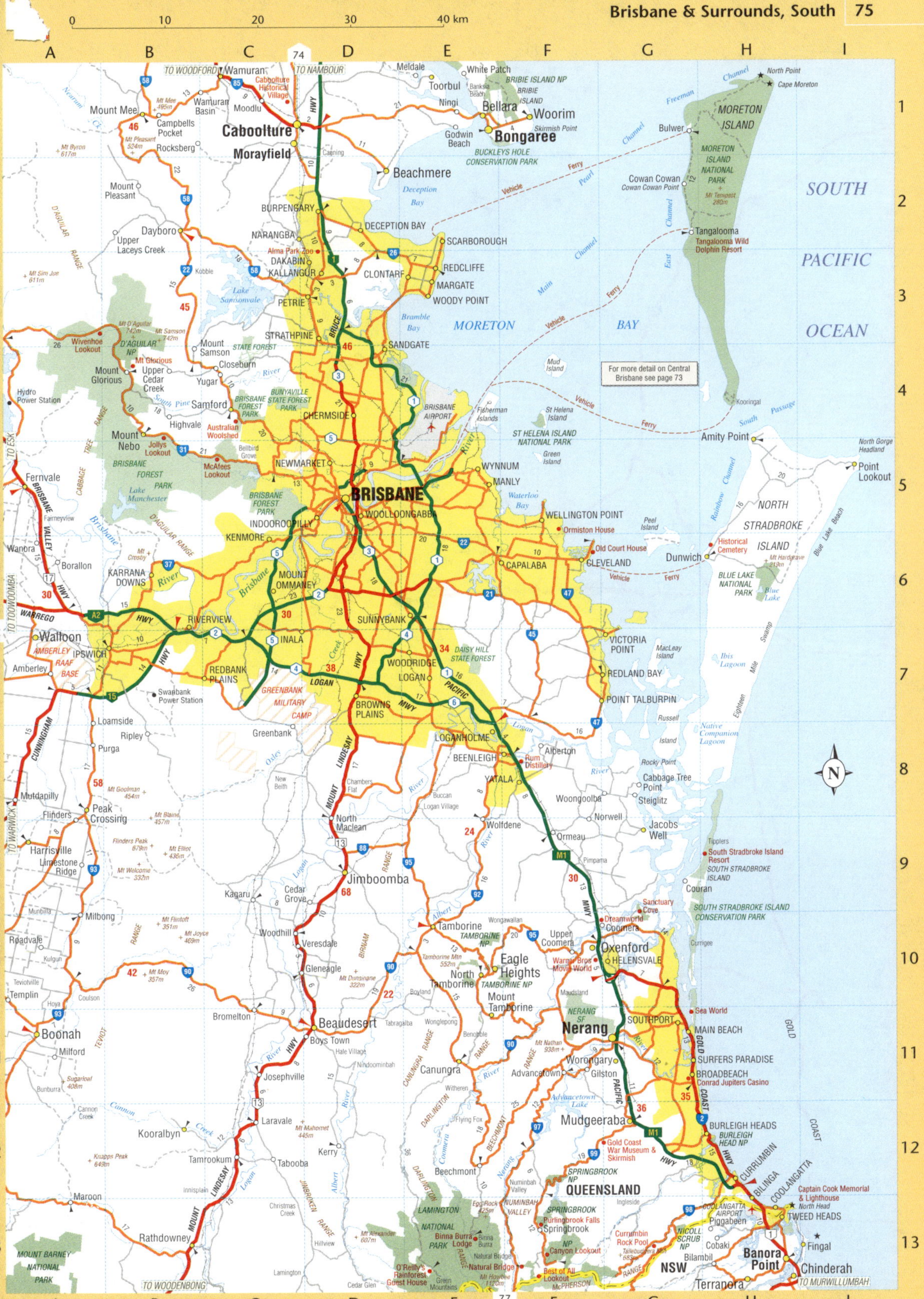
0 10 20 30 40 km
A B C D E F G H I
1 2 3 4 5 6 7 8 9 10 11 12 13
74
77
TO WOODFORD
TO NAMBOUR
TO ESK
TO TOOWOOMBA
TO WARWICK
TO WOODENBONG
TO MURWILLUMBAH
SOUTH PACIFIC OCEAN
MORETON BAY
MORETON ISLAND
MORETON ISLAND NATIONAL PARK
Mt Tempest 280m
North Point
Cape Moreton
Bulwer
Cowan Cowan
Cowan Cowan Point
Tangalooma
Tangalooma Wild Dolphin Resort
Kooringal
Freeman Channel
Pearl Channel
East Channel
Main Channel
South Passage
Vehicle Ferry
For more detail on Central Brisbane see page 73
BRIBIE ISLAND NP
BRIBIE ISLAND
White Patch
Banksia Beach
Bellara
Woorim
Skirmish Point
Bongaree
BUCKLEYS HOLE CONSERVATION PARK
Meldale
Toorbul
Ningi
Godwin Beach
Beachmere
Deception Bay
Wamuran
Wamuran Basin
Caboolture Historical Village
Moodlu
Caboolture
Morayfield
Caning
Mount Mee
Mt Mee 495m
Campbells Pocket
Mt Pleasant 524m
Rocksberg
Mt Byron 617m
Mount Pleasant
Dayboro
Upper Laceys Creek
D'AGUILAR RANGE
Mt Sim Jue 611m
Kobble
Lake Samsonvale
BURPENGARY
NARANGBA
Alma Park Zoo
DAKABIN
KALLANGUR
PETRIE
DECEPTION BAY
SCARBOROUGH
REDCLIFFE
MARGATE
WOODY POINT
CLONTARF
Bramble Bay
STRATHPINE
BRUCE
SANDGATE
Mount Samson
Closeburn
STATE FOREST
Mt D'Aguilar 742m
Mt Samson 742m
Wivenhoe Lookout
D'AGUILAR NP
Mt Glorious
Mount Glorious
Upper Cedar Creek
Yugar
Samford
South Pine River
BRISBANE FOREST PARK
BUNYAVILLE STATE FOREST PARK
Hydro Power Station
Highvale
Australian Woolshed
Mount Nebo
Jollys Lookout
McAfees Lookout
Bellbird Grove
CHERMSIDE
BRISBANE AIRPORT
Fisherman Islands
St Helena Island
ST HELENA ISLAND NATIONAL PARK
Mud Island
Green Island
Fernvale
BRISBANE VALLEY HWY
CABBAGE TREE RANGE
BRISBANE FOREST PARK
Lake Manchester
NEWMARKET
BRISBANE
WOOLLOONGABBA
INDOOROOPILLY
KENMORE
WYNNUM
MANLY
Waterloo Bay
WELLINGTON POINT
Ormiston House
Old Court House
CLEVELAND
CAPALABA
Peel Island
Amity Point
North Gorge Headland
Point Lookout
NORTH STRADBROKE ISLAND
Dunwich
Historical Cemetery
Mt Hardgrave 219m
BLUE LAKE NATIONAL PARK
Blue Lake
Brown Lake
Rainbow Channel
Blue Lake Beach
Fairneyview
Wanora
Borallon
Mt Crosby
KARRANA DOWNS
Brisbane River
MOUNT OMMANEY
RIVERVIEW
INALA
WARREGO HWY
Walloon
AMBERLEY RAAF BASE
IPSWICH
Amberley
REDBANK PLAINS
Swanbank Power Station
GREENBANK MILITARY CAMP
SUNNYBANK
WOODRIDGE
LOGAN
DAISY HILL STATE FOREST
PACIFIC MWY
BROWNS PLAINS
VICTORIA POINT
MacLeay Island
REDLAND BAY
POINT TALBURPIN
Russell Island
Ibis Lagoon
Native Companion Lagoon
Eighteen Mile Swamp
CUNNINGHAM HWY
Loamside
Ripley
Purga
Greenbank
LOGANHOLME
Logan River
Alberton
BEENLEIGH
Rum Distillery
YATALA
Rocky Point
Cabbage Tree Point
Steiglitz
Woongoolba
Norwell
Jacobs Well
Mutdapilly
Flinders
Peak Crossing
Mt Goolman 454m
Mt Blaine 457m
Flinders Peak 679m
Mt Elliot 436m
Mt Welcome 332m
Harrisville
Limestone Ridge
New Beith
Chambers Flat
MOUNT LINDESAY HWY
North Maclean
Buccan
Logan Village
Wolfdene
Ormeau
Pimpama
Tipplers
South Stradbroke Island Resort
SOUTH STRADBROKE ISLAND
Couran
SOUTH STRADBROKE ISLAND CONSERVATION PARK
Jimboomba
Kagaru
Cedar Grove
Munbilla
Milbong
Mt Flintoft 351m
Mt Joyce 469m
Roadvale
Kulgun
Woodhill
Veresdale
Gleneagle
BIRNAM RANGE
Mt Dunsinane 322m
Tamborine
TAMBORINE NP
Wongawallan
Tamborine Mtn 552m
North Tamborine
Eagle Heights
Mount Tamborine
Upper Coomera
Sanctuary Cove
Dreamworld
Coomera
Oxenford
HELENSVALE
Warner Bros Movie World
Curragee
Teviotville
Templin
Hoya
Coulson
Mt Moy 357m
Bromelton
Beaudesert
Boys Town
Hale Village
Tabragalba
Wonglepong
Boyland
Benobble
Nindooinbah
NERANG SF
Nerang
Maudsland
SOUTHPORT
Sea World
MAIN BEACH
SURFERS PARADISE
BROADBEACH
Conrad Jupiters Casino
GOLD COAST
Boonah
Milford
Sugarloaf 408m
Bunburra
Cannon Creek
TEVIOT
Josephville
CANUNGRA RANGE
Canungra
Witheren
Mt Nathan 938m
Worongary
Gilston
Advancetown
Advancetown Lake
Mudgeeraba
PACIFIC HWY
Kooralbyn
Laravale
Mt Mahomet 445m
Knapps Peak 649m
Tamrookum
Tabooba
Kerry
DARLINGTON RANGE
Flying Fox
BEECHMONT RANGE
Beechmont
Gold Coast War Museum & Skirmish
BURLEIGH HEADS
BURLEIGH HEAD NP
CURRUMBIN
BILINGA
COOLANGATTA
Captain Cook Memorial & Lighthouse
North Head
TWEED HEADS
COOLANGATTA AIRPORT
Innisplain
Maroon
Christmas Creek
JINBROKEN RANGE
Numinbah Valley
NUMINBAH VALLEY
Egg Rock 425m
SPRINGBROOK NP
QUEENSLAND
Ingleside
LAMINGTON NATIONAL PARK
Binna Burra Lodge
Mt Alexander 607m
Hillview
Rathdowney
MOUNT BARNEY NATIONAL PARK
Lamington
Cedar Glen
O'Reilly's Rainforest Guest House
Green Mountains
Natural Bridge
Mt Howard 1120m
SPRINGBROOK
Purlingbrook Falls
Springbrook
Canyon Lookout
Best of All Lookout
McPHERSON RANGE
Currumbin Rock Pool
Tallebudgera 683m
NICOLL SCRUB NP
Piggabeen
Cobaki
Bilambil
NSW
Terranora
Banora Point
Fingal
Chinderah

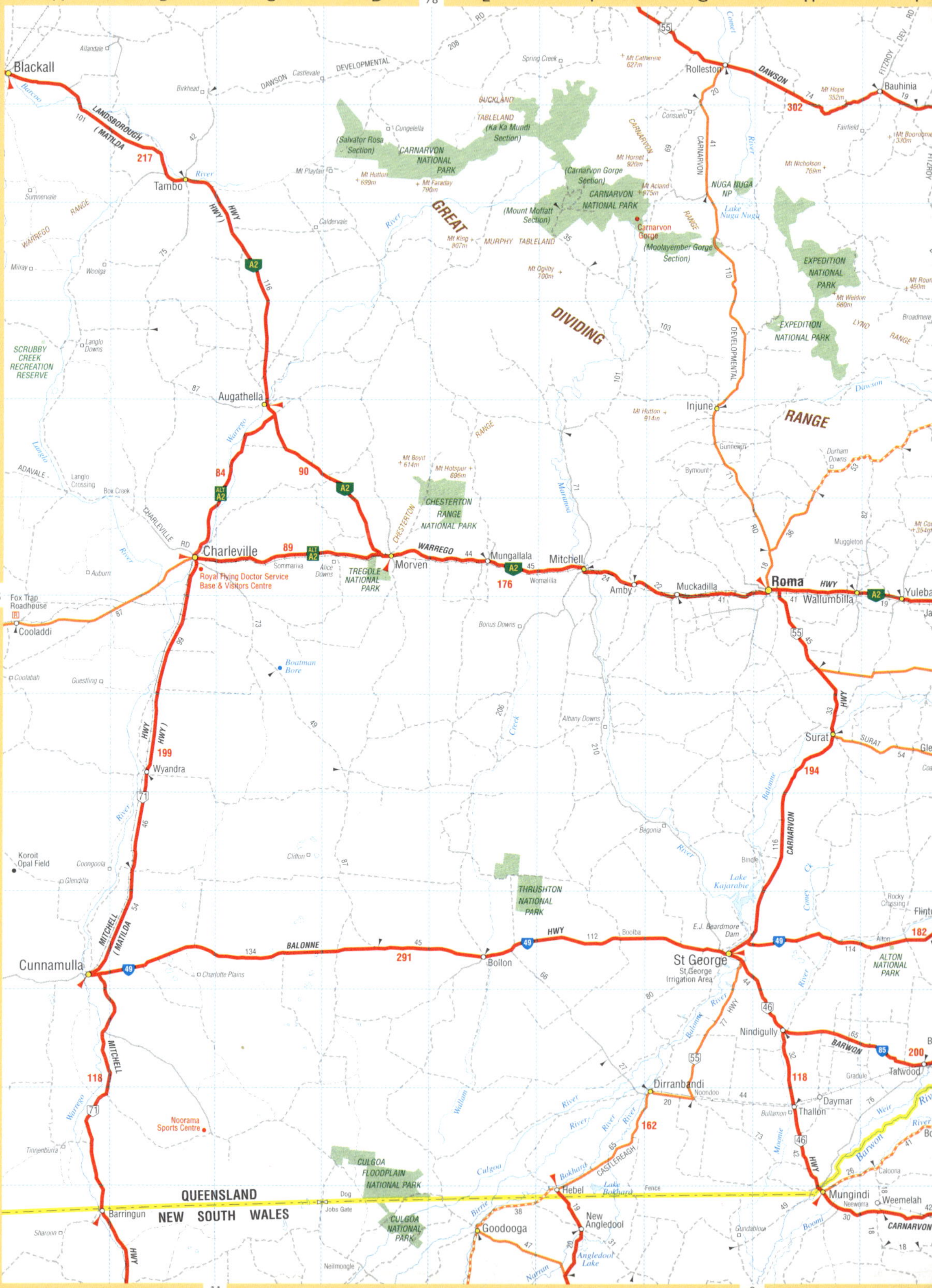

Blackall
Tambo
Augathella
Charleville
Morven
Mungallala
Mitchell
Amby
Muckadilla
Roma
Wallumbilla
Yuleba
Rolleston
Bauhinia
Injune
Surat
St George
Bollon
Cunnamulla
Wyandra
Nindigully
Dirranbandi
Thallon
Mungindi
Hebel
Goodooga
New Angledool
Barringun
Cooladdi
Talwood
LANDSBOROUGH (MATILDA) HWY
WARREGO HWY
BALONNE HWY
MITCHELL (MATILDA) HWY
CARNARVON HWY
DAWSON HWY
CARNARVON DEVELOPMENTAL RD
CARNARVON NATIONAL PARK
EXPEDITION NATIONAL PARK
CHESTERTON RANGE NATIONAL PARK
TREGOLE NATIONAL PARK
THRUSHTON NATIONAL PARK
CULGOA FLOODPLAIN NATIONAL PARK
CULGOA NATIONAL PARK
ALTON NATIONAL PARK
NUGA NUGA NP
SCRUBBY CREEK RECREATION RESERVE
GREAT DIVIDING RANGE
Royal Flying Doctor Service Base & Visitors Centre
Noorama Sports Centre
Fox Trap Roadhouse
Koroit Opal Field
QUEENSLAND
NEW SOUTH WALES

0 25 50 75 100 km
J K L M N O P Q R
1 2 3 4 5 6 7 8 9 10 11 12 13
79
SOUTH PACIFIC OCEAN
HERVEY BAY
FRASER ISLAND
GREAT SANDY NATIONAL PARK
Sandy Cape
Orchid Beach
The Cathedrals
Maheno Wreck
Kingfisher Bay Resort & Village
Eurong
Biloela
Thangool
Callide Coal Mine & Power Station
Callide Dam
KROOMBIT TOPS NP
Banana
Theodore
Moura
Cracow
PRECIPICE NP
ISLA GORGE NP
Glebe Weir
Monto
Moonford
Mulgildie
Abercorn
Eidsvold
Mundubbera
Gayndah
Biggenden
Childers
Howard
Torbanlea
Hervey Bay
Maryborough
Bundaberg
Bargara
Burnett Heads
Elliott Heads
Coonarr
Woodgate
Burrum Heads
Toogoom
River Heads
Gin Gin
Wallaville
Cordalba
Booyal
Mount Perry
Rosedale
Lowmead
Bororen
Miriam Vale
Nagoorin
Ubobo
Many Peaks
Builyan
Kalpowar
Mungungo
Bancroft
DEEPWATER NATIONAL PARK
LITTABELLA NP
CANIA GORGE NP
BURRUM RIVER NP
BURRUM COAST NP
GOODNIGHT SCRUB NP
COALSTOUN LAKES NP
MT WALSH NP
AUBURN RIVER NP
Aramara
Mungar
Tiaro
Bauple
Gundiah
Tin Can Bay
Rainbow Beach
Double Island Point
WIDE BAY MILITARY TRAINING AREA
Gympie
Kilkivan
Goomeri
Murgon
Wondai
Cherbourg
Proston
Kingaroy
Nanango
Kumbia
Yarraman
Blackbutt
Cooyar
Boreen Point
Tewantin
Noosa Heads
Sunshine Beach
Peregian Beach
Coolum Beach
Cooroy
Pomona
Eumundi
Nambour
Maroochydore
Mooloolaba
Buderim
Caloundra
Landsborough
Maleny
Beerwah
Glass House Mountains
Kenilworth
Imbil
Kilcoy
Woodford
Caboolture
Bongaree
Elimbah
MORETON ISLAND
MORETON ISLAND NATIONAL PARK
DECEPTION BAY
REDCLIFFE
Moreton Bay
BRISBANE
For more detail on Brisbane & Surrounds see pages 74–5
Point Lookout
CLEVELAND
Dunwich
NORTH STRADBROKE ISLAND
VICTORIA POINT
REDLAND BAY
LOGAN
BEENLEIGH
IPSWICH
Jacobs Well
SOUTH STRADBROKE ISLAND
HELENSVALE
MAIN BEACH
SURFERS PARADISE
BURLEIGH HEADS
CURRUMBIN
COOLANGATTA
TWEED HEADS
GOLD COAST
Nerang
Mudgeeraba
Beaudesert
Tamborine
Jimboomba
Boonah
Kalbar
Aratula
Rosewood
Laidley
Gatton
Grantham
Helidon
Withcott
Highfields
Crows Nest
Esk
Toogoolawah
TOOWOOMBA
Oakey
Pittsworth
Cambooya
Clifton
Allora
Warwick
Killarney
Stanthorpe
Wallangarra
Tenterfield
Texas
Inglewood
Goondiwindi
Boggabilla
Millmerran
Cecil Plains
Dalby
Jandowae
Chinchilla
Miles
Condamine
Tara
Moonie
Meandarra
The Gums
Wandoan
Kogan
Bell
Durong
QUEENSLAND
NEW SOUTH WALES
Murwillumbah
Chinderah
Kingscliff
Pottsville
Ocean Shores
Brunswick Heads
Mullumbimby
Byron Bay
Suffolk Park
Lennox Head
Ballina
Lismore
Alstonville
Wollongbar
Casino
Coraki
Woodburn
Evans Head
Kyogle
Nimbin
Tabulam
Drake
Bonalbo
GREAT DIVIDING RANGE
DARLING DOWNS
For more detailed coverage of localities in New South Wales see page 9
9

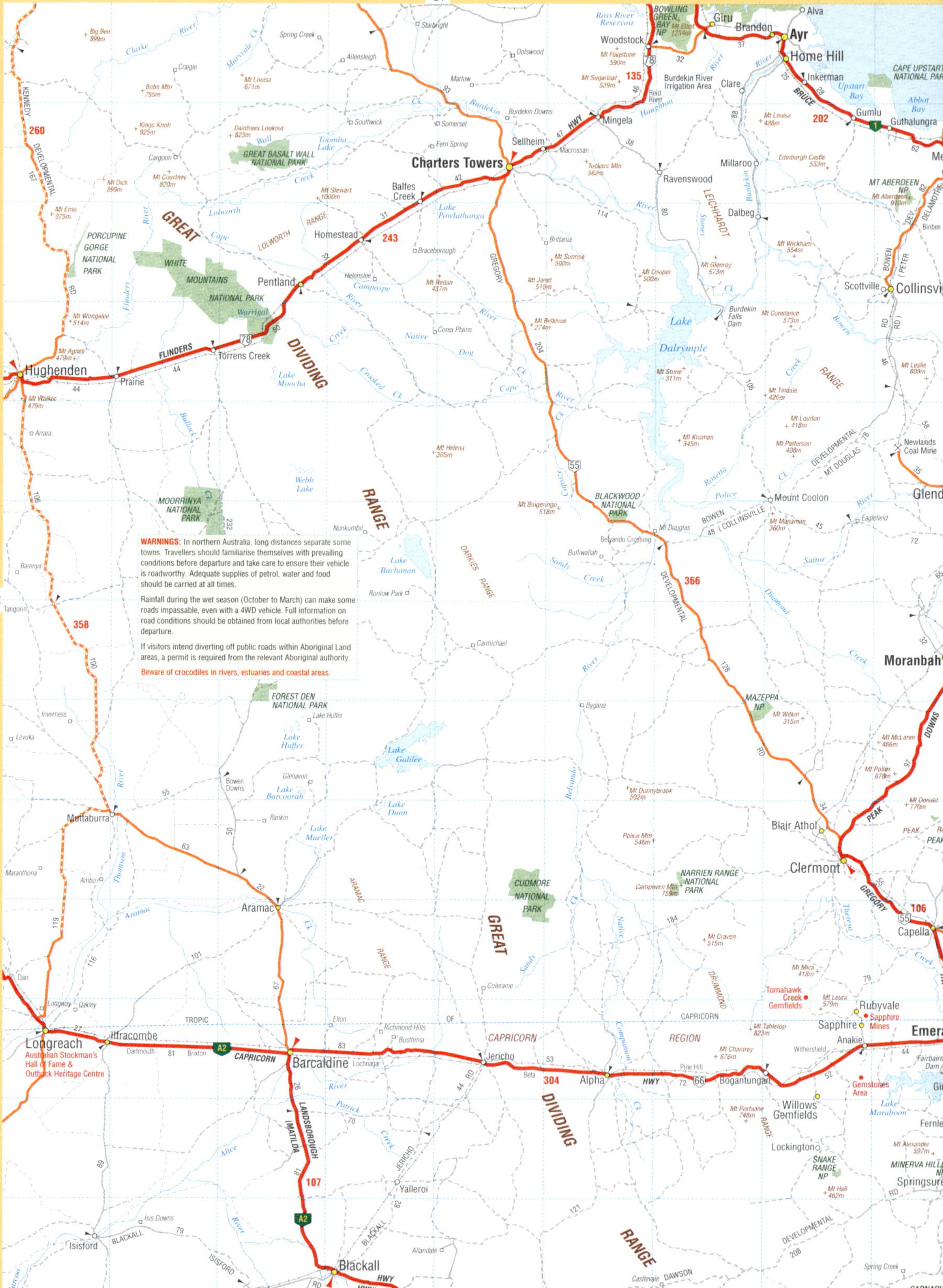
WARNINGS: In northern Australia, long distances separate some towns. Travellers should familiarise themselves with prevailing conditions before departure and take care to ensure their vehicle is roadworthy. Adequate supplies of petrol, water and food should be carried at all times.
Rainfall during the wet season (October to March) can make some roads impassable, even with a 4WD vehicle. Full information on road conditions should be obtained from local authorities before departure.
If visitors intend diverting off public roads within Aboriginal Land areas, a permit is required from the relevant Aboriginal authority.
Beware of crocodiles in rivers, estuaries and coastal areas.
A B C D E F G H I
1 2 3 4 5 6 7 8 9 10 11 12 13
81
85
87
76
Charters Towers
Hughenden
Prairie
Torrens Creek
Pentland
Homestead
Balfes Creek
Sellheim
Mingela
Ravenswood
Woodstock
Giru
Brandon
Ayr
Home Hill
Inkerman
Clare
Millaroo
Dalbeg
Gumlu
Guthalungra
Alva
Burdekin River Irrigation Area
Scottville
Collinsville
Mount Coolon
Glenden
Newlands Coal Mine
Moranbah
Blair Athol
Clermont
Capella
Rubyvale
Sapphire
Anakie
Emerald
Willows Gemfields
Lockington
Springsure
Fernlee
Muttaburra
Aramac
Longreach
Australian Stockman's Hall of Fame & Outback Heritage Centre
Ilfracombe
Barcaldine
Jericho
Alpha
Bogantungan
Yalleroi
Blackall
Isisford
Tomahawk Creek Gemfields
Sapphire Mines
Gemstones Area
PORCUPINE GORGE NATIONAL PARK
WHITE MOUNTAINS NATIONAL PARK
GREAT BASALT WALL NATIONAL PARK
MOORRINYA NATIONAL PARK
FOREST DEN NATIONAL PARK
BLACKWOOD NATIONAL PARK
MAZEPPA NP
CUDMORE NATIONAL PARK
NARRIEN RANGE NATIONAL PARK
SNAKE RANGE NP
MINERVA HILLS NP
CAPE UPSTART NATIONAL PARK
MT ABERDEEN NP
BOWLING GREEN BAY NP
GREAT DIVIDING RANGE
Lake Dalrymple
Burdekin Falls Dam
Lake Buchanan
Lake Galilee
Lake Huffer
Lake Barcoorah
Lake Dunn
Lake Mueller
Lake Moocha
Webb Lake
Lake Powlathanga
Toomba Lake
Lake Maraboon
Ross River Reservoir
Upstart Bay
Abbot Bay
FLINDERS HWY
GREGORY
DEVELOPMENTAL RD
KENNEDY DEVELOPMENTAL RD
LANDSBOROUGH (MATILDA HWY)
CAPRICORN HWY
BRUCE
PEAK DOWNS
LEICHHARDT RANGE
DARKIES RANGE
DRUMMOND RANGE
TROPIC OF CAPRICORN

0 25 50 75 100 km

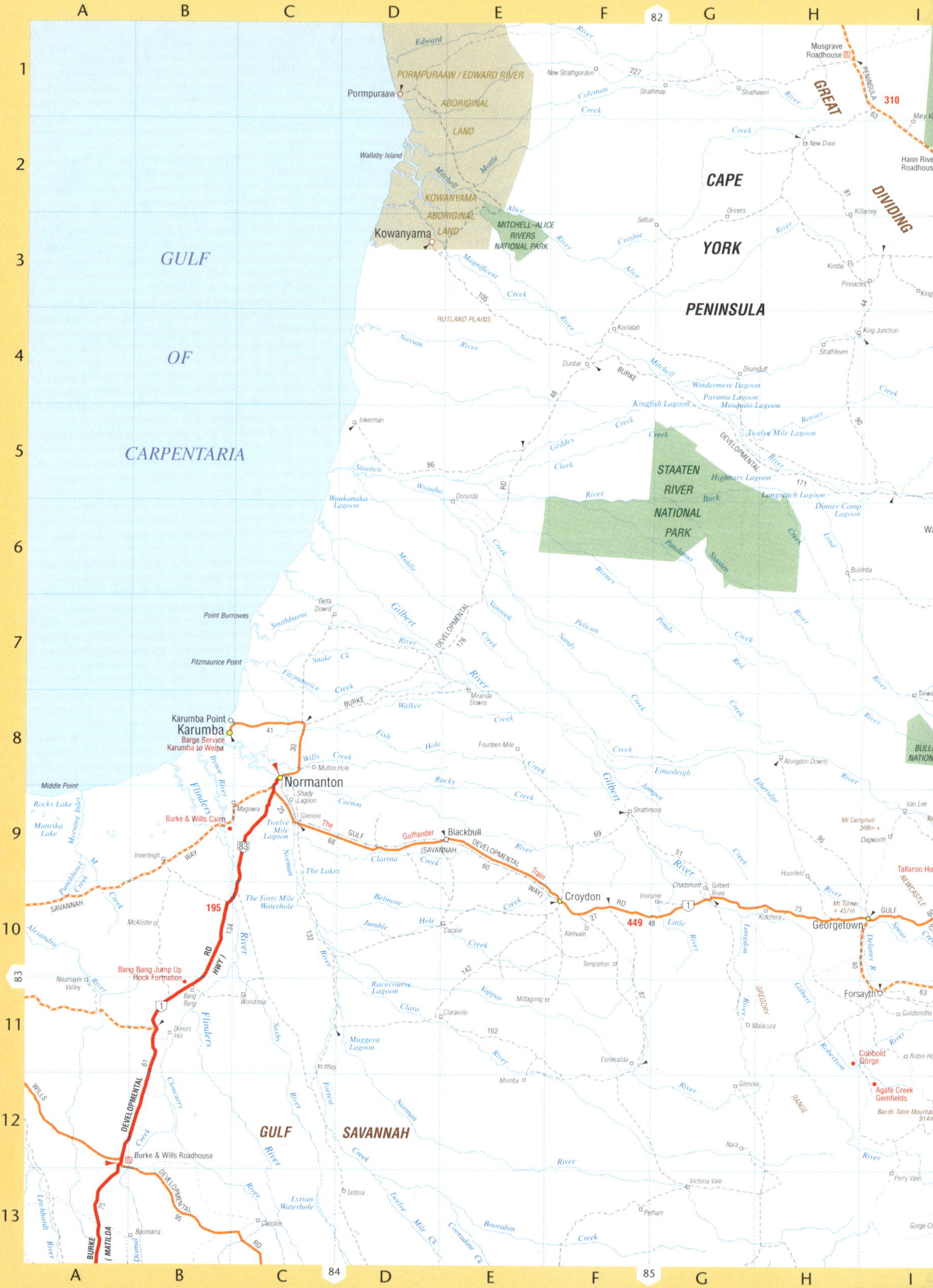
GULF OF CARPENTARIA
CAPE YORK PENINSULA
GREAT DIVIDING
POMPURAAW / EDWARD RIVER ABORIGINAL LAND
KOWANYAMA ABORIGINAL LAND
MITCHELL-ALICE RIVERS NATIONAL PARK
STAATEN RIVER NATIONAL PARK
RUTLAND PLAINS
GULF SAVANNAH
Pormpuraaw
Wallaby Island
Kowanyama
Musgrave Roadhouse
Hann River Roadhouse
New Strathgordon
Strathmay
Strathaven
New Dixie
Killarney
Oriners
Sefton
Kimba
Pinnacles
King Junction
Strathleven
Koolatah
Dunbar
Drumduff
Windermere Lagoon
Puruma Lagoon
Mosquito Lagoon
Kingfish Lagoon
Twelve Mile Lagoon
Highbury Lagoon
Longreach Lagoon
Dinner Camp Lagoon
Inkerman
Dorunda
Wuukanaka Lagoon
Bulimba
Delta Downs
Point Burrowes
Fitzmaurice Point
Miranda Downs
Karumba Point
Karumba
Barge Service Karumba to Weipa
Middle Point
Rocky Lake
Manrika Lake
Mutton Hole
Normanton
Shady Lagoon
Glenore
Magowra
Burke & Wills Cairn
Inverleigh
Twelve Mile Lagoon
The Lakes
The Forty Mile Waterhole
Fourteen Mile
Abingdon Downs
Strathmore
Gulflander
Blackbull
Croydon
Inorunie
Chadshunt
Gilbert River
Kutchera
Georgetown
Mt Turner + 457m
Mt Campbell 366m +
Dagworth
Huonfels
Tallaroo Hot
Van Lee
Forsayth
Goldsmiths
Cobbold Gorge
Agate Creek Gemfields
Bairds Table Mountain 914m
Robin Hood
McAlister
Curalie
Alehvale
Templeton
Bang Bang Jump Up Rock Formation
Neumayer Valley
Bang Bang
Wondoola
Donors Hill
Racecourse Lagoon
Mittagong
Claraville
Muggera Lagoon
Malacura
Iffley
Esmeralda
Momba
Glenora
Burke & Wills Roadhouse
Nara
Victoria Vale
Perry Vale
Taldora
Lyrian Waterhole
Canobie
Boomarra
Pelham
Gorge Creek
Torwood
GULF DEVELOPMENTAL RD
BURKE DEVELOPMENTAL RD
SAVANNAH WAY
The Gulflander Train
WILLS DEVELOPMENTAL RD
PENINSULA DEVELOPMENTAL RD
BURKE (MATILDA HWY)
GREGORY RANGE
NEWCASTLE
195
449
310
A B C D E F G H I
1 2 3 4 5 6 7 8 9 10 11 12 13
82
83
84
85

0 25 50 75 100 km
J K L M N O P Q R
1 2 3 4 5 6 7 8 9 10 11 12 13
82
85
78
WARNINGS: In northern Australia, long distances separate some towns. Travellers should familiarise themselves with prevailing conditions before departure and take care to ensure their vehicle is roadworthy. Adequate supplies of petrol, water and food should be carried at all times.
Rainfall during the wet season (October to March) can make some roads impassable, even with a 4WD vehicle. Full information on road conditions should be obtained from local authorities before departure.
If visitors intend diverting off public roads within Aboriginal Land areas, a permit is required from the relevant Aboriginal authority.
Beware of crocodiles in rivers, estuaries and coastal areas.
CORAL
SEA
GREAT
BARRIER
REEF
MARINE
PARK
LIZARD ISLAND NP
Lizard Island
Cape Flattery
STARCKE NP
MT WEBB NP
Cape Bedford
Hope Vale
ENDEAVOUR RIVER NATIONAL PARK
Cooktown
MT COOK NP
Laura
Split Rock & Gu Gu Yalangi Rock-art Site
Old Laura Homestead
Lion's Den Historic Hotel
Helenvale
Rossville
CEDAR BAY NP
Lakeland
Wujal Wujal
Ayton
DAINTREE NATIONAL PARK
Cape Tribulation
Noah Beach
Palmer River Roadhouse
Cow Bay
Daintree
Wonga
Miallo
Cooya Beach
Mossman Gorge
Mossman
Port Douglas
Craiglie
Mount Carbine
Maryfarms
Julatten
Oak Beach
Trinity Bay
Mount Molloy
Ellis Beach
Palm Cove
Smithfield
Kuranda
CAIRNS
Green Island
GREEN ISLAND NATIONAL PARK
Fitzroy Island
FITZROY ISLAND NATIONAL PARK
HANN TABLELAND NP
Lake Mitchell
Biboohra
Mount Mulligan
Mareeba-Dimbulah Irrigation Area
BARRON GORGE NP
Mareeba
Edmonton
Gordonvale
Aloomba
Walkamin
Chillagoe
CHILLAGOE-MUNGANA CAVES NP
Chillagoe Limestone Caves
Dimbulah
Mutchilba
Tinaroo Falls
Tolga
Kairi
WOOROONOORAN NATIONAL PARK
Fishery Falls
Deeral
FRANKLAND ISLANDS NP
RUSSELL RIVER NP
Atherton
Tinaburra
Yungaburra
Babinda
Bramston Beach
Almaden
Herberton
Petford
Watsonville
Malanda
Mirriwinni
Irvinebank
MT HYPIPAMEE NP
Millaa Millaa Falls
Topaz
ELLA BAY NP
Flying Fish Point
Innisfail
South Johnstone
Millaa Millaa
PALMERSTON HWY
Mourilyan
Millstream Falls
Ravenshoe
MILLSTREAM FALLS NP
Mena Creek
Mount Garnet
Innot Hot Springs
Cowley Beach
Silkwood
Kurrimine Beach
El Arish
Bingil Bay
Mission Beach
Dunk Island
FAMILY ISLANDS NP
Wongaling Beach
Tully
HULL RIVER NP
South Mission Beach
Bedarra Island
Koombooloomba Reservoir
Euramo
Tully Heads
EDMUND KENNEDY NP
Rockingham Bay
Murray Falls
Kennedy
Cape Richards
Cape Sandwich
O'Briens Creek Gemfields (Topaz)
FORTY MILE SCRUB NP
Mount Surprise
Undara Lava Tubes
UNDARA VOLCANIC NATIONAL PARK
Blencoe Falls
LUMHOLTZ NATIONAL PARK
Cardwell
HINCHINBROOK ISLAND
HINCHINBROOK ISLAND NP
Walters Plains Lake
Abergowrie
Lucinda
Halifax
Pelorus Island (Yanooa)
Orpheus Island (Goolboddi)
ORPHEUS ISLAND NP
Einasleigh
Wallaman Falls
Lannercost
Taylors Beach
Lake Lucy
Trebonne
Toobanna
Ingham
Saltern Lagoon
Great Palm Island
Forrest Beach
PALM ISLANDS
Extinct Volcano
PALUMA RANGE NATIONAL PARK
Jourama Falls
Bambaroo
Oasis Roadhouse
Greenvale Nickel Mine
PALUMA RANGE NP
Greenvale
Balgal
McClellands Lookout
Rollingstone
Jalloonda
MAGNETIC ISLAND NP
Magnetic Island
Horseshoe Bay
Nelly Bay
Bluewater
Picnic Bay
Cape Cleveland
Pallarenda
Cape Ferguson
TOWNSVILLE
Cape Bowling Green
BOWLING GREEN BAY NATIONAL PARK
THURINGOWA
Alligator Creek
Bowling Green Bay
Cungulla
Blue Water Springs Roadhouse
BOWLING GREEN BAY NP
Giru
Alva
Ross River Dam
Brandon
Woodstock
Ayr
Home Hill
GREAT DIVIDING RANGE
KENNEDY HWY
GREGORY DEVELOPMENTAL RD
BRUCE HWY
CAPTAIN COOK HWY

0 25 50 75 100 km
WARNINGS: In northern Australia, long distances separate some towns. Travellers should familiarise themselves with prevailing conditions before departure and take care to ensure their vehicle is roadworthy. Adequate supplies of petrol, water and food should be carried at all times.
Rainfall during the wet season (October to March) can make some roads impassable, even with a 4WD vehicle. Full information on road conditions should be obtained from local authorities before departure.
If visitors intend diverting off public roads within Aboriginal Land areas, a permit is required from the relevant Aboriginal authority.
Beware of crocodiles in rivers, estuaries and coastal areas.
TORRES STRAIT
BADU ISLAND
MOA ISLAND
St Pauls
Mount Earnest Island
Thursday Island
Horn Is
PRINCE OF WALES ISLAND
Cape York
Punsand Bay
Pajinka Wilderness Lodge
GULF OF CARPENTARIA
Endeavour Strait
Seisia
Injinoo
Bamaga
Newcastle Bay
Parslow Point
Vehicle Ferry
JARDINE RIVER NATIONAL PARK
Orford Bay
RICHARDSON RANGE
Vrilya Point
ABORIGINAL RESERVE
HEATHLANDS RESOURCE RESERVE
Captain Billy Landing
Jackson River
Shelburne Bay
GREAT BARRIER REEF
CORAL SEA
Cape Grenville
Mapoon
Red Beach
Bramwell
Bertiehaugh
GREAT DIVIDING RANGE
Temple Bay
Old Moreton Telegraph Station
Andoom Mine
Duyfken Point
UNINGAN NATURE RESERVE
Weymouth Bay
Albatross Bay
Weipa
Barge Service Weipa to Karumba
Napranum
Batavia Downs
IRON RANGE NP
Portland Roads
Cape Weymouth
Lockhart River
Cape Direction
PENINSULA
EMBLEY RANGE
LOCKHART RIVER ABORIGINAL LAND
Pera Head
Night Island
MARINE PARK
Aurukun
Table Mtn
Cape Sidmouth
Archer River Roadhouse
MUNGKAN KANDJU NATIONAL PARK
DEVELOPMENTAL RD
McILWRAITH RANGE
ABORIGINAL LAND LEASE AURUKUN
Meripah
CAPE YORK PENINSULA
Claremont Isles
Coen
Silver Plains
Port Stewart
FLINDERS GROUP NP
Flinders Island
Pipon Island
Cape Melville
Bathurst Bay
Princess Charlotte Bay
CAPE MELVILLE NATIONAL PARK
Barrow Point
PORMPURAAW / EDWARD RIVER ABORIGINAL LAND
Yarraden
Strathburn
Lily Vale
Marina Plains
Wakooka
Howick Island
Lotus Bird Lodge
Musgrave Roadhouse
Hann Crossing
LAKEFIELD NATIONAL PARK
New Strathgordon
Strathmay
Strathaven
Kalpowar Crossing
Pormpuraaw
STARCKE NP
A B C D E F G H I
1 2 3 4 5 6 7 8 9 10 11 12 13
80
81

0 25 50 75 100 km
A B C D E F G H I
1 2 3 4 5 6 7 8 9 10 11 12 13
GULF OF
CARPENTARIA
WARNINGS: In northern Australia, long distances separate some towns. Travellers should familiarise themselves with prevailing conditions before departure and take care to ensure their vehicle is roadworthy. Adequate supplies of petrol, water and food should be carried at all times.
Rainfall during the wet season (October to March) can make some roads impassable, even with a 4WD vehicle. Full information on road conditions should be obtained from local authorities before departure.
If visitors intend diverting off public roads within Aboriginal Land areas, a permit is required from the relevant Aboriginal authority.
Beware of crocodiles in rivers, estuaries and coastal areas.
Birri Fishing Resort
MORNINGTON ISLAND
ABORIGINAL LAND
Gununa
WELLESLEY ISLANDS
Bountiful Islands
FORSYTH ISLANDS
Bentinck Island
Allen Island
SOUTH WELLESLEY ISLANDS
Sweers Island Resort
Sweers Island
Point Burrowes
Delta Downs
Smithburne R
Snake Ck
Fitzmaurice Point
Fitzmaurice Creek
Wollogorang Station & Roadhouse
Gold Creek
495
59
Westmoreland
Settlement
Lagoon
Hells Gate Roadhouse
Buck Hill 258m
Cliffdale
Tarrant Point
Pascoe Inlet
Kangaroo Point
Karumba Point
Karumba
Barge Service Karumba to Weipa
41
30
Wills Creek
Mutton Hole
Normanton
Shady Lagoon
Glenore
Carron R
Twelve Mile Lagoon
CHINA WALL
WAANYI/GARAWA
Nicholson
ABORIGINAL
LAND TRUST
NORTHERN TERRITORY
QUEENSLAND
DOOMADGEE ABORIGINAL LAND
Walford
River
Doomadgee
4WD only
Bowthorn
Lily
Escott Barramundi Lodge
Burketown
The Lake
Albert River
Timor Lagoon
Rocky Lake
Dingo Dam
Manrika Lake
Morning Inlet
Middle Point
Flinders
Bynoe River
Magowra
Burke & Wills Cairn
WAY
Inverleigh
155
229
SAVANNAH
Punchbowl Creek
Wernadinga
NARDOO
Leichhardt
74
72
26
80
WILLS
DEVELOPMENTAL
Twelve Mile Creek
113
87
Almora
Floraville
Leichhardt Falls
Alexandra
BURKETOWN
34
McAllister
195
134
83
Norman
The Lakes
The Forty Mile Waterhole
132
River
Mussellbrook
Mt Oscar 115m
4WD
Creek
Millar
Neumayer Valley
River
Bang Bang Jump Up Rock Formation
RD
HWY
Springvale
Holly Ck
Mussellbrook Mining Camp
LAWN HILL NATIONAL PARK
CONSTANCE RANGE
Lawn Hill
Adels Grove
Archie
Gregory Downs
Gregory
Augustus Downs
35
73
1
Bang Bang
Wondoola
Donors Hill
Lawn
Hill
SMITHS RANGE
Gregory
RD
126
Ck
Cartridge
WILLS
64
Nardoo
141
Sandy Creek
Creek
Cloncurry
Flinders
Saxby
Muggera Lagoon
Iffley
Forrest
River
Riversleigh Fossil Site
Gregory
River
CAMOOWEAL
Fiery
Mitiguidi
77
DEVELOPMENTAL
61
DEVELOPMENTAL
GULF SAVANNAH
Burke & Wills Roadhouse
River
Creek
Gallipoli
Norfolk
O'Shanassy
Thornton
Creek
75
95
Lyrian Waterhole
Taldora
Canobie
Boomarra
Dismal
River
GREGORY DOWNS
Thorntonia
River
Gunpowder
Mistake
Creek
BURKE (MATILDA
Mammoth Mines
84
80

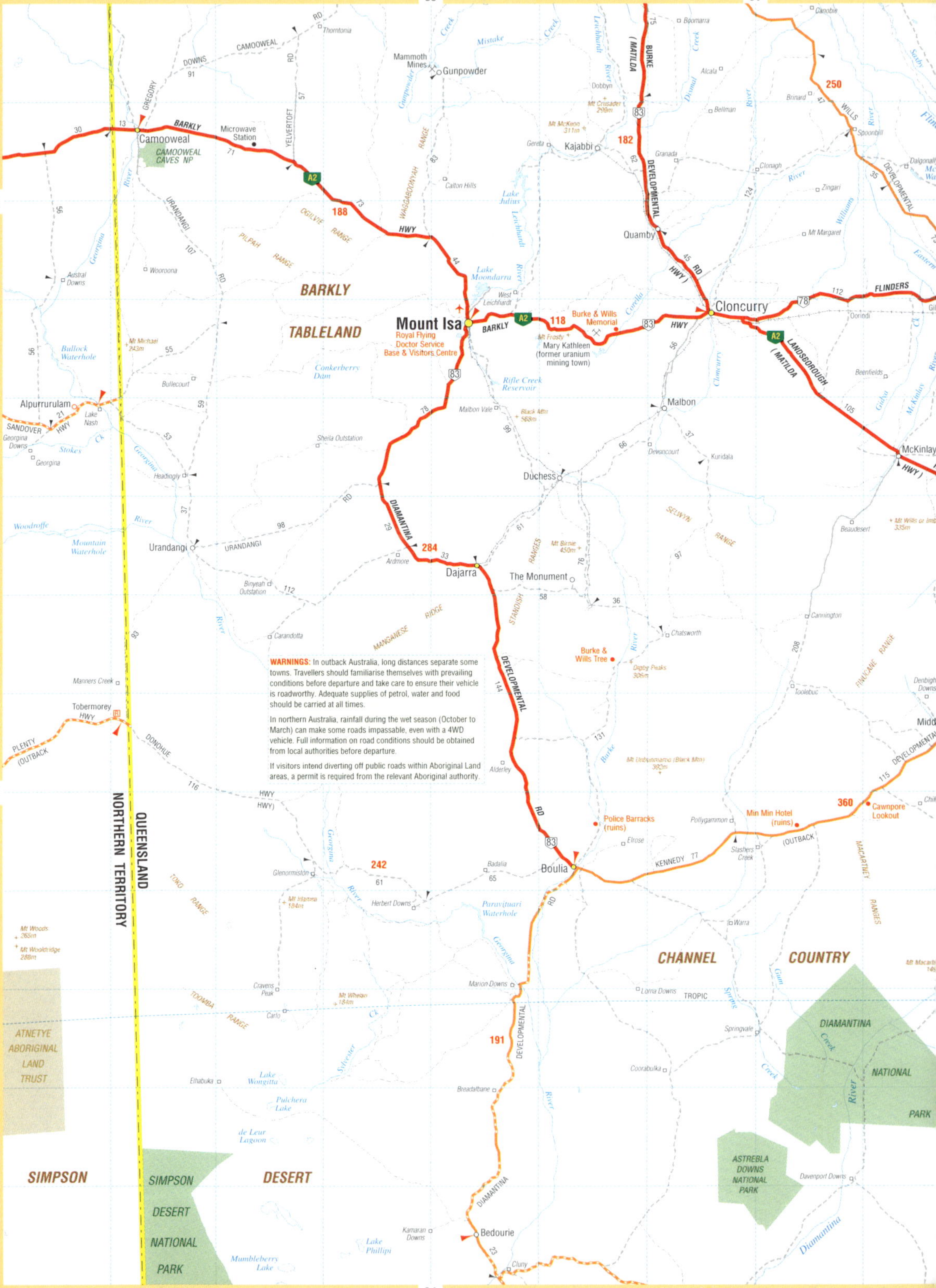

WARNINGS: In outback Australia, long distances separate some towns. Travellers should familiarise themselves with prevailing conditions before departure and take care to ensure their vehicle is roadworthy. Adequate supplies of petrol, water and food should be carried at all times.
In northern Australia, rainfall during the wet season (October to March) can make some roads impassable, even with a 4WD vehicle. Full information on road conditions should be obtained from local authorities before departure.
If visitors intend diverting off public roads within Aboriginal Land areas, a permit is required from the relevant Aboriginal authority.
Mount Isa
Royal Flying Doctor Service Base & Visitors Centre
Cloncurry
Camooweal
CAMOOWEAL CAVES NP
Microwave Station
Gunpowder
Mammoth Mines
Kajabbi
Quamby
Burke & Wills Memorial
Mary Kathleen (former uranium mining town)
Malbon
Duchess
McKinlay
Dajarra
The Monument
Urandangi
Alpurrurulam
Lake Nash
Burke & Wills Tree
Police Barracks (ruins)
Min Min Hotel (ruins)
Cawnpore Lookout
Boulia
Bedourie
BARKLY TABLELAND
CHANNEL COUNTRY
SIMPSON DESERT
SIMPSON DESERT NATIONAL PARK
DIAMANTINA NATIONAL PARK
ASTREBLA DOWNS NATIONAL PARK
ATNETYE ABORIGINAL LAND TRUST
NORTHERN TERRITORY
QUEENSLAND
BARKLY HWY
FLINDERS
LANDSBOROUGH (MATILDA HWY)
BURKE DEVELOPMENTAL RD
DIAMANTINA DEVELOPMENTAL RD
KENNEDY (OUTBACK) DEVELOPMENTAL
SANDOVER HWY
PLENTY (OUTBACK) HWY
DONOHUE HWY
URANDANGI

0 25 50 75 100 km

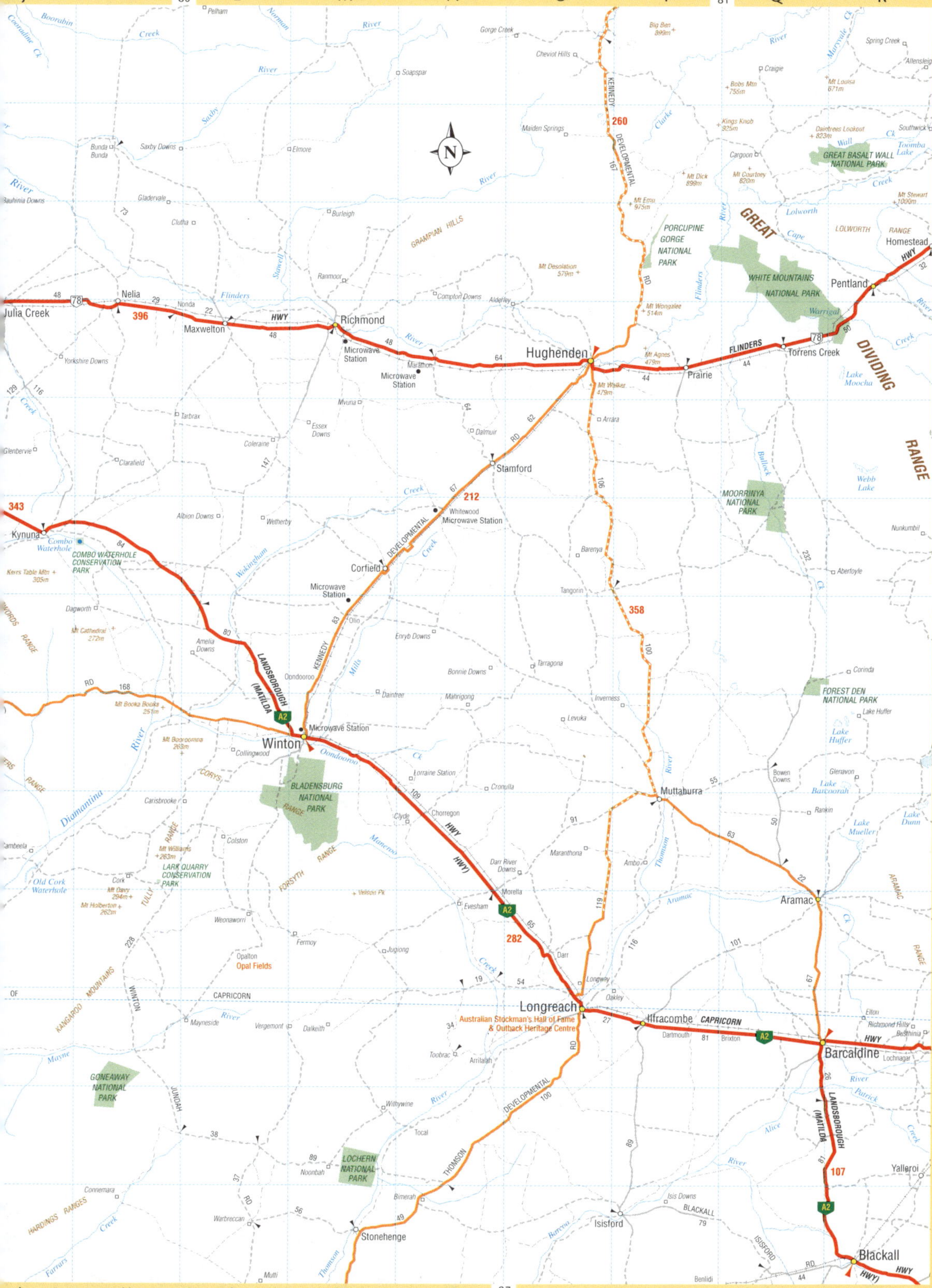

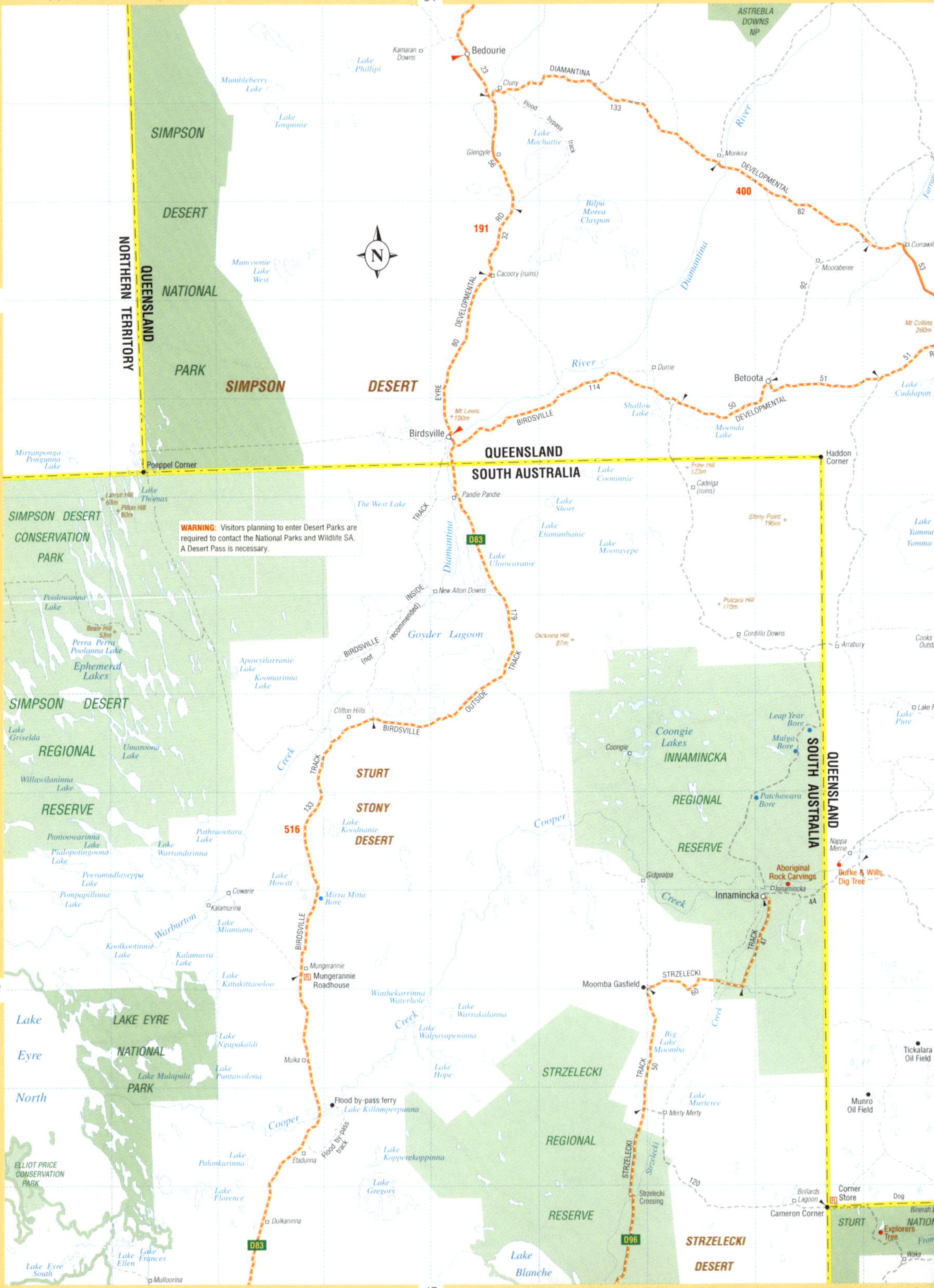
A
B
C
D
E
F
G
H
I
1
2
3
4
5
6
7
8
9
10
11
12
13
84
71
46
47
ASTREBLA DOWNS NP
Bedourie
Kamaran Downs
Lake Phillipi
Mumbleberry Lake
Lake Torquinie
Cluny
DIAMANTINA
Flood bypass track
133
Lake Machattie
Glengyle
Monkira
DEVELOPMENTAL
400
82
River
Bilpa Morea Claypan
191
RD
Currawill
Mooraberee
Muncoonie Lake West
SIMPSON DESERT NATIONAL PARK
NORTHERN TERRITORY
QUEENSLAND
Cacoory (ruins)
Diamantina
92
53
Mt Collins 260m
DEVELOPMENTAL
EYRE
SIMPSON DESERT
River
Durrie
Betoota
51
Lake Cuddapan
114
BIRDSVILLE
Shallow Lake
50
DEVELOPMENTAL
Moonda Lake
Mt Lehens 100m
Birdsville
QUEENSLAND
SOUTH AUSTRALIA
Haddon Corner
Mirranponga Pongunna Lake
Poeppel Corner
Lake Coominnie
Frew Hill 123m
Cadelga (ruins)
Lake Thomas
Larrys Hill 63m
Pillon Hill 50m
SIMPSON DESERT CONSERVATION PARK
WARNING: Visitors planning to enter Desert Parks are required to contact the National Parks and Wildlife SA. A Desert Pass is necessary.
The West Lake
TRACK
Pandie Pandie
Lake Short
Stony Point 195m
Lake Yamma Yamma
D83
Diamantina
Lake Etamunbanie
Lake Mooravepe
Lake Uloowaranie
INSIDE
New Alton Downs
(recommended)
Poolowanna Lake
179
Pulcara Hill 170m
Beale Hill 53m
Perra Perra Poolanna Lake
Ephemeral Lakes
BIRDSVILLE
(not
Goyder Lagoon
Dickinna Hill 87m
Cordillo Downs
Arrabury
Cooks Outsta
TRACK
Apaeyilarranie Lake
Koomarinna Lake
SIMPSON DESERT REGIONAL RESERVE
OUTSIDE
Clifton Hills
Lake Griselda
BIRDSVILLE
Lake Pure
Leap Year Bore
Coongie Lakes
Malga Bore
Coongie
INNAMINCKA REGIONAL RESERVE
Umaroona Lake
TRACK
Creek
STURT STONY DESERT
Willawilaninna Lake
133
Patchawarra Bore
SOUTH AUSTRALIA
QUEENSLAND
Lake Koodnanie
516
Pathraoutara Lake
Cooper
Pantoowarinna Lake
Pialopotingoona Lake
Lake Warrandirinna
Nappa Merrie
Aboriginal Rock Carvings
Burke & Wills Dig Tree
Gidgealpa
Innamincka
Peeramudlayeppa Lake
Lake Howitt
Cowarie
Mirra Mitta Bore
Pompapillinna Lake
Kalamurina
Creek
44
Warburton
Lake Miamiana
BIRDSVILLE
TRACK
47
Koolkootinnie Lake
Kalamurra Lake
Mungeranie
Mungerannie Roadhouse
Lake Kittakittaooloo
STRZELECKI
Moomba Gasfield
60
Wirrhekarrinna Waterhole
Lake Warrakalanna
Lake Eyre North
LAKE EYRE NATIONAL PARK
Creek
Lake Walpayapeninna
Lake Ngapakaldi
Big Lake Moomba
Creek
Tickalara Oil Field
Lake Mulapula
Lake Puntawolona
Mulka
Lake Hope
STRZELECKI REGIONAL RESERVE
TRACK
50
Munro Oil Field
Flood by-pass ferry
Lake Killamperpunna
Lake Murteree
Merty Merty
Cooper
Flood by-pass track
Lake Kopperekoppinna
ELLIOT PRICE CONSERVATION PARK
Lake Palankarinna
Etadunna
Lake Gregory
STRZELECKI
Strzelecki
120
Bollards Lagoon
Corner Store
Dog
Lake Florence
Strzelecki Crossing
Cameron Corner
Dulkaninna
STURT NATION
Explorers Tree
D83
D96
STRZELECKI DESERT
Lake Blanche
Lake Eyre South
Lake Ellen
Lake Frances
Mulloorina

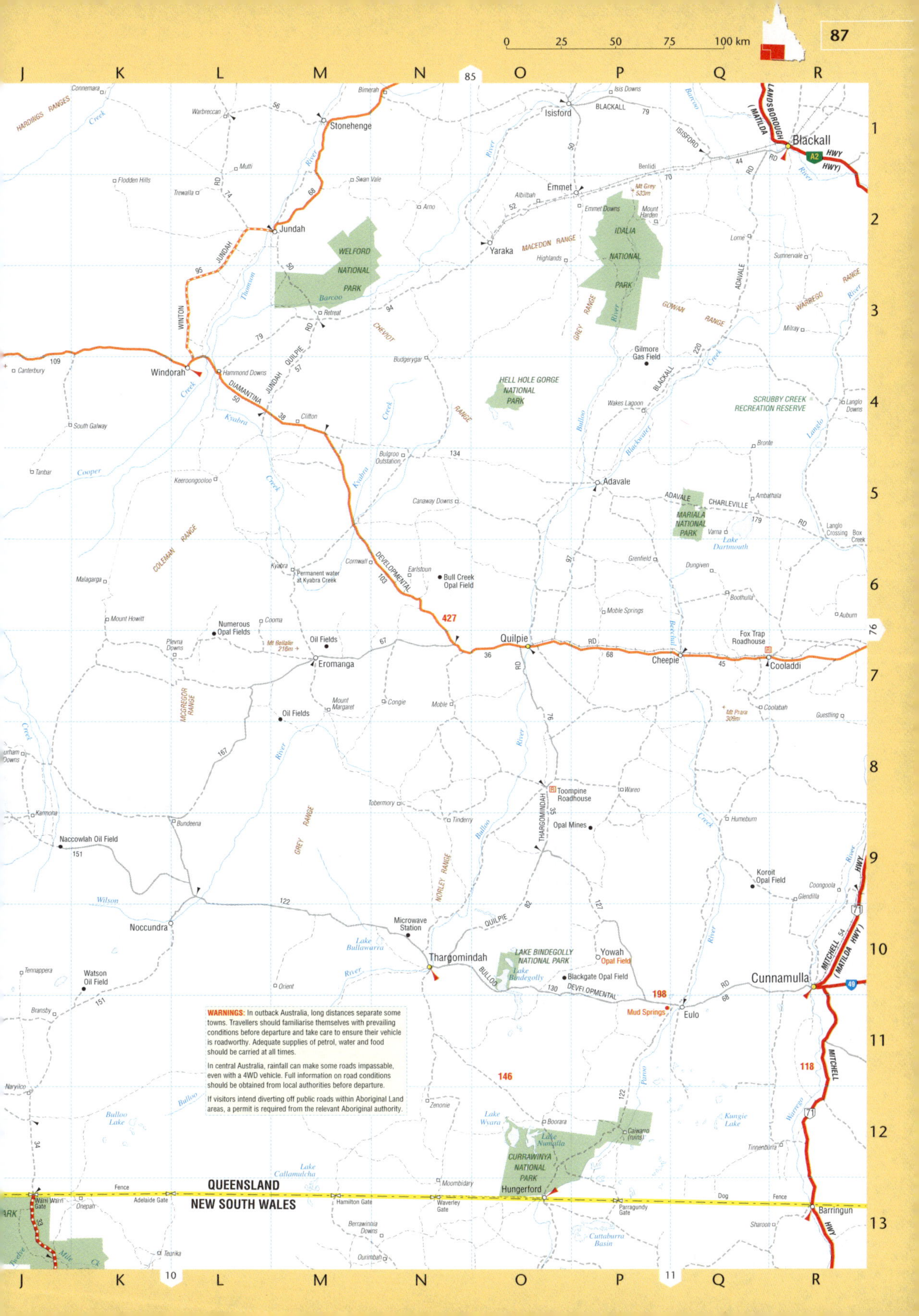

WARNINGS: In outback Australia, long distances separate some towns. Travellers should familiarise themselves with prevailing conditions before departure and take care to ensure their vehicle is roadworthy. Adequate supplies of petrol, water and food should be carried at all times.

In central Australia, rainfall can make some roads impassable, even with a 4WD vehicle. Full information on road conditions should be obtained from local authorities before departure.

If visitors intend diverting off public roads within Aboriginal Land areas, a permit is required from the relevant Aboriginal authority.

Tasmania

Location Map

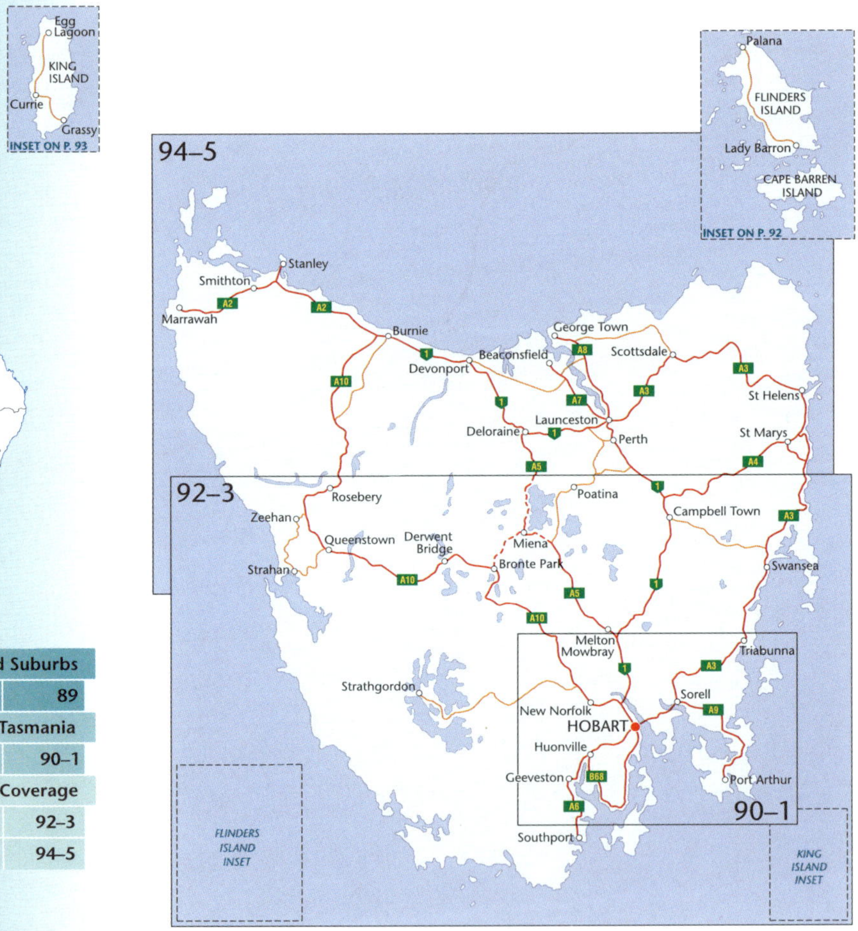

0 0.25 0.5 0.75 1 km
Accommodation
Barton Cottage 1 G9
Colville Cottage 2 G10
Country Comfort Hadleys Hotel 3 F8
Hobart Macquarie 4 E8
Hotel Grand Chancellor & Federation Concert Hall 5 G7
Lenna of Hobart 6 G9
Oakford on Elizabeth St Pier 7 G8
The Old Woolstore 8 G6
Salamanca Inn 9 F9
Note: Only a sample range of accommodation is listed; inclusion is not necessarily a recommendation.
General Information
Ferry/cruise departure point (incl. Cadbury cruises) 10 G8
General Post Office 11 F7
Hobart Transit Centre 12 E8
Metro Tasmania Bus Terminal 13 F7
Motoring Organisation (RACT) 14 D6
Police Headquarters 15 F6
Qantas Travel Centre 16 F7
Tigerline Coach Terminal 17 F6
Visitor Information 18 G7
Places of Interest
Antarctic Adventure 19 G9
Arthur Circus 20 G9
Cat and Fiddle Arcade 21 F7
Cenotaph 22 H6
Constitution Dock 23 G7
Elizabeth Street Mall 24 F7
Franklin Square 25 F7
Gasworks Shopping Village 26 G6
Government House 27 G3
Hope and Anchor Tavern 28 G7
Ingle Hall 29 F7
Kellys Steps 30 G9
Maritime Museum of Tasmania 31 G7
Parliament House 32 F8
Penitentiary Chapel & Historic Site (National Trust HQ) 33 F6
Queens Domain 34 F3
Salamanca Arts Centre 35 G9
Salamanca Place 36 G8
Signalling Station 37 H9
State Library / Allport Library & Museum of Fine Arts 38 E7
Tasmanian Museum & Art Gallery 39 G7
Theatre Royal 40 F6
Town Hall 41 F7
Van Diemen's Land Memorial Folk Museum (Narryna) 42 F9
Victoria Dock 43 G7
Wrest Point Hotel-Casino 44 H13
New Town
North Hobart
West Hobart
Glebe
HOBART
Battery Point
Sandy Bay
Dynnyrne
Royal Tasmanian Botanical Gardens
DOMAIN
QUEENS
DERWENT
RIVER
Sullivans Cove
Tasman Bridge
TO GLENORCHY
TO AIRPORT
TO CASCADES
TO TAROONA
University of Tasmania
Royal Yacht Club of Tasmania
Derwent Sailing Squadron
Wrest Point
Macquarie Point
Secheron Point
Pavilion Point
Short Beach
Ross Bay

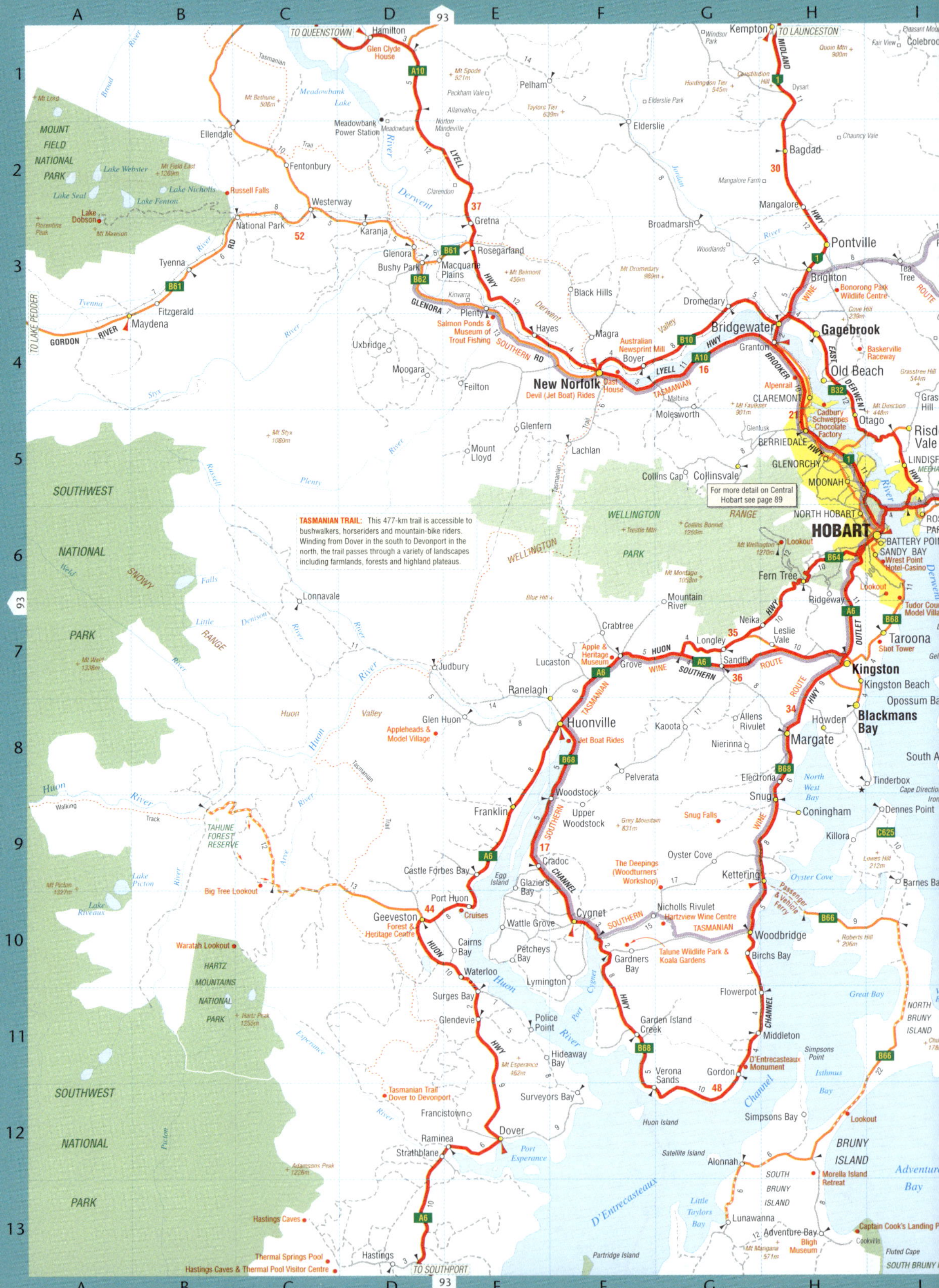
A
B
C
D
E
F
G
H
I
93
1
2
3
4
5
6
7
8
9
10
11
12
13
TO QUEENSTOWN
Hamilton
Glen Clyde House
A10
Kempton
TO LAUNCESTON
MIDLAND
HWY
Colebrook
Fair View
Quoin Mtn 900m
Windsor Park
Constitution Hill
Dysart
Huntingdon Tier 545m
Mt Spode 521m
Pelham
Peckham Vale
Allanvale
Norton Mandeville
Taylors Tier 639m
Elderslie Park
Elderslie
Chauncy Vale
Bagdad
30
Mt Lord
MOUNT FIELD NATIONAL PARK
Lake Webster
Mt Field East 1269m
Lake Nicholls
Lake Seal
Lake Fenton
Lake Dobson
Florentine Peak
Mt Mawson
Russell Falls
Mt Bethune 506m
Meadowbank Lake
Meadowbank Power Station
Ellendale
Fentonbury
Trail
LYELL
Clarendon
Derwent
Jordan
Mangalore Farm
Mangalore
Westerway
National Park
52
Karanja
37
Gretna
Broadmarsh
Pontville
Woodlands
Glenora
B61
Rosegarland
Bushy Park
Macquarie Plains
B62
Tyenna
Mt Belmont 456m
Mt Dromedary 989m
Black Hills
Dromedary
Brighton
Tea Tree
Bonorong Park Wildlife Centre
ROUTE
Cove Hill 239m
Tyenna
Fitzgerald
Maydena
TO LAKE PEDDER
GORDON RIVER
GLENORA
Kinvarra
Plenty
Salmon Ponds & Museum of Trout Fishing
Hayes
Magra
Valley
Bridgewater
Gagebrook
B10
Australian Newsprint Mill
Uxbridge
SOUTHERN RD
Boyer
Granton
BROOKER
Baskerville Raceway
A10
16
Old Beach
EAST DERWENT
Grasstree Hill 544m
Moogara
Feilton
New Norfolk
Oast House
Devil (Jet Boat) Rides
Styx
Malbina
TASMANIAN
Alpenrail
CLAREMONT
B32
Mt Faulkner 901m
Cadbury Schweppes Chocolate Factory
Molesworth
21
Mt Direction 448m
Otago
Grass Tree
Risdon Vale
Mt Styx 1080m
Glenfern
Glenlusk
BERRIEDALE
Mount Lloyd
Lachlan
GLENORCHY
LINDISFARNE
Collins Cap
Collinsvale
MOONAH
For more detail on Central Hobart see page 89
SOUTHWEST NATIONAL PARK
Plenty
Russell
TASMANIAN TRAIL: This 477-km trail is accessible to bushwalkers, horseriders and mountain-bike riders. Winding from Dover in the south to Devonport in the north, the trail passes through a variety of landscapes including farmlands, forests and highland plateaus.
WELLINGTON RANGE
Trestle Mtn
Collins Bonnet 1269m
NORTH HOBART
HOBART
BATTERY POINT
SANDY BAY
Wrest Point Hotel-Casino
WELLINGTON
PARK
Mt Wellington 1270m
Lookout
B64
Weld
SNOWY
Falls
Mt Montagu 1058m
Fern Tree
Derwent
Lonnavale
Blue Hill
Mountain River
Ridgeway
Lookout
Tudor Court Model Village
Little
Denison
RANGE
Crabtree
Neika
A6
B68
Mt Weld 1338m
Apple & Heritage Museum
Longley
35
Leslie Vale
OUTLET
Taroona
Shot Tower
Judbury
Lucaston
HUON
Grove
WINE
A6
SOUTHERN
Sandfly
ROUTE
36
Kingston
Kingston Beach
Ranelagh
Opossum Bay
Huon
Valley
Glen Huon
Allens Rivulet
34
Howden
Blackmans Bay
Appleheads & Model Village
Huonville
Kaoota
Margate
Jet Boat Rides
Nierinna
South Arm
B68
Pelverata
Electrona
North West Bay
Tinderbox
Cape Direction
Huon
River
Walking Track
Woodstock
Upper Woodstock
Snug
Coningham
Dennes Point
TAHUNE FOREST RESERVE
Franklin
Grey Mountain 831m
Snug Falls
Killora
C625
Arve
17
Oyster Cove
Lowes Hill 212m
Mt Picton 1327m
Lake Picton
Castle Forbes Bay
A6
Cradoc
The Deepings (Woodturners' Workshop)
Kettering
Oyster Cove
Barnes Bay
Lake Riveaux
Big Tree Lookout
Egg Island
Glaziers Bay
CHANNEL
Passenger & Vehicle Ferry
Port Huon
44
Cruises
Geeveston
Forest & Heritage Centre
Cygnet
Nicholls Rivulet
Hartzview Wine Centre
B66
Waratah Lookout
Wattle Grove
Woodbridge
Roberts Hill 206m
HARTZ MOUNTAINS NATIONAL PARK
Hartz Peak 1255m
Cairns Bay
Petcheys Bay
Gardners Bay
Talune Wildlife Park & Koala Gardens
Birchs Bay
Waterloo
Lymington
Surges Bay
Flowerpot
Great Bay
NORTH BRUNY ISLAND
Glendevie
Police Point
Port Cygnet
Garden Island Creek
Middleton
Esperance
Hideaway Bay
B68
Simpsons Point
Mt Esperance 462m
D'Entrecasteaux Monument
Verona Sands
Gordon
Isthmus Bay
B66
SOUTHWEST NATIONAL PARK
48
Tasmanian Trail Dover to Devonport
Surveyors Bay
Channel
Francistown
Huon Island
Simpsons Bay
Lookout
Picton
Dover
Raminea
Strathblane
Port Esperance
BRUNY ISLAND
Satellite Island
Alonnah
SOUTH BRUNY ISLAND
Morella Island Retreat
Adventure Bay
Adamsons Peak 1226m
D'Entrecasteaux
Little Taylors Bay
Hastings Caves
A6
Lunawanna
Captain Cook's Landing Place
Adventure Bay
Bligh Museum
Cookville
Mt Mangana 571m
Thermal Springs Pool
Hastings
Fluted Cape
Partridge Island
Hastings Caves & Thermal Pool Visitor Centre
TO SOUTHPORT
SOUTH BRUNY

0 5 10 15 20 km
93
MILITARY TRAINING AREA
TO SWANSEA
Triabunna
Woodstock
Okehampton
Mt Hobbs 823m
Levendale
Craigbourne Dam
Mt Bains 334m
Stonehurst
Bluff River
Cape Bougainville
Louisville
Eastcoaster Resort
Point Horne
Orford
Prosser Bay
Quarry Point
Shelly Beach
Spring Beach
Ferry
Isle du Nord
Cape Boullanger
MARIA ISLAND NP MARINE EXTENSION
Darlington
Historic Penal Settlement
Painted Cliffs
Bishop and Clerk
Brown Mountain 792m
Brockley
Prosser River
Court Farm
Three Thumbs 549m
TASMAN
Buckland
Historic Church
Sally Peak
Whitemarsh
Runnymede
Campania
Campania House
Mt Morrison 469m
Johnsons Point
Rheban
Carrickfergus Bay
Mercury Passage
Lachlan Island
Ringrove
MARIA ISLAND NATIONAL PARK
Mt Maria 709m
Mistaken Cape
Prosser Sugarloaf 647m
Earlham
Byton Tops
Point Des Galets
Shoal Bay
Walking Track
Riedle Bay
Cockle Bay
Nugent
MARIA ISLAND
Richmond
Richmond Bridge (Australia's Oldest Bridge)
Park View
Orielton
Pawleena
Cape Bernier
Cape Maurouard
Wattle Hill
Hillcrest
Mt Lord 279m
Penna
SOUTHERN
Sorell
Gordon SL 415m
Carlton River
Benders Hill 404m
Cape Peron
Kellevie
Pitt Water
Midway Point
Forcett
ARTHUR
TASMANIAN
Bream Creek
Marion Bay
HWY
HOBART AIRPORT
WINE
Copping
Museum
Marion Bay
Cambridge
Lookout
Seven Mile Beach Protected Area
Lewisham
Dodges Ferry
Mt Rumney 378m
Seven Mile Beach
Tiger Head
Park Beach
Carlton
ROUTE
Blackman Bay
Cape Paul Lamanon
North Bay
Cape Frederick Hendrick
Rokeby
Carlton Bluff
Connellys Marsh
Dunalley
Denison Canal
Lauderdale
Primrose Point
Primrose Sands
Frederick Henry Bay
Dunalley Bay
Fulham Island
Mt Forestier 320m
Humper Bluff
FORESTIER PENINSULA
High Yellow Bluff
Sandford
Green Head
Smooth Island
Lime Bay
Cremorne
Sloping Island
LIME BAY NATURE RESERVE
Whitehouse Point
King George Island
Murdunna
Cape Surville
Cape Deslacs
Clifton Beach
Mt Stewart 180m
Norfolk Bay
Flinders Bay
FLINDERS BAY CONSERVATION AREA
Macgregor Peak 591m
North West Head
Gwandalan
Coal Mines Historic Site
EAGLEHAWK BAY CONSERVATION AREA
Pirates Bay Lookout
Tessellated Pavement
TASMAN
Cape Contrariety
Deer Point
Saltwater River
Eaglehawk Bay
Pirates Bay
Dart Island
Halfway Bluff
Eaglehawk Neck
Penzance
Tasman Blowhole
Betsey Island
Mt Communication 344m
Outer North Head
Premaydena
Tasmanian Devil Park
Doo Town
Tasmans Arch
Devils Kitchen
Taranna
Koonya
TASMAN NATIONAL PARK
Waterfall Bay
ROARING BEACH COASTAL RESERVE
O'Hara Bluff
Nubeena
Storm Bay
Wedge Bay
Mt Koonya 488m
White Beach
TASMAN
PENINSULA
Oakwood
Thumb Point
Wedge Island
STEWARTS BAY STATE RES
Bush Mill Steam Railway
Fortescue Bay
SEA
Cape Hauy
Highcroft
Port Arthur
Port Arthur Historic Site
Mt Arthur
Stormlea
Palmers Lookout
TASMAN NATIONAL PARK
Munro Bight
Salters Point
Remarkable Cave
West Arthur Head
Raoul Bay
Maingon Bay
Black Head
Cape Pillar
Cape Raoul
Tasman Island
A3
A9
B37
B33
62
73
26
54
44
J K L M N O P Q R
1 2 3 4 5 6 7 8 9 10 11 12 13

94
SOUTHERN
OCEAN
Granville Harbour
Renison Bell
Melba Flats
Rosebery
Williamsford
Montezuma Falls
Mt Murchison 1275m
Anthony Power Station
Zeehan
West Coast Pioneers Memorial Museum
Dundas
Mt Dundas 1158m
MURCHISON
ZEEHAN
HWY
A10
31
B27
Mt Agnew 846m
Trial Harbour
Remine
Henty
Lake Margaret
Mt Lyell Mine
Gormanston
Queenstown
Linda
LYELL
B24
Ocean Beach
Strahan
Strahan Visitors Centre
Regatta Point
Point Hibbs
Cape Sorell
Lynchford
King River Power Station
King River Forest Drive
The Wilderness Railway
Mt Owen 1146m
Mt Jukes 1168m
Darwin Dam
Mt Sorell 1144m
Mt Darwin 1031m
Macquarie Harbour
Gordon River Cruise
Sloop Point
Gorge Point
Pillinger
Sarah Island
Birthday Bay
Heritage Landing
Mt Discovery 680m
Mt Lee 734m
Hibbs Bay
Point Hibbs
SOUTHWEST
Spero Bay
Endeavour Bay
Wanderer
CONSERVATION
AREA
High Rocky Point
Mt Osmund 369m
Frederick Hill 518m
Low Rocky Point
Elliott Bay
Elliott Hill 209m
Hardwood Hill 412m
Nye Bay
Mulcahy Bay
Wreck Bay
Kelly Basin
Payne Bay
Point St Vincent
Port Davey
Stephens Bay
Island Bay
Window Pane Bay
SOUTHWEST CONSERVATION AREA
CRADLE MOUNTAIN–
LAKE ST CLAIR
NATIONAL PARK
Lake Rolleston
Lake Burbury
Mt Ossa 1617m
Mt Pelion East 1461m
Mt Gould 1491m
Mt Olympus 1447m
Mt Hugel 1307m
Mt Rufus 1402m
Mt Gell 1439m
Mt Arrowsmith 981m
Lake St Clair
108
HWY
Frenchmans Cap 1443m
Mt King William I 1324m
FRANKLIN–GORDON
WILD RIVERS
NATIONAL
PARK
KING WILLIAM RANGE
PRINCE OF WALES RANGE
Mt Curly 1039m
Mt Humboldt 1079m
Mt Wright 1119m
Gordon PS Dam
Strathgordon
Serpentine Dam
Lookout
Lake Gordon
Mt Sprent 1058m
GORDON RIVER
B61
126
Creepy Crawly Nature Trail
Mt Bowes 957m
Mt Wedge 1146m
Mt Mueller 1234m
Maydena
FRANKLAND RANGE
Serpentine Reach
Lake Pedder
SCOTTS PEAK RD
Mt Anne 1425m
Mt Gibson 879m
Scotts Peak Dam
Edgar Dam
SOUTHWEST
NATIONAL
PARK
Mt Gaffney 586m
Mt Hean 747m
Mt Orion 1119m
Mt Bradley 729m
ARTHUR RANGE
Mt Picton 1327m
Mt Norold 978m
Mt Rugby 771m
Bathurst Harbour
Melaleuca
Mt Counsel 800m
Mt Melaleuca 595m
Cox Bight
New Harbour
South West Cape
Karamu Bay
Louisa Bay
Ile du Golfe
De Witt Island
Flat Witch Island
MAATSUYKER GROUP
Maatsuyker Island
Prion Bay
Surprise Bay
New River Lagoon
Rowallan Power Station
Lake Rowallan
WALLS OF JERUSALEM
NATIONAL
PARK
CENTRAL PLATEAU
CONSERVATION
Derwent Bridge
A10
33
B1
Bronte Park
Lake King William
Clark Dam
Butlers Gorge Power Station
Butlers Gorge
Tarraleah
Tarraleah Power Station
Liapootah Power Station
Wayatinah
Mt Field West 1439m
MOUNT FIELD NATIONAL PARK
Adamsfield
Clear Hill 1198m
FLINDERS ISLAND
Hobart
Inner Sister Island
Stanley Point
Palana
Blyth Point
Killiecrankie Bay
Killiecrankie
Cape Frankland
Marshall Bay
Lughrata
Emita
Wybalenna Historic Site
Memana
72
C803
Arthur Bay
Prime Seal Island
Long Point
Whitemark
Parry's Bay
B85
Ranga
Trousers Point
Loccota
Lady Barron
STRZELECKI NP
Mt Chappell Is
Badger Is
Anderson Is
Long Is
Franklin Sound
Vansittart Is
Puncheon Point
Cape Barren Island
Mt Munro 716m
CAPE BARREN ISLAND
Mt Kerford 499m
Preservation Is
Sloping Pt
Kent Bay
Cape Barren
Clarke Island
Passage Is
Forsyth Is
Lookout Heads
Moriarty Point
BANKS STRAIT
BASS STRAIT
Babel Is
Sellars Lagoon
Cameron Inlet
FURNEAUX GROUP
0 10 20 km

0 10 20 30 40 50 km
J K L M N O P Q R
1 2 3 4 5 6 7 8 9 10 11 12 13
95
Liffey Falls
Liffey
Cressy
Blackwood Creek
Poatina
Poatina PS
Cramps
GREAT WESTERN TIERS
Tods Corner PS
Flintstone
Arthurs Lake
Wilburville
Shannon
Waddamana
CONSERVATION AREA
Lake Sorell
Interlaken
Powranna
Epping Forest
Cleveland
Conara
Campbell Town
Auburn
Goldsmith
Ross
Female Factory Historic Site (Prison)
Tunbridge
TURNBRIDGE TIER CONSERVATION AREA
Lake Crescent
Storys Creek
Rossarden
Fingal
Avoca
Llewellyn Siding
Royal George
Lake Leake
Meetus Falls
Gray
Seymour
Long Point
DOUGLAS-APSLEY NATIONAL PARK
Lookout
East Coast Birdlife & Animal Park
Waubs Harbour
Bicheno
Cape Lodi
Apslawn
Cranbrook
FREYCINET NATIONAL PARK
Freycinet Marine Farm
Swanwick
Coles Bay
Cape Tourville
The Hazards
Wineglass Bay
Swansea
The Swansea Bark Mill
Great Oyster Bay
Cape Forestier
FREYCINET PENINSULA
Schouten Island
Cape Degerando
Cape Baudin
Cape Sonnerat
Isle des Phoques
Pontypool
Little Swanport
Triabunna
Louisville
Eastcoaster Resort
Orford
Shelly Beach
Spring Beach
Darlington
Historic Penal Settlement
MARIA ISLAND
MARIA ISLAND NATIONAL PARK
Rheban
Cape Peron
York Plains
Oatlands
Nala
Pawtella
Lemont
Andover
Inglewood
Mount Seymour
Stonehenge
Whitefoord
MILITARY TRAINING AREA
Tunnack
Rhyndaston
Woodsdale
Eldon
Levendale
Buckland
Runnymede
Bothwell
Apsley
Lower Marshes
Convict-built Mud Walls
Jericho
Parattah
Stonor
Tiberias
Baden
Melton Mowbray
Kempton
Colebrook
Hamilton
Langloh
Hollow Tree
Pelham
Elderslie
Bagdad
Mangalore
Broadmarsh
Pontville
Rekuna
Campania
Brighton
Bridgewater
Gagebrook
Old Beach
Richmond
Orielton
Pawleena
Wattle Hill
Nugent
Kellevie
Bream Creek
Marion Bay
Fentonbury
Westerway
Gretna
Glenora
Bushy Park
Plenty
Hayes
Magra
Boyer
Black Hills
Dromedary
Uxbridge
Moogara
New Norfolk
Granton
CLAREMONT
BERRIEDALE
Otago
Risdon Vale
LINDISFARNE
Sorell
Penna
Midway Point
Lewisham
Dodges Ferry
Carlton
Primrose Sands
Dunalley
Feilton
Glenfern
Mount Lloyd
Lachlan
Collinsvale
GLENORCHY
HOBART
ROSNY PARK
HOWRAH
Cambridge
Seven Mile Beach
Rokeby
Lauderdale
Sandford
Cremorne
Clifton Beach
WELLINGTON PARK
Fern Tree
Mountain River
Crabtree
Lucaston
Judbury
Ranelagh
Glen Huon
Huonville
Longley
Leslie
Grove
Sandfly
Neika
Taroona
Kingston
Opossum Bay
Howden
Blackmans Bay
Kaoota
Margate
Tinderbox
South Arm
Dennes Point
Pelverata
Snug
Coningham
Franklin
Woodstock
Castle Forbes Bay
Port Huon
Oyster Cove
Kettering
Killora
Barnes Bay
Geeveston
Cygnet
Nicholls Rivulet
Woodbridge
Birchs Bay
Gardners Bay
Flowerpot
Garden Island Creek
Middleton
Gordon
Verona Sands
Waratah Lookout
Waterloo
Surges Bay
Glendevie
Lymington
Police Point
Francistown
Surveyors Bay
Raminea
Strathblane
Dover
Hastings
Lune River
Ida Bay
Southport
Scenic Railway
Southport Lagoon
Lady Bay
Catamaran
Cockle Creek
Moss Glen
South East Cape
Recherche Bay
Simpsons Bay
BRUNY ISLAND
NORTH BRUNY ISLAND
Storm Bay
Alonnah
Adventure Bay
Lunawanna
Cape Connella
SOUTH BRUNY ISLAND
SOUTH BRUNY NATIONAL PARK
Tasman Head
Cloudy Bay
Great Taylors Bay
Murdunna
FORESTIER PENINSULA
Cape Surville
Cape Frederick Hendrick
Eaglehawk Neck
Taranna
TASMAN NP
TASMAN PENINSULA
Saltwater River
Premaydena
Koonya
Nubeena
White Beach
Highcroft
Stormlea
Port Arthur
Port Arthur Historic Site
Fortescue Bay
Cape Hauy
TASMAN NATIONAL PARK
Cape Pillar
Tasman Island
Cape Raoul
Raoul Bay
Maingon Bay
Wedge Island
Betsey Island
Norfolk Bay
TASMAN SEA
For more detail on Hobart & Surrounds see pages 90–1
KING ISLAND
Hobart
Cape Wickham
Cape Farewell
Phoques Bay
Egg Lagoon
Lavinia Point
LAVINIA NATURE RESERVE
New Year Is
Christmas Is
Whistler Point
Yambacoona
Reekara
BASS STRAIT
Sea Elephant
Loorana
King Island Dairy
Sea Elephant Bay
Naracoopa
Currie
Pegarah
Parenna
Fitzmaurice Bay
Yarra Creek
Lymwood
Bold Head
Grassy
Cataraqui Point
Pearshape
Seal Point
Surprise Point
Seal Bay
Surprise Bay
Stokes Point
0 10 20 km

BASS
SOUTHERN
OCEAN
Spirit of Tasmania ferries Devonport to Melbourne
Three Hummock Island
THREE HUMMOCK ISLAND NATURE RESERVE
Cape Adansan
Hunter Island
HUNTER ISLAND CONSERVATION AREA
Cuvier Bay
Hope Channel
Hunter Passage
Walker Channel
Walker Island
Trefoil Island
Cape Grim
Valley Bay
Woolnorth
Robbins Island
Ransonnet Bay
Robbins Passage
Cape Elie
Perkins Island
Perkins Bay
North Point
West Point
Half Moon Bay
Highfield Point
Stanley
The Nut
Circular Head
Sawyer Bay
Studland Bay
West Montagu
Montagu
Mella
Mowbray Park
Smithton
Wiltshire Junction
Forest
Black River
Port Latta
Brickmakers Bay
Rocky Cape
ROCKY CAPE NATIONAL PARK
Mt Cameron West 168m
West Point
Marrawah
ARTHUR-PIEMAN CONSERVATION AREA
Redpa
Togari
Christmas Hills
Brittons Swamp
South Forest
Crayfish Creek
Edgcumbe Beach
Detention River
Hellyer
Irishtown
Mengha
Alcomie
Lileah
Edith Creek
Nabageena
Rocky Cape
Montumana
Sisters Beach
Birdland Native Gardens
Boat Harbour Beach
Boat Harbour
Table Cape
Table Cape Lookout
Mawbanna
Sisters Creek
Myalla
Moorleah
Flowerdale
Wynyard
Seymour Hill 134m
Arthur River
Cruise
Gardiner Point
Roger River
Roger River West
Trowutta
Dip Falls
Milabena
Lapoinya
Somerset
Camdale
Cooee
Burnie
Wivenhoe
Chasm Creek
Heybridge
Howth
Sulphur Creek
Penguin
Ulverstone
Turners Beach
Devon
Lower Mount Hicks
Oldina
Upper Mount Hicks
Elliott
Yolla
East Yolla
West Ridgley
Ridgley
Upper Stowport
Stowport
Cuprona
Natone
West Pine
Ferndene
Calder
Kellatier
Preolenna
Meunna
Takone
West Takone
Henrietta
Tewkesbury
Highclere
Upper Natone
Riana
North Motton
South Riana
Gawler
Forth
Abbotsham
Spalford
Kindred
Don
Quoiba
Spreyton
Hampshire
Gunns Plains
Heka
Preston
Sprent
Central Castra
Warringa
Castra
Upper Castra
Loyetea
Peak Hill Farm
Lower Barrington
Barrington
Paloona
Melrose
Sheffield
Nietta
Narrawa
Wilmot
Loongana
South Nietta
Roland
Stoodley
Paradise
Staverton
Claude Road
Gowrie Park
Erriba
Wilmot PS
Cethana PS
Moina
Daisy Dell
Lorinna
Liena
Mayberry
Mole Creek
King Solomons Cave
Marakoopa Cave
MOLE CREEK KARST NP
Chudleigh
Caveside
Lemonthyme Power Station
Fisher Power Station
Rowallan Power Station
Lake Rowallan
Lake Parangana
Nelson Bay
Couta Rocks
Temma
Temma Harbour
Kaywood
Balfour
Mt Frankland 433m
ARTHUR-PIEMAN CONSERVATION AREA
Mt Hazelton 671m
Mt Norfolk 759m
Mt Hadmar 762m
Sandy Cape
LAKE CHISHOLM FOREST RESERVE
MILKSHAKE HILLS FOREST RESERVE
JULIUS RIVER FOREST RESERVE
WES BECKETT FOREST RESERVE
Frog Hill 338m
Mt Fittolani
SAVAGE RIVER NATIONAL PARK
HELLYER GORGE STATE RESERVE
Parrawe
Guildford
Waratah
Luina
Cleveland Mine
Bronzite Hill 488m
Mt Cleveland 856m
Hazelwood
Savage River
Mt Pearse 1001m
Mt Meredith 792m
Mt Ramsey 855m
Mt Charter 889m
Bulgobac
Lookout
Cradle Mountain Lodge
Waldheim Chalet
Cradle Valley
Cradle Mtn 1545m
Charles Peak
Rupert Point
Pieman Head
Hardwick Bay
Corinna
Ferry
Cruises
Reece Power Station
Dam
PIEMAN RIVER STATE RESERVE
Ahrberg Bay
Lake Pieman
Bastyan PS
Mackintosh Power Station
Lake Mackintosh
Lake Rosebery
Tullah
Granville Harbour
Renison Bell
Melba Flats
Rosebery
Williamsford
Montezuma Falls
Mt Murchison 1275m
Anthony Power Station
SOUTHWEST CONSERVATION AREA
CRADLE MOUNTAIN–LAKE ST CLAIR NATIONAL PARK
WALLS OF JERUSALEM NATIONAL PARK
Mt Agnew 846m
Zeehan
Dundas
West Coast Pioneers Memorial Museum
Mt Dundas 1158m
Trial Harbour
Remine
Lake Murchison
Lake Rolleston
Mt Ossa 1617m
Mt Pelion East 1451m
Mt Oakleigh 1000m
Mt Jerusalem 1458m
Lake Margaret
Mt Lyell Mine
Gormanston
Linda
Queenstown
Lake Burbury
Mt Gould 1491m
Mt Ida 1158m
Mt Owen 1146m
Ocean Beach
Strahan
Strahan Visitors Centre
Lynchford
King River PS
Regatta Point
Point Hibbs
Cape Sorell
King River Forest Drive
The Wilderness Railway
Mt Jukes 1168m
Darwin Dam
FRANKLIN–GORDON WILD RIVERS NATIONAL PARK
Mt Olympus 1447m
Mt Hugel 1307m
Mt Rufus 1402m
Mt Gell 1439m
Mt Arrowsmith 981m
Derwent Bridge
Lake St Clair
Lake King William
Mt King William I 1324m
Frenchmans Cap 1443m
Mt Sorell 1144m
Mt Darwin 1031m
Macquarie Harbour
Sloop Point
Butlers Gorge PS
Clark Dam
Butlers Gorge
BASS HWY
MURCHISON HWY
ZEEHAN HWY
LYELL HWY
A2
A10
B22
B23
B24
B26
B27
B18
B17
B15
B14
B12
C102

92

0 10 20 30 40 50 km

J K L M N O P Q R

1 2 3 4 5 6 7 8 9 10 11 12 13

J K L M N O P Q R

93

INDEX

Explore Australia Publishing Pty Ltd
12 Claremont Street
South Yarra, Victoria 3141, Australia

First edition published by Explore Australia Publishing Pty Ltd, 2003

10 9 8 7 6 5 4 3 2 1

Printed and bound in China by Midas Printing (Asia) Ltd

Publisher's note: Every effort has been made to ensure that the information in this book is accurate at the time of going to press. The publisher welcomes information and suggestions for correction or improvement. Write to the Publications Manager, Explore Australia Publishing, 12 Claremont Street, South Yarra, Victoria 3141, Australia or email explore@hardiegrant.com.au

Disclaimers: The publisher cannot accept responsibility for any errors or omissions. The representation on the maps of any road or track is not necessarily evidence of public right of way.

Design: Adrian Saunders
Writing: Ingrid Ohlsson
Editing: Astrid Browne, Rachel Pitts
Cartography: Bruce McGurty; Paul de Leur, Claire Johnston

Photographs:
Front cover: Uluru, Northern Territory (John Meier)
Back cover: Sydney Harbour, New South Wales (Explore Australia Publishing/Nick Rains)
Title page: Daintree National Park, Queensland (Tourism Queensland)
Contents pages: Cape du Couedic Lighthouse, South Australia (Rachel Pitts); Flinders Ranges, South Australia (Geoff Murray)
Destination Guide: Three Sisters, New South Wales (Explore Australia Publishing/ Gary Lewis); Parliament House, Australian Capital Territory (Explore Australia Publishing/JP & ES Baker); Twelve Apostles, Victoria (John Meier); Barossa Valley, South Australia (South Australian Tourism Commission); The Pinnacles, Western Australia (Explore Australia Publishing/JP & ES Baker); Kata Tjuta, Northern Territory (Explore Australia Publishing/Nick Rains); Palm Cove, Queensland (Tourism Queensland); Cradle Mountain–Lake St Clair National Park, Tasmania (Explore Australia Publishing/JP & ES Baker).
Practical Guide: Floriade, Australian Capital Territory (Explore Australia Publishing/JP & ES Baker); Great Ocean Road, Victoria (Explore Australia Publishing/Ken Stepnell); The Pilbara, Western Australia (Explore Australia Publishing/Don Skirrow); *Spirit of Tasmania* ferry (courtesy *Spirit of Tasmania*); Holiday Hub Beach Resort, New South Wales (courtesy of the resort); Crocodile warning sign, Northern Territory (Stock Photos/Bill Bachman); Australian currency (courtesy Reserve Bank of Australia)